A TANK GUNNER'S STORY

Cpl Gruntz of the 712th Tank Battalion

LOUIS G. GRUNTZ, JR.

Fonthill Media Limited
Fonthill Media LLC
www.fonthillmedia.com
office@fonthillmedia.com

First published in 2013

Copyright © Louis G. Gruntz Jr., 2013

ISBN 978-1-62545-023-4

All rights reserved. No part of this publication may be reproduced, stored in a retrieval system or transmitted in any form or by any means, electronic, mechanical, photocopying, recording or otherwise, without prior permission in writing from Fonthill Media Limited

Typeset in 10pt on 13pt Sabon LT
Printed and bound in England

Connect with us
facebook.com/fonthillmedia  twitter.com/fonthillmedia

CONTENTS

Dedication and Acknowledgments   4
Introduction   5
Prologue: World War II to a Baby Boomer   7
1. The Flight – Journey to the Past   23
2. Training for War   32
3. The Sherman Tank   58
4. The Beaches of Normandy   67
5. The Hedgerows   76
6. The Breakout   95
7. The Purple Heart – August 7, 1944   108
8. Return to Action – Fortress Metz   122
9. The Mud of Lorraine   133
10. The Battle of the Bulge   152
11. The Siegfried Line and into Germany   175
12. V-E Day and Occupation   186
13. Alsace and Ancestors   210
14. The Last Time I Saw Paris   212
15. Going Home   217
16. Other Casualties and a Never Ending War   224
17. The Final Battle   241
    Epilogue: Thanks Dad   248
    Endnotes   251
    Bibliography   262

Dedication and Acknowledgments

Dedicated to my family – my parents who lived the story and witnessed the inception of this book but did not live to see it published – my children and grandchildren for their enthusiastic support that Paw-Paw's story be told and who will become, what Henri Levaufre describes as, "Keepers of the Flame".

Special thanks to Aaron Elson, whose father was in the 712th Tank Battalion, for his journalistic expertise, his critical review and his unceasing encouragement to bring this work to print.

Introduction

The palest ink is better than the best memory.

Chinese Proverb

Many World War II veterans have gone to their graves with their individual wartime experiences remaining untold. With America's "Greatest Generation" rapidly fading into history, the sadness of their loss is compounded by their stories disappearing with them. Sixty years after World War II, the surviving veterans of that great conflict were passing away at the rate of 1,200 per day. My father, Louis Gruntz, was among the 1,200 veterans who answered the final roll call on February 7, 2004.

Throughout my boyhood and early adulthood, my father rarely talked about his experiences during the war. Despite my questioning, Dad's answers never contained any graphic details about his combat actions. I knew only very basic information about Dad's days as a soldier – he was in a tank in Europe and was once wounded.

For over forty-seven years, most of these details would remain a mystery to me, but in 1994 Dad's years of silence ended. He and I spent thirteen days in Europe retracing the battle route of his unit, the 712th Tank Battalion. Each night of our trip, I made journal entries regarding the stories he related to me that day.

We returned to Europe in June of 2000 for a monument dedication ceremony in Périers, France. The monument was in honor of the 90th Infantry Division and the 712th Tank Battalion's liberation of Périers in 1944. My mother and my two youngest children accompanied Dad and me on this second trip as we again retraced his battle route of 1944-45. Once more Dad recounted his experiences at different points along the way. This time my son and I recorded and videotaped Dad's stories.

Subsequent to these trips, Dad talked more freely to the family about the war. All of my children urged him, "Paw-Paw, you should write a book about the war." Dad politely declined. Instead he entrusted his story to me orally with instructions for me to reduce it to writing.

While many artifacts and the official histories of World War II are being maintained, professional historians also recognize the importance of preserving for future generations the stories of the individual veterans of that war. As an avid amateur genealogist, I also recognize the importance of preserving Dad's story for future generations of my family.

This is primarily an account of Dad's story told to me during our 1994 trip. It also touches on my continuing journey to learn about Dad's experiences, which did not end after that thirteen day trip, and my research for the accounts of others that witnessed these same events. I began this task prior to Dad's death and he reviewed much of the early transcripts for accuracy.

As with any journey for knowledge, my journey to learn of my father's wartime experiences would also teach me just how much I didn't know. I would discover that there is much more that I will never know or fully appreciate about his days in combat. But, with respect and love, I have undertaken his charge to me. This undertaking is not only for preserving for future generations the story of one veteran, but also for my children, grandchildren and generations of my descendants yet to come in order that the story of their ancestor, Cpl Louis G. Gruntz of the 712th Tank Battalion, will be remembered.

PROLOGUE

World War II to a Baby Boomer

> To be ignorant of what occurred before you were born is to remain always a child.
>
> Marcus Tullius Cicero, 46 BC

American soldiers of World War II returning home had a profound effect upon their country – a marked increase in the birth rate. By 1947, the year I was born, the post-war baby boom was shifting into high gear. Several years later the moniker Baby Boomer was used to describe children of my age, and this generational name has been applied to us Boomers ever since.

Dad was 28 years old when I was born, and as I reflect back on our life as a family, I realize he always seemed older than his years. I truly believe his experiences in combat produced this effect. Dad, like many veterans in the late '40s and early '50s, tried to forget the war, but as all of the veterans would discover there were some things they could not forget. The veterans who returned home to civilian life in 1945 were not the same boys they were on December 6, 1941. Their experiences and memories of World War II became part of them and would remain with them all of their lives. Their life experiences impacted their actions and behavior in the '50s and '60s as we Baby Boomers grew. Perhaps it is for this reason that we, the children of World War II veterans, continue to have a fascination with the events that occurred in those years before we were born, and the desire to pass this fascination to our children.

Upon Dad's discharge from the Army on November 1, 1945, he came home with a uniform and small box of wartime souvenirs. The uniform was packed away with moth balls and the cardboard box was tucked away in the corner of the top shelf in the bedroom closet. That box laid secluded for almost a decade since Dad was anxious to resume his civilian life, start a family and put the memories of wartime experiences behind him. The story of my parents' lives during the war years, like that box in their bedroom closet, was beyond my reach for much of my early life.

Hi-Way Cleaners. (*Author's collection*)

After their wedding in 1942, Mom and Dad had lived at Dad's family home on Bauvais Street in Metairie, Louisiana. When Dad entered the service, Mom, moved back to her home with her parents on Brooklyn Avenue in the adjacent neighborhood in Jefferson Parish. After his discharge, there was no separate residence for Mom and Dad to call home. Although my Aunt Clare still lived at home with my grandparents, there was still room enough for Mom and Dad, consequently, they established their marital residence, temporarily, at the Casteix family home at 478 Brooklyn Avenue.

Immediately after the war, there was, naturally, a down turn in the military industries. Dad's pre-war job at the shipyard was no longer available. He took the civil service exam and applied for a position with the United States Post Office. After waiting several weeks with no reply, he decided to go into the laundry and dry cleaning business with my maternal grandfather, Ernest Casteix. After all the paperwork had been completed for this business partnership, the postal service responded with a job offer, but by then it was too late, the laundry business was underway. Dad declined employment with the post office.

My grandfather and Dad did not have a long commute to work. The cleaners was located in the rear yard of their home and fronted on Jefferson Highway,

Living Room photograph. (*Author's collection*)

a major thoroughfare from the city to the only bridge in the area that crossed the Mississippi River, the Huey Long Bridge. The partnership operated under the name Hi-Way Cleaners.

After I came along in 1947, the household was beginning to get crowded. Mom and Dad purchased property up the street, in the 300 block of Brooklyn Avenue, not far from the dry cleaners/laundry. Dad spent several months building our future family home.

My earliest recollections of childhood are in that home that Dad built. Even though Dad rarely mentioned the war, it seems as though I always knew Dad was in the Army; perhaps because of the military photograph that hung in the living room of our home. Mom purchased a 16x20 lithograph patriotic photo mat and frame for Dad's picture taken in his uniform. I never recall a time when the photo was not displayed.

At the end of the war, my mother had also purchased a book entitled *The Fighting Men of Louisiana*, published in 1946 by the Louisiana Historical Institute. This leather bound book, similar to a college yearbook, contained photographs of men from Louisiana who served in the military during World War II. In 1950 I somehow got hold of this book, along with a pencil. I began to exercise my three-year-old artistic talents on many of the photographs in that book, with the exception of Dad's photograph. I don't recall the incident or discipline meted out for that transgression, but I am sure it was impressive. Even now, I refrain from making notations on pages of books I own.

In 1954, I was seven years old, the age of reason. It was about that time I began to ask my father the question heard by just about every father of that day, "What did you do during the war, Daddy?"

Dad's answers were usually short, with little detail or he usually changed the topic and talked about incidents that usually did not involve combat. Dad's wartime experiences were otherwise rarely mentioned, although he did tell me that he was in a Sherman tank in Europe during the war. On a few of those occasions when I inquired about the war, he went to his closet and retrieved the box that had been stored since 1945. The box of souvenirs contained French and German coins, a Nazi flag, German binoculars, along with some photos taken during training and after the war. During the 1950s, the Bronze Star Medal, the Purple Heart Medal, and his other World War II decorations were stored in that box in the closet, along with a German P-38 pistol and a German bayonet Dad obtained toward the end of the war.

To me the most curious contents of the box were two pieces of fragmented metal. When I asked about these, Dad told me the pieces were from his tank – when it was hit by a German bazooka and he was wounded. I asked if the doctors had removed these pieces from his wounds and given them to him. He said "No, if I had been hit by such large fragments, I would have been killed." Dad found those large chunks of shrapnel in his personal belongings in his

Mom and her young artist. (*Author's collection*)

knapsack, retrieved from the damaged tank. When I asked if he had any scars from his wounds, Dad then showed me his back which was peppered with black powder burns where small pieces of shrapnel had lodged.

Even during these accounts, Dad never went into any great detail about the events surrounding combat. I have since discovered that this was a common occurrence by the men in those days who had been on the battlefield just ten years earlier.

I remember asking Dad if he had learned how to speak German during the war. He indicated knowing only a few phrases. Due to their frequent requests, the German children taught Dad and other GIs the phrase, "Haben Sie Sie Schokolade?" ("Have any chocolate?").

Prior to Hurricane Katrina, the name New Orleans was mostly synonymous with Mardi Gras. When people from other parts of the United States discovered we are New Orleanians, the conversation inevitably shifts to our annual pre-Lenten celebration. Rex and his Krewe rule our city each Mardi Gras Day as the organization parades through the streets of our city. The festivities have become so popular that there are numerous organizations (krewes) which parade on different days for approximately two weeks prior to Mardi Gras Day; these other krewes frequently adopt the names of mythical Greek or Roman gods.

It is hard to imagine life in our city without this annual celebration occurring.[1] Yet, during the years of World War I and World War II, all Mardi Gras parades in New Orleans were cancelled. With most of the men off to war, the merriment and mirth of the remaining citizens in the "City that Care Forgot" was replaced by the care and concern for the war effort. The historians of our city refer to Mardi Gras Day during these years as being ruled by the Krewe of Mars (the god of war) in lieu of the Krewe of Rex.

It was during the Mardi Gras season of 1954, when Dad joined the Krewe of Carrollton, that I first recall Dad talking with others about the war. After Dad's initial parade ride, my Uncle Charlie, Dad's brother-in-law, asked him, what did it feel like to be riding high atop the parade float traveling through the huge crowds in the street. Dad said the throngs of joyous people, shouting along the parade route, reminded him of when his tank rolled through the liberated towns in France. The newly liberated French were celebrating wildly. When American soldiers came through such towns, the townspeople greeted them with wine or cider. They were yelling deliriously, waving flags and banners, and throwing flowers on the tanks and other American vehicles as they came by. Even after ten years, while celebrating a joyous Mardi Gras event, Dad could not escape memories and flashbacks of the war.

In the mid-1950s Baby Boomers were in grammar school, it was also the golden age of television. Being a typical middle class household – Dad worked and Mom was a housewife – we soon had one of those electronic marvels in our living room.

My initial boyhood perceptions of war came mainly from TV portrayals of the military, albeit the military in the nineteenth century. The cavalry soldiers of Fort Apache in the Adventures of Rin Tin Tin, were my first introduction to military ranks. But my introduction to the glory and valor of combat was the battle of the Alamo and the figure who was idolized by all boys of that day, Davy Crockett, King of the Wild Frontier.

Each day when signing on and signing off, the television stations would play the National Anthem and show newsreel combat footage from WWII. The image that sticks out in my mind the most was the film of the flag raising on Iwo Jima.

During the mid to late 1950s, one of my favorite childhood traditions was going to the movies at our neighborhood theater, the Arrow Theater on Jefferson Highway. Every Saturday night the parents in the neighborhood had an automatic baby-sitter; all the kids in our area went to the movies. Horror movies were in vogue, as well as westerns and, of course, war films.

It was about this time that I also became fascinated with another war, the Civil War. Being a Louisianian, I wondered if any of my ancestors had fought for the Old South. Dad advised that no one from the Gruntz family was in the Civil War; they had not emigrated to America from Alsace until the late 1800s.

All of these movies of my youth, whether Civil War or World War II, usually had the same moral theme, the good guys wore white hats and good always triumphed over evil. Naturally, we rooted for the American soldiers in all of those John Wayne World War II movies. One of the earliest war movies I remember was Audie Murphy's autobiographical account of war, *To Hell and Back*.

The other boys in my class watched the same TV series and movies that I watched. We reenacted many a battle on the playground at school. When we were shot, we fell to the ground with all the dramatics of any Hollywood actor.

Many New Orleanians in the '50s, as well as decades before and since, have tried to escape the hot and muggy summers of the city by going to the north shore of Lake Pontchartrain or to the Mississippi beaches to enjoy the cooler breezes off of the Gulf of Mexico. My parents purchased a small parcel of property on Merritt Lane in Waveland, Mississippi for such purposes; my maternal grandparents had a similar small lot of land in Slidell, Louisiana. Dad and Mom, as well as my grandparents, bought Higgins Huts for their respective vacation homes and weekend retreats. During the war, Higgins Industries in New Orleans, owned by Andrew Higgins, manufactured the D-Day landing crafts for the military. These landing crafts were made primarily of plywood. In addition to these landing crafts, Higgins also utilized his factory to manufacture plywood housing kits for use by the military. The housing kits, known as Higgins Huts, were inexpensive, relatively light and mobile and easy to erect. After the war, Higgins industries sold the pre-fabricated house kits to the public for approximately $250.00. A finished Higgins Hut consisted of two bedrooms, one bath and a living room and kitchen area. Our cabin in the country was Dad's retreat from the toil and pressures of the workplace.

The post-war purchase of military Higgins Huts by civilians was not an isolated business occurrence, as many businesses and individuals purchased surplus war materials during the 1950s. I remember the advertising gimmick used by stores to attract attention to a grand opening or other event in those days before television became widespread. Huge rotating search lights mounted on trailers shot beams of light into the night sky. There is no doubt that this enterprising advertising device in the 1950s brought back memories to many veterans, recalling the wartime use of these devices during air raids.

I was always fascinated by the fact that the small light source in front of the giant parabolic mirror produced such an intense beam of light and how these white shafts of light extended far into to the dark heavens and danced across the skies. During all of these occasions, however, Dad never mentioned to me the military uses for which these lights were originally built.

While Dad and Mom would enjoy this escape from daily life, being an only child, I had a different perspective on our weekend sojourns. Although I usually enjoyed our weekends once in Waveland, I often dreaded these trips as the weekends drew near. Going to Mississippi meant my friends were back home in Louisiana, to make matters worse, there was very poor TV reception in Waveland. Additionally, in those days before the interstate highway system had been constructed, US Highway 90 was the only road that led eastward out of the city, it was a long two-hour ride in our 1952 Ford Sedan between our home the western side of New Orleans and our weekend home in Waveland.

Every child has an imagination, it is said to be an important part of a child's development. I was certainly no different in that respect from other children. I suppose I compensated for the lack of friends and TV in Mississippi by kicking my imagination into high gear to pass the time away. This process began with the two-hour drive.

Our trek took us through the city streets and then past the Industrial Canal in eastern New Orleans, near one of Higgins' shipyards. I recall Dad speaking of his pre-war work in the nearby shipyards, but never any mention of the war itself

Once past the eastern New Orleans suburbs, the road narrowed to two lanes through the narrow strait of marsh and swamp that separates Lake Pontchartrain from Lake Borgne and the Gulf of Mexico. The route took us past two nineteenth century forts, Fort Pike and Fort Macomb, erected on the Rigolets Pass and Chef Menteur Pass respectively. These large brick fortifications were erected on these two waterways, connecting Lake Pontchartrain and the Gulf of Mexico, to prevent enemy forces from entering Lake Pontchartrain and launching a rear attack on New Orleans. Fort Macomb was closed to the public and in a deteriorating condition. Fort Pike, on the other hand, was maintained by the state park service. A two hour drive was boring for any child, I was no exception and although Mom and Dad were anxious to reach our final destination, on one or two occasions we stopped and toured Fort Pike. My imagination went wild from the moment we crossed the bridge across the moat into the entrance of the fort – I was immediately transported back into history. Whether peering from one of the gun ports or overlooking the adjacent waterways from the upper parapets I was repelling an imaginary enemy attacking my home town. Despite the resemblance between Fort Pike and some of the forts that comprised the Maginot Line surrounding the French city of Metz where Dad fought, there was no mention of World War II. Perhaps it was still too fresh in Dad's memory and he had not yet considered it as achieving the status of 'history'. To Dad, World War II was still merely old news.

Once past the Rigolets and into St Tammany Parish, Highway 90 enters the Honey Island swamp along the narrow ridge that was an ancient Indian trail and then utilized by French and Spanish settlers to travel between Mobile and New Orleans in the 1700s. It is still known as the Old Spanish Trail. There was not a single thing along this foreboding and desolate stretch of road with the exception of the White Kitchen Restaurant built in 1933 at the junction of US Highway 190 and US Highway 90. It was the midway point between New Orleans and the Mississippi Gulf Coast and was open 24 hours a day for weary travelers. Its landmark sign was an Indian Brave kneeling and holding a skewered fowl over a campfire. We occasionally stopped at the White Kitchen because no matter how much Mom and Dad exhorted me to go to the bathroom before we left home, that two-hour ride was just too long.

Exiting the Honey Island Swamp as we crossed the East Pearl River into Mississippi, we began to see a few semblances of civilization, but we still had another half hour drive through the pine woods of southern Mississippi to reach our weekend home. I would imagine an invisible enemy lurking behind every tree ready to attack as our car, the lead vehicle in an imaginary military convoy, proceeded along the highway.

Summers in Waveland also meant swimming at the beach. My imagination would transform the beaches of the Mississippi Gulf Coast into the D-Day beaches of Normandy; as I waded ashore in waist deep water, the imaginary bullets whizzed past me striking the water. Upon reaching the shore, I would zig-zag across the sand avoiding the enemy fire from an imaginary machine gun until I safely reached the three foot high concrete seawall.

My youthful imagination was fed by the movie and TV images of that era. As I look back on those films of my childhood, I realize how much those movies of the '50s and '60s portrayed a sanitized and glamorized image of warfare. When soldiers were killed in action in the movies, death was painless and instantaneous with one bullet. There was no blood, no maiming or prolonged suffering depicted in those films. I did not realize until my journey with Dad, just how much these early movies not only shaped, but shaded my perception of war and combat.

War had become a game to us Baby Boomers. During one school picnic all the boys played an early version of today's paint ball. Armed with water pistols loaded with red Kool-Aid, we separated into two armies and entered the wooded area of the camp grounds and began our war. A red stain on our T-shirt indicated that we had been wounded by the opposing side and we were out of the game, we had to return to the main picnic camp site. The group with the most unstained shirts at the end of the game was declared the winner of the war.

In 1957, my grandfather, Ernest Casteix, suffered a debilitating stroke that left him partially paralyzed. The father-in-law/son-in-law business was dissolved and the dry cleaning business fell solely on Dad's shoulders.

During this period, Dad also began several real estate ventures on the side that proved quite successful. We sold the Higgins Hut on Merritt Street and purchased an older sturdier residence on Jefferson Davis Boulevard in Waveland. Our new vacation home included a large tract of land to the rear. Dad had a road installed, subdivided the tract into lots and sold them to other New Orleanians seeking a weekend or vacation retreat.

As a sole proprietor, Dad's business began to prosper. He remodeled and modernized the cleaners. Dad was determined that I would not be deprived of any educational opportunities. With their additional income, Mom and Dad transferred me from public school to St Agnes Parochial School.

One night in the late '50s we had a special dinner guest. My mother was scurrying around getting the good china, polishing the silver, and setting the table in our dining room. It was the first time I ever recall that we would be using it for dinner rather than show. The guest that night was Joe Roush, one of Dad's friends from the 712th Tank Battalion. Joe lived in Oklahoma but was in New Orleans on business for several days.

At no time during the night did either Joe or my father talk about their war experiences. The closest thing discussed was Joe's desire to have a reunion of the soldiers from B Company of the 712th Tank Battalion and to regain contact with all of their Army buddies. In 1962, Joe eventually published an inaugural newsletter and began making plans for a reunion of B Company veterans in Milwaukee, scheduled for 1964.

Meanwhile as I entered my teens, my early childhood perceptions of war as a glamorous adventure were reinforced by the epic films of the 1960s. Although death was depicted, there was no blood or gore or agonizing death scenes in such films as *The Longest Day, The Guns of Navarone, Bridge on the River Kwai, The Great Escape, Von Ryan's Express, The Dirty Dozen,* and by TV programs, such as *Combat* and *The Gallant Men*. The entertainment industry further skewed baby boomers' perceptions of war by making comedies such as *McHale's Navy* and *Hogan's Heroes.*

I no longer needed to ask Dad anything about the war. After all, I had been granted the same omniscience granted to all teenagers; these films and TV series merely reinforced my misconceptions.

My high school years, from 1961 to 1965, coincided with the twentieth anniversary dates of America's involvement in World War II; it also marked the centennial of the Civil War. I continued my fascination with this era in American and Louisiana history. I drew a confederate flag on one of my notebooks with the initials CSA. Mom was mortified that I had adorned my notebook with such initials. She had not realized that I had intended the CSA to be an abbreviation of Confederate States of America. She explained that CSA was the initials for a derogatory name that the residents called our neighborhood. With its history of being dairy farms and housing cattle barns, many of the people living in our area referred to Brooklyn Avenue as Cow Shit Alley. That revelation tarnished the allure those initials had for me.

During the early '60s, there were no memorial tributes like today, I do not recall any specific news or media coverage of any of the World War II events, with perhaps the brief news announcements commemorating Pearl Harbor. Americans became fixated on space exploration and our newest heroes – the Astronauts. We looked to the future, not the past. I imagine Dad welcomed the respite from my juvenile questions about World War II.

I entered Jesuit High of New Orleans, which had the very first junior ROTC program in the country. The entire student body wore khaki uniforms in the early fall and late spring and winter Marine wool uniforms from December through March. Close order drill was substituted for physical education twice a week. The Jesuit priests believed close order drill was an important method of instilling discipline as well as an important method of teaching teens the leadership skills necessary for adult life. With Dad in the dry cleaning business, my uniforms had crisp military creases on a daily basis. Although Dad had given me some tips on drill, there was still never any discussions about his combat experience.

Then in November 1963 President John F. Kennedy was assassinated. The only reference to World War II that I recall from that period was Kennedy's heroics on PT 109 in the Pacific.

1964 marked the twentieth anniversary of D-Day. I was 17 years old and not particularly interested in hearing Dad's stories about World War II, after all, I had learned everything there was to know from the movies and TV during my early teens. In August of that year, my parents and I were traveling to Milwaukee for the first reunion of B Company of the 712th Tank Battalion. As boring as that may sound for a seventeen year old, I didn't mind going. Having only rarely traveled beyond 100 miles of New Orleans, this trip seemed adventurous and certainly the other veterans of the 712th would have kids my age. We traveled to and from Milwaukee by train. Despite being summer, the Milwaukee weather seemed cool to us thin blooded southerners from New Orleans.

Dad quickly renewed friendships with his old wartime comrades and Mom quickly formed new friendships with their wives. I do not recall the men talking of their war experiences during this reunion, instead they talked about what had transpired in their lives in the twenty years since the end of the war – their jobs and professions, their hobbies, and their families.

The younger generation kept to ourselves and were not interested in the Allied invasion of Europe. Our interest was in the British invasion of America… by the Beatles and the other British rock groups. After the reunion we traveled home again on the Illinois Central train that has since become legendary in song, 'City of New Orleans'.

Curiously, the most outstanding memory of this reunion, occurred one morning at breakfast in the diner in the Milwaukee train station. When I told the waitress I wanted an order of grits for breakfast, she said "Grits! What is that?" I had forgotten I was north of the Mason-Dixon line.

By 1965, Baby Boomers were entering college. In the fall of 1965, I enrolled in the School of Engineering at Tulane University. College life is a period of new found freedoms, and my generation pushed those freedoms to the limits. During the latter part of the 1960s, neither I nor probably any other early Baby Boomer had any interest in hearing about our parents' military experiences. Furthermore, having just completed four years of military style discipline and drill in high school, I wasn't interested in ROTC at Tulane, I declined all the recruiting overtures.

The second reunion for the 712th was scheduled for the summer of 1967 in New Orleans; this reunion included all of the 712th Tank Battalion veterans, not just B Company. Being in our hometown, Dad chaired the reunion. After the 1967 reunion the bonds of friendship that had been rekindled became even stronger, many of these veterans visited my parents in the succeeding years and vice versa. They were John and Rose Ockenga, from Ohio, the 712th cluster from Wisconsin – Bob and Arlone Kellner, Bob and Kathleen Gaulke, Al and Lucy Helland, Ted and Clara Ballman, Wally and June Kubert, Orin and Caren Bourdo. From other locales were Ed and Irene Swierczyk, Ziggy and Regina Kaminski, and Chester and Margaret Martin from Pennsylvania, Jim and Emma Armstrong and John and Gladys Essenburg from Michigan, Juel and Billye Winfrey from Oklahoma and Roy and Eva Bardo from Kansas City.

At the time of the 1967 reunion, I was going steady with my future wife, Cora. She came to the reunion and we both helped with the behind the scene details that an event like this requires, such as registration of attendees, making name tags, and the like. If any of these old army buddies were telling any war stories, I didn't hear them, Cora and I were only interested in spending time together.

By 1967, the conflict in Vietnam had grown significantly from a small amount of military advisors to over 365,000 American troops. Some of the children of World War II veterans were learning firsthand the reality of war. The rest of us witnessed the fighting taking place in Southeast Asia by extensive coverage of the war in the nightly newscast on TV. It was also a time when we Baby Boomers began to question authority, and protests began against the Vietnam conflict. While some from my generation were fighting and dying in Vietnam, others were protesting in the streets and on campuses across this county. For still others, like myself, the events of the era seemed to bypass us. Always conscious of the possibility of eventually being drafted, I received a student deferment from the draft and throughout my undergraduate studies concerns about Vietnam were avoided.

Tulane University was not immune to the anti-war protests, but they were relatively small and generally limited to a small group of students. The arch-conservative student body of the engineering schools generally paid little attention to these demonstrations as we were buried in our books.

The typical engineering student of the '60s had short hair, horned rim glasses, and carried a slide rule to class. Admittedly, I fit the stereotyped image of such an engineering student. The stress of studying was offset by my membership in Pi Kappa Alpha Fraternity. The global politics and the Vietnam war were not in the forefront of my daily concerns.

Cora and I married during the summer before my senior year in 1968. After graduation in May of 1969, I was employed as a mechanical engineer in a local chemical industry. Life was great and in October of 1969 my first son, Louie, was born.

Working as an engineer during the day, I attended Loyola Law School's evening division. My penchant for expanding my education was instilled within me at an early age by my father. He would always tell me, "It is easier to earn a living with your brain than it is to earn it with your brawn." I am sure his attitude was borne out of the educational opportunities denied to him as a youth.

When I eventually received a draft notice in early 1970, I went for my induction physical examination. During my physical, the doctor discovered a minor medical problem. I received a medical deferment and, consequently, any concerns I had about combat vanished. Furthermore, my second son, Cory, was born in 1970 and my thoughts were concentrated on my job and earning a living. I never had to give much thought about the reality of combat. My perception and opinion on war remained stagnated in the cinematic images of World War II that I acquired in my youth and were unaffected by the realities of the late 1960s and early 1970s in southeast Asia.

It was also around that time, the movie *Patton*, starring George C. Scott, was released. This is when I first learned from Dad that the 712th Tank Battalion was part of the Third Army under the command of Gen. George S. Patton Jr. Dad saw the movie and recalled many of the areas and the events that were depicted in the movie. But he still refrained from initiating any detailed discussion regarding his own personal wartime experiences.

During the scene involving Patton's prayer before the Battle of the Bulge, Dad said the prayer actually existed and copies of it were distributed to all members of the Third Army; Dad's copy was tucked away someplace in his box of memorabilia in his closet.

This film, like those produced in the 1940s, 1950s and 1960s had a patriotic theme, and had the effect of reinforcing many of my misconceptions of actual combat. This was a golden opportunity for me to learn more about Dad's wartime experiences, but I let it slip by. The rigors of working as an engineer during the day and attending law school at night made spare time a commodity that I could only spend on my own personal Paper Chase.[2]

In 1974, the 30th anniversary of D-Day, I had just finished law school and was about to embark on a legal career. The last thing on my mind during those days was to sit down with my father and discuss his war experiences. During this period, Dad joined and became active in the American Legion. It was also during this period that a then unknown professor from the University of New Orleans was soliciting World War II veterans in the New Orleans area for interviews regarding their experiences during the war. Dad declined these invitations to talk about the war, later stating that he did not want to tell a stranger the stories he had kept to himself for so long. The university professor was none other than Stephen E. Ambrose.

In 1982, Mom and Dad took a trip to Europe and visited many of the locations where Dad had been during the war. Although I would have enjoyed going on that the trip, such a vacation at that time was simply out of the question. I was employed as an Assistant Parish Attorney for Jefferson Parish, my daughter Rochelle, was born in 1976, and Cora was expecting our fourth child, David. Needless to say, I was busy with the affairs of my family.

During this trip Mom and Dad met Henri and Janet Levaufre in Périers, France. The 712th Tank Battalion had been attached to the 90th Infantry and both had fought in Périers during the war. Henri was only thirteen years old in 1944 and after the troops had left his town, he and his younger brother explored the battlefields around the town. As an adult, Henri had to again explore these fields in connection with his job in the power industry. He discovered many artifacts and began collecting them. He also became curious about the military engagements that had taken place all around his locale. He soon became an authoritative historian on these battles and the 90th Infantry Division that had fought in them. Henri and Janet have visited the United States frequently in the intervening years and during each visit they would come to New Orleans and spend a few days in the Gruntz household.

In 1984, my youngest child, Becky was born. That year also marked the 40th anniversary of D-Day. During the late 1980s, and especially after meeting Henri, Dad's shell began to crack and he was receptive to requests to discuss his wartime experiences. He became active in the American Legion and shared war stories with other veterans. Unfortunately, with everything going on in my life, I was not able to pursue the questions I had asked Dad as a child. Dad was ready to talk but I was not able to listen.

In 1985, the 712th Tank Battalion Association returned to New Orleans for another reunion. Clegg "Doc" Caffery of Franklin, Louisiana served as the host. My duties as an Assistant Parish Attorney prevented me from attending any of the formal functions, but I briefly attended an informal gathering of Dad's close friends at Mom and Dad's home after the reunion had ended. The number of Dad's friends who were present are too numerous to remember, but I recall Caffery being there, along with Lt-Col. Edward S. Hamilton (ret.) of the 357th Regiment of the 90th Infantry Division and Henri Levaufre and his wife Janet. Once again, an opportunity to question Dad about his war years slipped past me.

In 1994, my marriage of twenty-five years was ending in divorce. I attempted to avoid the emotional upheaval that divorce brings by pursing hobbies such as researching my family's genealogy.

My fascination in history, which began in my childhood, continued. My childhood questions of what, if any, role any of my ancestors may have played in historical events were rekindled. Were any of my ancestors, knights in shining armor, did the Gruntz family have a coat of arms, did anyone in my ancestral lineage participate in either the Revolutionary War or the Civil War? I took a course in genealogy at a community college and began tracing my Gruntz family ancestry back to the 1600s. In searching for interesting facts, details and tidbits about my ancestors, however, I had overlooked the most interesting ancestor of all, my father, who was a combatant in the largest conflict in the history of the world.

That year also happened to be the fiftieth anniversary of D-Day. In an effort to lift my spirits, Dad invited me on a trip to Europe to retrace his battle route and tell me about his experiences during the war on the sites where they occurred. Thus, the time had come at last when my boyhood questions regarding Dad's military service would be answered; Dad was ready to talk and I was ready, willing and able to listen.

Above and below: The journey begins.

CHAPTER 1

The Flight – Journey to the Past

One of the greatest joys known to man is to take a flight into ignorance in search of knowledge.

Robert Lynd (1892-1970)

June 6, 1944, was a day that changed the world. From the time the Nazis swept across the European Continent in 1939, the people in the occupied countries waited, hoped, and prayed for the day the Allies would come. D-Day was that day. The joy of liberation from the Nazis had not been dimmed by the passage of time and to mark the fiftieth anniversary of their liberation the French government planned memorial events throughout the year. On June 6, 1994, numerous ceremonies were planned at each of the five invasion landing beaches. Heads of State from the various Allied countries were invited; 45,000 American veterans were invited to the ceremonies at Omaha Beach alone. With all this hoopla, Dad was not interested in going to Europe in June with all of the crowds. Our trip was scheduled for October, 1994.

Neither was Dad interested in taking a tour, instead we booked our own flights to Paris and rented a car. Mom stayed at home, and was enthusiastic that Dad and I were traveling alone. I was forty-seven and Dad was seventy-five. This was the first time in our lives that we were going on a vacation together, just the two of us.

In preparation for our trip, one night several weeks before out departure, Dad retrieved the box of war memorabilia from the closet. I had remembered that box from my youth and it had been many years since I had seen it and perused its contents. Dad was looking for his copy of the History of B Company, of the 712th Tank Battalion, which listed not only the names and locations of the various battles but also the various villages where the B Company Headquarters (HQ) were established during the progress of the war. From this and Dad's memory of the events, we set our own itinerary and schedule.

Mom, Dad and I also looked through some of the photographs, particularly those taken while Dad was in training in 1943, when Mom had the opportunity to be with him. They both recounted times and places whose significance escaped me at that time but I would come to appreciate later.

The day of our departure arrived, our transatlantic flight lifted off in the evening light. We were flying from twilight into the dark night sky by the time we had reached the Atlantic Ocean, somewhere over Newfoundland. As we began crossing over Atlantic Ocean, Dad had remembered back sixty-seven years, when he was eight years old. He had a small crystal radio set; he listened to the news reports on that radio of Lindburgh's historic first solo flight across the Atlantic in 1927. Now, here we were, on a jumbo jet, making that same journey. Dad's recollection of that fact was my prompt to begin asking questions about his boyhood.

I asked Dad to tell me about his father, whom I never knew. I wanted to know what Dad's life was like as a boy, and to fill many of the blanks I had in our family's history. As he began his narrative, and throughout the next two weeks of our travel, he recalled the events of the 75 years of his life as if they had happened yesterday.

Dad was born on May 10, 1919, the second of three children and the only son of Louis Henry Gruntz and Mary Ellen Dwyer. My grandfather was a first generation American of Alsatian and German descent, my grandmother was a redheaded colleen, born in the Irish Channel neighborhood of New Orleans. Both the Gruntz family and the Dwyer family had a strong work ethic, a trait that my Dad had all of his life. He also inherited the stubbornness of his Gruntz Germanic ancestry, the quick temper and sharp tongue of his Dwyer Irish heritage.

In the early 1900s, the area of New Orleans known as the Irish Channel was divided into two distinct ethnic neighborhoods – the residents of Irish descent in one and the German-speaking immigrants and their descendants in the other. Although both of these groups were predominately Roman Catholic, each had their own church. St Mary's Assumption Catholic Church on Josephine Street ministered to the German speaking community. Around the corner on Constance Street, St Alphonsus Church ministered to the Irish Catholics. Both of my ancestral families had deep rooted religious beliefs and their respective Catholic churches were the focal points of their lives. The melting pot of foreign immigrants that was New Orleans in the late 1800s and early 1900s and the proximity of these churches and neighborhoods explains my family's mixed heritage.

It seems our family had very little originality in naming the male members in my lineage. Dad's paternal grandfather, also named Louis Gruntz, owned a tract of land in the rural environs of New Orleans known as Metairie where he operated a dairy farm. Dad's grandmother, Emma Ohr Gruntz, was the sister of the renowned potter of that era, George Ohr, the Mad Potter of Biloxi. She did not care for the country life and the family also maintained a home in the city.

Dad's father was an artist who earned a living as a sign painter. In 1921, when Dad was two years old, the younger Gruntz Family moved to rural Metairie, near the site of Dad's grandfather's old dairy farm. It was in Metairie that Dad and his older sister Alma and younger sister Emily lived until adulthood. As a young boy, Dad had fun exploring and hunting for small animals in the wooded areas near his home with the other boys that lived nearby.

Dad's idyllic childhood, however, was cut short. In 1925, when Dad was six years old, my grandfather was committed to a mental institution after suffering a severe mental breakdown. I had a general knowledge of this aspect of our family history but it wasn't until I asked Dad about his childhood during our flight that I learned a great deal more. He and I spoke at length about his childhood and his memory of his father.

Treatment for the mentally ill was abysmally poor during that era. In those days the principal state mental health facility was located in Jackson, Louisiana, about 110 miles from New Orleans. Dad had few opportunities to see his father after my grandfather's hospitalization; automobile travel in America and particularly Louisiana during the 1920s was challenging to say the least. One newspaper article of that day described both situations:

> The highway system was a series of muddy lanes with antique ferries and narrow bridges with high toll charges. [...] Families north of New Orleans were forced to pay an $8 toll to cross Lake Pontchartrain into New Orleans and return.
>
> State institutions constituted a disgrace. The insane were strapped, put into stocks and beaten.[1]

Dad vividly remembered the few visits he had with his father. Dad's uncle, William Dwyer Jr., brought him, his mother and two sisters to visit his father at the mental hospital. He remembered an all-day drive over hot and dusty gravel roads in the backseat of a Model A Ford to get to the hospital in Jackson.

Dad looked forward to this visit for some time, and when they arrived they were kept waiting in the visiting area. When his father eventually came out, Dad was taken aback by my grandfather's appearance. My grandfather's clothes were disheveled and he was unshaven and sporting a beard stubble of several days. He was not the alert and energetic father that Dad had remembered. Although he was happy to see his family, my grandfather was sluggish and apparently under medication.

On the way home from the hospital, Dad tearfully wished he could personally care for his father; he desperately wanted to be old enough to remove him from that wretched place and bring him back home to New Orleans. But such was not to be, my grandfather never returned home and he died in the mental hospital after several years of confinement. I could tell by the crackle in Dad's voice, in relating this story, how this experience deeply affected him. I realized how much he had missed having a father as he was growing up, and how lucky I was to have Dad during my youth.

With the loss of my grandfather's income, my grandmother, Mary Dwyer Gruntz, was forced to obtain employment to raise Dad and his two sisters. In order to save on household expenses, my grandmother joined households with her parents, William and Delia Dwyer. They all lived as one family in Metairie. Grandma Dwyer cared for the children while Dad's mother was at work.

While living with his grandmother, Dad experienced his first taste of battle. Dad attended Ella Dolhonde Elementary School, about two blocks from his home. There was no school lunch program at that time; the children who lived near school went home for lunch, others brought their lunch to school. Dad went home every day and Grandma Dwyer fixed lunch for him and his two sisters. One day, on his way home for lunch, two bullies jumped Dad and administered a pretty fair beating. Dad ran home crying. As an adult, Dad stood 5 foot 4 inches tall; naturally, as a boy he was small in stature, which prompted the larger bullies to think he was easy prey.

Grandma Dwyer was a tough first generation Irish American. She fixed Dad's lunch, but, as Dad was leaving to return to school, she scolded him for running away from the bullies. She told Dad to go back and take care of those two hooligans; if he didn't, she was going to give him a whipping when he came home from school that afternoon.

Armed with that warning, Dad located the two bullies. He attacked the most aggressive of the two first. As soon as he did, the other kid ran away. Dad meted out the appropriate retribution on the first bully and when he was finished, he searched for the second one. A short while later he found the second bully and the schoolyard justice was complete. Dad learned his first important tactic of warfare that afternoon – divide and conquer.

The combined Gruntz-Dwyer households experienced another misfortune after only a few years, Grandma Dwyer died in 1928. That family loss, coupled with the onset of the Great Depression in 1929, caused the Gruntz family struggles to continue. My grandmother found employment as a nurse's aide in Charity Hospital in downtown New Orleans. Her elderly father, William Dwyer Sr., cared for her children while she was at work. Although there was little money, the back and side yards of their home were sufficient to provide a family garden and to raise a few chickens which kept enough food on the table during those tough economic times. Grandpa Dwyer, a retired carpenter, also did a few odd jobs to supplant the family funds.

As Dad continued the stories of his boyhood, I was learning that he had been a bit of rapscallion. As a boy, he had a tendency to get into mischief, sometimes with injurious consequences. Laughingly, Dad told me that one day, while playing with friends, he called another kid a derogatory name. The other kid got angry and, "He then chased me into the street and I got hit by a Model T Ford." On another occasion Dad was a bit rambunctious while playing in a tree. He lost his grip, fell out of the tree and broke his arm. Since that day, he has had a fear of heights.

Dad's neighborhood in Metairie was bordered on the north by Lake Pontchartrain and on the south by the Mississippi River. Being not far from the Mississippi River, most of the boys in the area would hike to the river during the summer months. Dad, as well as the other boys, were forbidden to go swimming in the Mississippi River because the dangerous currents caused many drownings. Despite this, on several occasions, Dad went swimming in the Mississippi River. Swimming in Lake Pontchartrain was a little safer, but it was a longer walk. Dad recounted. "We walked to the lake to go swimming and usually brought our lunch along with a bottle of milk. But with the summer heat, by the time we reached the lake, the milk was sour." Hence the choice for choosing the river as a swimming hole.

Many times on their journey to the Mississippi River, the route brought the boys near the Colonial Country Club, and on several occasions they sought jobs as caddies. Dad would earn 65 cents for caddying a round of golf.

In 1934, when Dad was fifteen years old, tragedy once again befell the household. On Saturday, September 8, my grandmother left home around 6:00 a.m. for her job as a nurse's aide at Charity Hospital in New Orleans. Shortly after her shift began, she was summoned to the emergency room to assist with a gunshot victim. Upon entering the treatment area, she was horrified to learn that the victim was her sister, Alma. The shock only deepened as she began to learn the details of the happenings of that morning.

Dad's Aunt Alma and her husband, Willie, had a marital dispute earlier in the week and Alma and her three children spent several days at my grandmother's home. Shortly after my grandmother left for work that morning, Willie came to the Gruntz household to talk to Alma and attempt a reconciliation.

Alma arose and prepared a pot of coffee and the husband and wife talked for several minutes. After a few moments, Willie pulled a pistol out of his pocket, shot Alma and then turned the gun on himself. He died instantly. Grandpa Dwyer hurried to the kitchen to investigate the disturbance and discovered his gravely wounded daughter and his son-in-law dead on the floor. Grandpa Dwyer ran out of the house and hailed a passing motorist and brought Alma, who was wounded in the neck, to the hospital. The wound, however, was mortal and she died in the operating room.

Alma and Willie's three small children – ages nine, seven, and four – who were in the adjoining bedroom during the entire horrific event were now fatherless and motherless. Grandpa Dwyer refused to allow his three young grandchildren to be placed in an orphanage – he obtained legal custody and along with my grandmother took them into their home. Mary Dwyer Gruntz raised her niece and two nephews as her own children. The cousins, William 'Brother', Shirley Mae, and Alvin became younger brothers and sister to Dad and his two sisters.

The tragic events of that day turned out to be a pivotal point in Dad's life.

Cpl Gruntz's grandfather and mother, William Dwyer and Mary Dwyer Gruntz. (*Author's collection*)

With my grandmother having a household of eight people, Dad's adolescence was abruptly ended. He quit school and become an additional bread winner to supplement the family's meager income during the height of the Great Depression.

Dad's first steady job was that of a newsboy selling newspapers at the Jefferson Racetrack. Selling the morning newspaper required an early rise and shine. While walking through the racetrack's stable area, the barns would be pitch black. As he went through and yelled "Newspaper!", one by one, the trainers and horse handlers would light a lantern and come out and buy a paper. The winner of the previous day's race, whose name was in the headlines would usually pay Dad one dollar for the paper and tell Dad to keep the change as a tip. Dad said he usually made fourteen dollars per week as a newsboy. Although these earnings seem paltry by today's standards, Dad's earnings as a newsboy exceeded the income of many grown men who had fallen upon hard times during the Depression.[2]

Each morning, on the way to the racetrack with his stack of newspapers, Dad had to pass a gas station, owned by Mr Stanley. Mr Stanley lived on Severn Avenue near Dad's house and knew Dad from the neighborhood. One morning, about 3 a.m., as Dad was passing the station, everything was wide open. The station had been burglarized. Dad ran to Mr Stanley's house to awaken him and tell him of the robbery. This act by Dad did not go unrewarded.

The daily newspaper that Dad sold once ran a contest for its paper carriers. The prize was a seven day cruise to Central America, Belize and Honduras. Dad was one of eight carriers that won the trip. Stanley gave Dad $20.00 to spend on his trip. Dad had very little money to take with him and he very much appreciated the $20.00 gift. Dad spent much Mr Stanley's largesse on a rare luxury – new clothes for himself. He bought new silk shirts for $1.00 each.

As Dad grew older, his job selling newspapers at the racetrack led to other employment. He worked with the horse trainers and exercised the horses. Dad's height of 5 foot 4 inches made him a little too tall to become a jockey. With all the sordid characters that hung around racetracks in the 1930s, my grandmother was not very happy with this line of work. Rather than face the wrath of his Irish mother, Dad soon sought other employment.

1940 found Dad employed at a local factory that made corrugated cardboard boxes earning $0.35 per hour, and working nights as a bartender at Gennaro's Bar and Restaurant in Metairie. The owner's son was Peter Gennaro, one of Dad's friends.

In early 1941, Dad boasted to his family and friends how he was going to remain a bachelor, "The girl I'm going to marry isn't born yet, and her mother is dead." His status as a confirmed bachelor did not last very long. In May of 1941 he attended a dance, he noticed Audrey Casteix, a slender brunette about three years younger than him across the dance floor. Both worked at the box manufacturing factory and they had seen each other during work but were never formally introduced.

I recalled Mom telling me how she and Dad met. Mom was dating another fellow at the time and attended the dance with him. Mom was sitting with some other girls when she saw Dad approaching the group. She thought to herself, "I sure hope he asks me to dance." He did and after the dance, Dad asked if he could bring her home. Mom, however said no, she came with a date and was obligated to have him bring her. Dad asked if he could see her the following Sunday. Mom already had a date with the other fellow for that Sunday evening. Dad, however, was persistent, and Mom tentatively agreed to their first date that Sunday afternoon, provided she received parental permission.

After securing permission to see this brash new boy, Mom saw him at work and confirmed the date. Dad arrived for Mom early that Sunday afternoon. When the afternoon was drawing to a close, Mom really didn't want to end the date, but she had made a commitment and didn't want to break it. When it was time to bring Mom home, mindful of the fact that she was going out with the other fellow that night, Dad said jealously, "I hope it rains all night long." Shortly after Dad brought Mom home, the skies opened up with one of those typical New Orleans summer deluges. The streets flooded and her date for that night was cancelled. Mom and Dad dated only each other after that.

Mom and Dad often double dated with Dad's friend, Peter Gennaro. Peter

Bride and Groom with parents of the Bride. (*Author's collection*)

was the life of the party and a remarkable dancer. In the 1950s and 1960s, Peter gained fame as a Broadway and Hollywood dancer and choreographer, winning a Tony Award in 1977. But in that summer of 1941, as twenty-two year olds, there were all carefree kids.

By the end of summer, Dad popped the big question and on September 7, 1941, Mom's nineteenth birthday, she received an engagement ring. They immediately began plans for a spring wedding. Little did they realize that exactly three months later, on December 7, 1941, world events would impact their lives and the lives of millions of other Americans.

Despite America's entrance into World War II, my parents proceeded with their wedding plans and were married on May 10, 1942. In addition to being their wedding day, it also happened to be Dad's twenty-third birthday. The bride and groom danced their first dance to the strains of "I'll Be With You in Apple Blossom Time", the popular song recorded by the Andrew Sisters in 1941.

Prior to the wedding, Dad spent several months constructing an additional bedroom on the Gruntz family home on Bauvais Street in Metairie and the newlyweds moved in after a short honeymoon. With the number of residents now totaling nine, Dad's paycheck was important for the household. After December 7, 1941, the defense industries began to blossom in the New Orleans area. Dad sought higher-paying employment at Delta Shipyards earning $1.00 per hour.

Mom and Dad entered marriage with the same hopes and dreams of all newlyweds. Even though Dad was now married, my grandmother had been under the belief that Dad, as the oldest male wage earner in the family, would be considered head of the household and, therefore, not be susceptible to the military draft.[3] But, my grandmother's hopes to have her only son remain out of harm's way were soon dashed and Mom and Dad's "Apple Blossom Time" was short-lived. Six months and one day after the wedding, Dad received his Order to Report for Induction into the United States Army. His induction notice was dated November 11, 1942, the twenty-fourth anniversary of the Armistice of World War I, which prior to then had been characterized as "the war to end all wars".

Mom got the impression that my grandmother began to regret that the wedding proceeded so soon after the start of the war. My grandmother was convinced that the members of the local draft board took notice of Dad's change in family status after the wedding announcement appeared in the newspaper and was announced in church. Instead of being the head of a household of eight people, he was now considered merely a young husband with only his wife as a dependent and who was capable of entering the armed forces.

The family income suffered a severe reduction with Dad's entry into the Army. Plans were made for Mom to move back home to her parents; several days prior to leaving for the service, Dad moved Mom, her belongings, and their bedroom set back to the Casteix home on Brooklyn Ave.

With both Dad and Mom leaving, the crowded living quarters on Bauvais Street were becoming relatively spacious. Dad said, "Brother Felder couldn't wait for us to get out so he could get the bedroom. I gave him my car too. I owed money on it so I told him to take it over and make payments, he could have it. A blue Chevrolet. I was a big dog going to get your Momma in that beautiful blue Chevrolet."

On November 28, 1942, Dad left on a train bound for Camp Claiborne near Alexandria, Louisiana. Dad's cousin, Bill Dwyer, drove Mom and Dad to the train station, for them to say their last goodbyes before Dad officially entered the service. As the train left the station to travel west, Bill and Mom jumped in Bill's car and drove along Airline Highway, which ran adjacent to the railroad tracks. Bill tried to keep pace with the train for as long as he could, while Dad waved to Mom from the train window, and Mom, with tears streaming from her eyes, waved to Dad from the car window.

Upon arrival at camp, the induction personnel took notice of not only Dad's horse riding skills but also his employment background – operating machinery at the box factory. The Army determined that he was an excellent candidate for training at Fort Benning, Georgia, where the horse cavalry units were being converted into mechanized units and trained in tank warfare. Two days after his induction, Dad was again on a train leaving Louisiana and on his way to Fort Benning, Georgia for tank training.

CHAPTER 2

Training for War

If I had eight hours to chop down a tree, I'd spend six sharpening the axe.

Abraham Lincoln

The guns of World War I were silent a mere twenty-one years when war once again erupted in Europe as Germany invaded Poland in September, 1939.

At the outset of this new European conflict, a vast majority of Americans opposed becoming involved in another European war.[1] Following World War I, the United States had again turned to isolationism. The United States' military budget dwindled and by 1939 the US Army was only the eighteenth largest in the world.

Between September 1939 and December 1941, England was alone in the fight against Nazi Germany. Although the United States was technically a neutral country, it aligned itself with Great Britain. Emerging from the grip of the Great Depression, American industry turned to the production of war materials and began furnishing supplies, materials, and weapons to the British under the Lend Lease Program. President Franklin Roosevelt referred to the United States as the Arsenal of Democracy.

Although the public sentiment was against war, military leaders saw the war clouds on the horizon and fully believed that the United States would eventually be drawn into the war in Europe. Preparation and transformation of the military was needed. The daunting task of transforming the small US Army of 1939 into an army capable of fighting and defeating Nazi Germany fell to Gen. George C. Marshall, the US Army Chief of Staff. Marshall and a small cadre of military officials were the only experts capable of determining the size of the military needed, the number of divisions, the number and type of weaponry, and developing the logistics needed to implement it.[2]

A massive reorganization of the US Army took place in early 1942, in the months before Dad entered the service. The War Department grouped units of the Army into three main elements. The Army Ground Forces (AGF), under the command of Maj.-Gen. Lesley McNair, was responsible for combat training. The Army Air Forces (AAF) directed the aviation segment. The Army Service Force (ASF) looked after supplies and supporting services.[3] The Allied Powers of the United States, Great Britain and the Soviet Union were committed to the defeat of the Axis Powers – Nazi Germany, Japan and Italy.

Both before and after Japan attacked Pearl Harbor, Allied plans called for the defeat of Germany first and then Japan. Stephen Ambrose wrote that Marshall "created the US Army of World War II with a campaign in Northwest Europe in mind. He had designed the Army to take on the Wehrmacht in France, to defeat it in battle, to drive it out of France and destroy it in the process."[4] But, in early 1942, it had been determined that it would take no less than one year to assemble the manpower necessary to accomplish this. To convert the Army's horse cavalry units into mechanized armored divisions and create new infantry divisions by transforming civilian recruits into a fighting force would take at least a year of training. The initial assessment indicated a European invasion could not begin before 1943.

America's entrance into the war on two fronts, the Pacific and Europe, also highlighted the severe shortage of ships large enough to transport troops and supplies and supporting units to both combat theaters. This was a prime factor for further delaying the invasion of Europe until 1944. To alleviate the shipping problem, all military units were directed to eliminate unnecessary vehicles and excess noncombatants.

Army officials recognized that the manpower pool in America was not limitless. Recruiting and drafting too many able bodied men from the industrial and farming sectors in the United States would adversely impact the production of needed supplies. Therefore, only eighty-nine of the originally envisioned 213 divisions were created. The relatively small US Army of 1939 would grow from 400,000 to over 8 million for the European Campaign.[5] Manpower shortage was partially alleviated by American females entering the workforce.

The logistic problems of shipping coupled with the timetable established for an invasion in Europe, forced the Army to abandoned the traditional practice of every unit bringing all of its equipment and supplies with it when it moved, particularly into battle. A different approach was utilized, in order to expedite the build-up of Allied Forces in England. In 1942 and 1943, while training of the various units was being conducted in the US, all the equipment, guns, tanks, trucks, and so on, being manufactured in the US were shipped to and stored in England. When the troops arrived in England in the months and weeks before D-Day, their training equipment was left behind in the states and the troops were issued all the new equipment that had been stockpiled in England.

The progenitor of the 712th Tank Battalion was the 11th Cavalry. On December 7, 1941, the 11th Cavalry was stationed at Camp Morena and

```
                    TRIP PASS
                 ENLISTED MAN'S PASS
     Gruntz, Louis G         Pvt           38373076
     ----------------------  -----------   ---------------
           (Name)            (Grade)       (Army serial No.)
     is authorized to be absent from his post—

     From ____1800 Daily_____

     To   ____0700 Daily_____

     To visit _Columbus, Ga._____

     Signed  William C Riley       Capt. Cav.
                                   Company commander
                          (OVER)
                 This Pass Expires April 30, 1943
```

These pages: Dad's Pass. (*Author's collection*)

Camp Seeley, California near San Diego. In June of 1942, in accordance with Army reorganization, the men of the 11th Cavalry transferred to Fort Benning, Georgia. On July 15, 1942, the 11th Cavalry was inactivated as a horse mounted unit, all personnel and equipment were transferred to the 11th Armored Regiment, a new vacant regiment constituted on July 11. The 11th Armored Regiment was assigned to the 10th Armored Division, which also had been activated on July 15.

The 10th Armored Division was nicknamed the *Tiger Division* by Maj.-Gen. Paul Newgarden, the division's first commander. The nickname was picked because a tiger has soldierly qualities, including being clean and neat and the ability to maneuver and surprise his prey.

Upon arrival at Fort Benning in November of 1942, Pvt. Louis Gruntz was assigned to Company H of the 11th Armored Regiment, of the 10th Armored Division.

From November 28, 1942, the day Dad left for boot camp, Mom, now back with her parents at the Casteix household, cried every day that Dad was gone. Dad learned that married men were allowed to live with their wives in housing off base. At Christmas time, Dad called Mom and told her to come to Columbus, Georgia.

Mom caught a train for Georgia on Christmas Day. My maternal grandmother, Gertrude Casteix, spent all of Christmas morning ironing

In accepting this pass, I understand that—
1. I am a soldier at all times and subject to both civil and military control.
2. I must be temperate and not do anything in public to disgrace myself or the Army.
3. I must be polite to all people I meet, whether they are in uniform or civilian clothes.
4. A pass is a privilege, and I may not get another one if I do not conduct myself properly.

I have read the above rules of conduct and will obey them.

(Signature)

W. D., A. G. O. Form No. 7
September 8, 1942

☆   GPO   16—30563-1

cotton dresses. This was Mom's first trip away from home, but remarkably my grandmother was not upset with her youngest daughter moving out of town. My grandmother said that she never thought that she would be so happy putting her daughter on a train on Christmas Day. Now she would not have to listen to that crying all day long.

Columbus, Georgia – Fort Benning

After Mom arrived in Columbus, Georgia, Mom and Dad rented a room in a boarding house at 810 Third Avenue. Because he was married, Dad was given a daily pass to leave the base each night, provided he was back the next morning for reveille.

Dad would ride the city bus to and from camp each morning and night. One day, one of the recruits developed measles and the whole barracks was quarantined. Dad pleaded with the sergeant to let him leave, "My wife just got in town," he said. "I can't leave her alone like that." The sergeant gave Dad the OK, but told Dad not to get caught. That night, Dad boarded the bus and sat toward the rear. A few minutes later, as luck would have it, the commander that issued the quarantine order entered the bus on his way home. Dad crouched down in his seat as far as he could without looking suspicious and prayed that the commander would not notice him. Fortunately, the commander's bus stop was before Dad's and he exited the bus without noticing Dad.

When several of the men noticed Dad had the opportunity to leave base every night because he was married, they soon questioned him about it. They had fiancées back home and wanted to get married and bring their wives near the base.

While in the Army, Dad became very good friends with Sgt John R. (Richard) Williams. Although Dad was three years older than Richard, Richard out ranked Dad. Richard was born in 1922 and had enlisted in the Army on July 10, 1940, shortly after his eighteenth birthday.

"I think plenty of the guys in the outfit thought I was a Chaplain or something because they confided in me," Dad said. "Richard was a good friend of mine. He used to confide in me; he wanted to go home to Kentucky and get married (to Opal Rodgers)." Richard asked Dad what he thought about the idea. Dad encouraged him. "Richard came to me and said 'How do you do it Louie, how do you get a place to stay? I want to bring Opal back with me.' I said, 'OK, come on back and you can get one (an apartment) right around me.' He went home (on a furlough) and got married and he brought Opal back with him."

Mom, Dad, Richard and Opal were the best of friends while they lived in Columbus, Georgia, when Dad and Richard were training at Fort Benning. That friendship continued when the battalion was transferred to Fort Jackson in Columbia, South Carolina. Opal and Mom remained friends for many years after the war; they corresponded by mail and Aunt Opal came to our house in Louisiana on several occasions.[6]

After several months of marriage in 1943, however, Richard and Opal, started having marital difficulties, as Dad explained, "Opal loved him, but she enjoyed making him jealous. Which was the wrong thing to do and that made them fight with one another. He loved her and she loved him." But, they separated during training and although they reconciled briefly before the troops shipped overseas, their marriage was still rocky.

Dad mentioned that while he was in training during the day, Mom found employment. When he recounted this fact, I remembered the conversation the three of us had, while looking through photographs a few days before Dad and I departed for Paris. Mom remembered her employment during 1943. "I worked most of the time, I worked a good while. I worked at Tom's Peanuts in Columbus, Georgia. I used to catch the bus early in the morning, it was pitch black, I wasn't scared. Now, I would die but you could do those things then."

I asked both of them to describe living in a strange town without any other family members around. Dad said, "That was a romantic time of our lives – traveling." But there was little money to do any entertaining. "I used to get $66 per month from the Army. But I had to pay room and board. Mom worked and she got a few bucks. We went to the movies and took walks."

Above: Louis, Opal and Richard. (*Author's collection*)

Right: Louis, Audrey and Richard. (*Author's collection*)

Mom added, "We went to the show, we went for walks. We didn't have any money. My Grandpa died on March 1 (1943), my mother didn't have any money to send me train fare to come home for the funeral. She said don't worry about it." Mom's grandfather was buried while she remained in Georgia.

"It was cold." she explained, "I stayed in a cold apartment one day. Dad had to borrow money to buy some kerosene for the heaters and lamps. And then I got sick and had to quit (my job). It was a hard life."

Dad sighed, "I always regret – they (the Army) made a picture of H Co. and sold it for $1 but I never bought one I didn't have the money. We could live for a day on $1."

When I asked Dad about boot camp, he related one of the first lessons he learned – Never Volunteer! "They told you when you get in the Army, never volunteer. Once there was a group of soldiers gathered and the sergeant asked 'Who knows how to drive?' Three or four raised their hands. The sergeant then said, 'Ok you, you and you, drive those wheelbarrows over there and pick up that dirt.'"

During basic training, although Dad spent the nights with Mom in the boarding house in town, he still had a bunk space in the barracks at camp. "We had about thirty guys in one barracks together. I had to be in there each morning for inspection and in the daytime if I had to go in there for something." Ed Swierczyk, Richard Grable, Clifton Booth, and Floyd McBride were friends with Dad. "We were in the barracks together, these guys bunked right next to me." McBride was the oldest guy in the outfit, he was forty-two years old when he was drafted.

In addition to being a primary base for tank training, Fort Benning was also a primary base for training paratroopers. The tankers, however, considered themselves the toughest soldiers in camp. It was not unusual for the troops who got passes on Saturday nights to often seek liquid refreshments. After too many of these beverages, a few soldiers would occasionally become embroiled in fisticuffs. Dad said that the officers counseled the tank crews about such situations and advised them, "If you see two paratroopers fighting with one tanker don't get involved, it's an even fight."

Dad trained in Company H throughout his period at Fort Benning and on June 14, 1943, was promoted to the rank of corporal.

Shortly after Dad's promotion, after approximately seven months of training, the entire 10th Armored Division went on maneuvers in Tennessee under the command of the Second Army. During the period of the maneuvers, from June 24, 1943, to September 2, 1943, Dad's unit was still Co. H, 11th Armored Regiment of the 10th Armored Division. As Dad explained, "We were at Fort Benning first and we were there a good while, all through basic training and then we went on maneuvers in Tennessee."

Prior to leaving for Tennessee, Dad received a furlough for a few days. The wives were not able to accompany the troops while they were in Tennessee, consequently Mom and Dad scraped up enough money to come back home to New Orleans for Dad's furlough. Mom would stay home during this period in order to undergo surgery to have her tonsils removed. She planned on rejoining Dad when the unit returned to Fort Benning at the conclusion of the maneuvers.

In 1942 and 1943 reports were circulating throughout New Orleans of German U-Boats patrolling the Gulf of Mexico near the mouth of the Mississippi River and sinking many Merchant Marine vessels.[7] These news reports also fueled an atmosphere of suspicion and speculation that coastal residents and fishermen were aiding the U-boats with shipping information or supplies.

While Dad was home on furlough, his friends told him that Mr Stanley, the service station operator that had befriended Dad when he was a newsboy, was no longer operating the service station near Dad's boyhood home. His sudden and unexplained absence from the neighborhood fueled the gossip that he was a Nazi collaborator or spy.

When Dad heard this news he recalled how Mr Stanley had always acted strangely, he never trusted anyone. He remembers being in a nearby café when Mr Stanley ordered a ham and cheese sandwich. He wanted it without any mayonnaise or butter, just plain and dry. When he received the sandwich, he took all the ham and cheese off and examined each piece to make sure no one had tampered with it.

Although there were no confirmed reports of any such Nazi agents in southeast Louisiana, rumors of Nazi spies and saboteurs in the southeast Louisiana persisted. Dad was never sure if the rumors about his old benefactor were true, but his recollections of Mr Stanley's idiosyncrasies and paranoid tendencies definitely added credence to the scuttlebutt.

"Somewhere in Tennessee" – Maneuvers

Maneuvers were war games in which the various military units participated in mock battles. Dad explained, "We had red and blue teams." These teams engaged in mock combat to review and test training methods and the proficiency of the commanders and the troops. Senior Army officials served as umpires, they measured and graded the performance of participating units. The hilly farmland of Tennessee was chosen because of its similarity to the terrain American forces would encounter in France. To achieve realistic combat conditions in these simulated engagements, the military units traveled across the countryside and farm fields of Tennessee the same as they would during actual battle.

Dad said that these simulated battles did not always sit well with the local citizenry, "The farmers had stone fences made of slate. When the tanks hit those fences, stones went flying everywhere. The farmers would come out raising forty kinds of hell. We told them, 'Call your governor, the government will pay for it.'"

Maneuvers were, in fact, intended to reveal all aspects of actual combat, including mechanical breakdowns in the equipment. "If the tank broke down we stayed wherever the tank broke down until somebody came around to fix it. When we broke down they just left us there because they were going on with the maneuvers. Two of us stayed with the tank. They came back later and rounded up the stragglers."

Dad's tank broke down near Alexandria, Tennessee, close to the farmhouse of Walter Reeves. Dad fondly remembered the Reeves' eight-year-old son, Joe Mack, and the days he spent on Reeves farm. "We stayed by this ... house about three or four days. (Reeves) had about eleven cows and he had two kids, him and his wife. Every morning and every evening he milked those cows. He had those five gallon (milk) cans; he'd take the cans and drop them down in the well. The well kept the milk cold. The next morning he'd pull the cans up from the well and carry them down the hill to the road and put on the side of the road for the dairy truck to come by and pick them up. That's what he made his living off of."

Little Joe Mack was fascinated by all of the military equipment and soldiers conducting maneuvers near his home. During those few days, Joe Mack befriended Dad. Dad reciprocated and let Joe Mack get inside the tank and showed him how everything worked. Dad gave him his C-rations and other small items. Joe Mack was exuberant with all the Army souvenirs. After the tanks were repaired and moved on with the maneuvers, Joe Mack wrote Dad several letters and sent pictures. Dad responded a few times before he was shipped overseas to Europe. Unfortunately, while being transported overseas he lost Joe Mack's address and never communicated with him again. Dad still had the two pictures of Joe Mack in his box of mementos. He often wondered what had become of little Joe Mack.

While on maneuvers, the Army supplied everything the soldiers needed in the field; they instructed the troops not to buy anything in the local stores because the stock in the stores was low due to the war and the goods were being rationed to the local citizens. These shortages, however, did not dampen the southern hospitality of the Tennessee farmers, who often treated soldiers to home cooked meals.

"Another time our tank broke down outside of Murfreesboro, Tennessee. We were stuck there for several days. They left us behind and we didn't see anyone else in the Army, they all went on to another location. The people on that area were real nice, they brought food every day, like fried chicken. They brought us fresh milk every day. Harold Slayton was in the tank with me and every time he drank that fresh milk he'd get the shits; he would grab the

Joe Mack Reeves. (*Author's collection*)

shovel and go run into the woods."

In an article published in the *Tigers' Tale*, the 10th Armored Division's Newspaper, a soldier described the conditions on maneuvers in a dense forest "Somewhere in Tennessee".

During tactical operations the troops were not allowed to have tents up during the day and at night had to operate in total blackout. Such conditions made it necessary to put tents up after dark with only the sense of touch to guide. "It is fairly easy to pick out an area which is not covered with underbrush or blackberry vines, but not always easy to see just what we are getting into. We'll never forget the night we picked a cozy little place, which had a nice carpeting of 'something' to protect us from the hard ground, and awoke the next morning to find we had spent the night in a growth of poison ivy under which reposed a neat little ant hill. However, the ant bites and a slight case of poison ivy which resulted didn't bother as much as we could hardly distinguish these from the chigger and mosquito bites which already covered large areas of our body."[8]

Sherman Tank. (*Company B photograph*)

Les Vink and Louis Gruntz. (*Company B photograph*)

Sgts Les Vink, Warren Willinger and Orin Bourdo. (*Company B photograph*)

Top L-R: Les Vink, Warren Willinger, Orin Bourdo, unknown, Ed Swierzyck. *Bottom:* Roy Bardo, unknown. (*Company B photograph*)

Above: Company "H" 11th Armored Regiment, 10th Armored Division. Eighteen months after Dad passed away, I learned that Eva Bardo had discovered a copy of the Company "H" photograph among the belongings of her late husband, Roy Bardo. Eva graciously sent me a copy. (*Company B photograph*)

Left: Louis and Audrey. (*Author's collection*)

Augusta, Georgia – Camp Gordon

After the completion of the Tennessee maneuvers, the 10th Armored Division was transferred to Camp Gordon, outside of Augusta, Georgia, where training continued. Mom rejoined Dad in Augusta where they again found a room in a boarding house.

The 10th Armored Division, activated in July of 1942, was among the several established at the beginning of the war. The establishment of these new armored units was accomplished by converting the horse mounted cavalry force to armor. The old cavalry organization structure followed through to the new armored divisions.

Sherman tanks manned by Americans first entered the war in Tunisia, North Africa with disastrous results. Between Christmas 1942 and February 1943 over 110 Sherman tanks were wiped out by enemy forces. The debacle, involving elements of the 1st and 2nd Armored Divisions in North Africa, pointed out many command and organizational problems with maintaining the old cavalry organizational framework; the new armored divisions had an excess of tank personnel and too few supporting infantry forces.

Consequently, in September 1943, the War Department adopted Gen. McNair's recommended revised organizational structure for armored divisions. Three tank and armored infantry battalions in the armored division replaced the regimental structure of the old cavalry. Each tank battalion included one light and three medium tank companies, also included was a service company to perform maintenance. These new service companies replaced the former regimental headquarters and service units.

This move fit in with Gen. McNair's pooling theory, which was adjunct to his theory on streamlining, wherein battalion size units of field artillery, engineers, tanks, tank destroyers, and other forces were planned to be used by the corps level commanders and attached to various combat divisions on an as needed basis. The tank companies sliced off of the old regiments after this reorganization were allocated into separate and independent battalions to be attached to infantry divisions when needed.

712th Tank Battalion Activated

As a result, on September 20, 1943, less than 3 weeks after arriving at Camp Gordon, the 712th Tank Battalion officially came into existence, as one of these independent battalions. It was formed out of the 3rd Squadron of the old 11th Cavalry (3rd Battalion of the 11th Armored Regiment). By General Orders No. 18 of the 10th Armored Division, the following companies of the 11th Armored Regiment were re-designated:

Old Designation	**New Designation**
HQ Company, 3rd Battalion, 11th Armored Regiment	HQ Company, 712th Tank Battalion
Company "G", 11th Armored Regiment	Company "A", 712th Tank Battalion
Company "H", 11th Armored Regiment	Company "B", 712th Tank Battalion
Company "I", 11th Armored Regiment	Company "C", 712th Tank Battalion
Company "B", 11th Armored Regiment	Company "D", 712th Tank Battalion[9]

Companies "A", "B", and "C" of the 712th were equipped with the M4 Sherman tanks; "D" Company was a light tank company equipped with M5 Stuart tanks. A newly activated Service Company was also included within the newly formed tank battalion.

Major William E. Eckles was named acting Battalion Commander and assumed immediate command. On September 30, 1943, Lt-Col. S. Whitside Miller, Commanding Officer of the 2nd Battalion, 11th Armored Regiment on detached service with XII Corps, was assigned to the Battalion as Commanding Officer, however, he did not immediately assume command – he remained on detached service. From September 30 through December 31, Capt. Vladimir Kedrovsky and then Maj. Baxter Davis commanded the Battalion. Lt-Col. Miller assumed command on New Year's Eve, 1943.

Officially relieved from assignment to the 10th Armored Division, the 712th became one of sixty-three independent tank battalions created by the Army under this reorganization plan. Thirty-two of these independent battalions, including the 712th, were assigned to the European Theater of Operations (ETO).

The remainder of the 11th Armored Regiment was also reorganized. The personnel and equipment of the former 1st and 2nd Squadrons of the old 11th Cavalry was combined to form the newly designated 11th Tank Battalion and remained assigned to the 10th Armored Division.[10]

Columbia, South Carolina – Fort Jackson

Very soon after the re-designation, the 712th Tank Battalion moved from Camp Gordon to Fort Jackson in Columbia, South Carolina. The relocation of the battalion to Fort Jackson also meant another move for Mom as well. In Columbia, they found an apartment in town at 1219 Calhoun Street.

While in Columbia Mom had a very surprising encounter. "I had a job at a dime store in town. One time in the middle of the day, I was walking down one side of the street and coming in the opposite direction was a high school classmate, Vernon Richardson. I said, 'Vernon it's so good to see you.' He was in the Army too and was stationed in South Carolina. We chatted on the sidewalk for a little while. When you are in a strange faraway place and you see a familiar face from home, it is almost like being back home."

Mom and dad celebrated Christmas 1943 in South Carolina. B Company of the 712th Tank Battalion had a full Christmas dinner complete with turkey and dressing, which Dad also attended. It was on the mind of everyone that for some of the members of B Company, it would be their last Christmas on American soil.

Fort Knox, Kentucky

Shortly after the holidays, Dad was among several soldiers from the battalion ordered to Fort Knox, Kentucky for more advanced tank training. "I went

Christmas Card, 1943. (*Author's collection*)

Opposite above: Joe Roush, KP King. (*Company B photograph*)

Opposite below: L-R: Clifton Booth, Chester Martin, Fred Bieber, Joe Roush, Homer Miller, Gerald Thomas, Floyd McBride, Ben Woods. (*Company B photograph*)

Joe Blaha and Stanley Gagat.

L-R foreground on ladder and sitting: Joe Roush, Fred Bieber, Floyd McBride, William Hogue, Elza Sullivan, Roy Bardo, Ben Woods, Jose De La Garza. *Standing in middle:* Ernest Proctor, William Knowlton, Leo Lolli, J. Williams, Chester Martin. *Standing on balcony:* Bob Hodges, Theodore Ballman, William Siggins.

L-R: Francis James, Stanley Muhich, Joe Cavalieri, Gunther Jahnke, and David Dickson. (*Company B photograph*)

to the Armored Forces School at Fort Knox in January, 1944 right before we shipped out to go overseas. There was only about two or three of us in school. Everett Roberts (also from Co. B) was with me at Fort Knox. Your mother and I traveled together by train to Fort Knox. It was cold, it was so cold there when we arrived, there was a huge icicle hanging from the train's water tower (in Elizabethtown, Kentucky)."

Dad and Mom rented a room in a boarding house in Elizabethtown. "Each room had a wood burning heater or fireplace all connected to a common chimney. I was going to bank the fire at night (pile up plenty wood) before going to bed so in the morning it would still be burning. That was the only heat we had. So I banked it at night and, the next morning, I banked it too good and all the wood hadn't caught fire. So I threw some kerosene on it. It went *whooomp!*"

When Mom and Dad came out of their room, Dad continued, "The landlady said, 'I don't know what happened, I heard a terrible noise this morning and there is soot all upstairs in all the rooms.' The explosion had cleaned out the flues."

Mom later related the same incident, "I said 'Oh my God!' and went back into my room without saying anything I was so embarrassed. Dad's eyebrows were singed and everything."

Dad also related what happened when they got orders to ship overseas, "We went to Fort Knox from Fort Jackson. We were only at Fort Knox about thirty days. We had not yet quite finished when they called me back to Fort Jackson because we were going overseas. Then back to Fort Jackson and then we went up to Camp Miles Standish."

When the orders came to Fort Jackson for the 712th to ship overseas, the Battalion was deployed to Camp Miles Standish outside of Boston. All of the married men had to tell their wives goodbye at Fort Jackson, since the Battalion would only be in Boston for a few days. "Mom had to go home from South Carolina, around the middle of February, because we were shipping out."

Mom remembered, "Opal was so mad with me. She was so mad because I knew they were leaving and she didn't know it. 'You know everything,' she said. 'Richard doesn't tell me anything.'"

The married troops were allowed to take their wives out to dinner the night before the battalion deployed to Boston. The next morning the wives were allowed on base for their last kiss and embrace before their husbands left. "I told Dad goodbye at Fort Jackson." Mom then boarded a train for the lonely and tearful journey back to New Orleans.

Troops on board SS *Exchequer*. (*The History of the 712th Tank Battalion*)

Joe Roush and friends deliver mail in Chiseldon. (*Company B photograph*)

Dad then said, "We left in February to go overseas, we shipped out on Feb 28, 1944. We were only in Boston a short time. It was cold and rainy – miserable.

"All the guys from up north, when we were at Fort Benning complained about the heat. They said the Indians didn't want that land that's why they gave it to the Southerners. When we got to Boston, I told them, 'You said when we were in Georgia that the Indians didn't want it. Well they sure in hell didn't want this mess you have up here.'" Those Yankees weren't too fond of Dad's reverse needling.

England

On February 27, the troops were loaded on the SS *Exchequer* and the ship sailed at dawn the next day. Once at sea, the ship joined a convoy for the Atlantic crossing. Dad described the trip to England. "The voyage took nine days. I was one of the only few that did not get sea sick. I didn't drink too much liquids. They (the seasick) were all four high (in bunks) puking and shitting – slipping all over the boat. I got out and went on deck most of the time. Then you'd go down to the galley to eat and you'd smell that food, it smelt so bad you'd get out of there."

The History of the 712th Tank Battalion described the voyage as having

Lt-Col. Samuel Whitside Miller. (*Turner Publishing Co.*)

"many unreconstructed landlubbers" who were a "happy bunch that welcomed land on 8 March as the Battalion debarked at Gouroch, Scotland to the skirl of bagpipes..." The Battalion spent the next three months engaged in further training in England.

The 712th Tank Battalion along with several other US military units were stationed at Camp Chiseldon, an old British World War I army base just south of the village of Chiseldon near Swindon, England. The old World War I camp, like many other camps all over England, was greatly expanded to house the great influx of American soldiers arriving for the invasion of Europe. Chiseldon is north of the city of Southampton, the port from which the 712th and numerous other American units would embark in 1944 on their voyage across the English Channel to their destinies on the European continent.

Dad described his days in England. "We landed up in Scotland and we had to take the train down to Chiseldon. I was amazed to see women working on the railroad tracks with pick axes. In Chiseldon they put us up in Quonset huts and every now and then we would get an air raid and we had to run outside and jump in a trench, the buzz bombs (V-1 Rockets) were coming over."

The V-1 bombings of London were being reported in the newspapers back in the United States. These random bombings were causing not only massive property damage but were inflicting casualties on the English civilian population. Mom was so worried about Dad that she wrote and begged him not to go into London for fear that he would be accidentally killed in one of these bombing raids.

"I went to Wales. Slayton and I took a train and went to Cardiff, Wales. We went sightseeing and stayed one night and left the next day. (On the way to

Cardiff) we got on the wrong train and it took us to a coal mine at the end of the line. They had a turnaround and headed back. That's the first time I saw the digging for coal right off the top of the ground."

Before the invasion, daily army life continued; Dad mentioned an incident when he needed dental work. "I was still in England. That's when I went to the dentist, a captain, and he made me a bridge. And he said, 'Come back tomorrow they'll be ready.' I went back the next day. He said 'OK we got 'em.' And I put them in and I couldn't stand them they hurt me so bad. I said, 'Captain, these don't fit.' He said, 'Don't worry about it, take them. They are going to last as long as you're going to last where you are going.' And as I went outside, I mumbled, 'You no good son of a bitch,' and all the other nice words I learned in the army. I still have that partial plate in that box upstairs in the closet."

Lt-Col. S. Whitside Miller, at the age of thirty-seven, had assumed command of the 712th Tank Battalion on New Year's Eve, 1943, a little over a month before the 712th had shipped out to England. Whitside Miller, named Samuel Whitside Miller[11] after his maternal grandfather, Brig.-Gen. Samuel Marmaduke Whitside, was a descendant of President William Henry Harrison, and the son of 1st Lieutenant Archie Miller of the 6th Cavalry, who was awarded the Congressional Medal of Honor for service during the Philippine Moro Campaign in 1909.

Whitside Miller's father was killed in a plane crash when Whitside was thirteen years old. Whitside then attended a series of military schools before obtaining an appointment to West Point. After graduation in 1929, he expressed his desire to follow in the footsteps of his father and grandfather. "It has long been my cherished ambition to become as great a cavalryman as my father and grandfather, so that they would have been justly proud of me had they lived." His desire to be a cavalryman was fulfilled and he held the rank of captain in the 11th Cavalry when Japan attacked Pearl Harbor.

When the 11th Cavalry was transferred to the 11th Armored Regiment of the 10th Armored Division at Fort Benning, Miller was promoted to the rank of Lt-Col. and placed in command of the 2nd Battalion.[12]

Military leaders make decisions quickly, always focusing on completing the mission successfully, and show respect for their subordinates and other military officers. They are judged by their ability to make decisions on their own and bear ultimate moral responsibility for those decisions. Despite his military pedigree, Lt-Col. Miller did not display these requisite skills to instill confidence as a combat commander to the subordinate officers and men of the 712th.

> Whitside was an inadequate, obsessive compulsive neurotic replete with facial tics, and picking at his fingernails.
>
> Unfortunately, his behavior disorder was almost disastrous for the battalion.

He imposed unrealistic training goals, unrealistic physical training standards, and inappropriate reprimands.

He had no sense of delegation of duties. He personally rechecked all requisitions, reports, including dental and immunization records and spectacle prescriptions.[13]

He repeatedly chastised and reprimanded subordinate officers in front of enlisted men. In one instance a soldier came into the officer's mess to advise Miller that he had a telephone call. The colonel spent ten minutes chewing out the soldier for interrupting his meal. When he finished berating the messenger and went to answer the phone the caller had hung up. This led to another reprimand.

When Capt. Forrest Dixon sought counsel of another colonel because Miller had threatened him with court-martial for not installing blackout lights on tanks (a practical impossibility), the colonel brought Dixon to Gen. Middleton's Headquarters. The staff officer hearing Dixon's complaint stated, "You know, I wouldn't pay any attention to what you're telling me if yesterday we didn't get a petition signed by a bunch of men from the 712th Tank Battalion..."

Fearful of the terrible consequences that would have unfolded if Miller had been left in charge to command the battalion in combat, several of the officers in the battalion sent letters to the commanding general complaining of Miller's idiosyncrasies.

Gen. Middleton investigated the complaints and presented Miller with the letters written by the men to give Miller the opportunity to talk to his men and see if they would change their minds. The subordinate officers and men that had complained to Gen. Middleton held to their convictions and shortly thereafter Miller was transferred. Eventually Miller was attached to the 29th Infantry Division as a G-3 staff officer.

Lt-Col. George B. Randolph was named commander of the 712th on the eve of combat as the battalion was readying to cross the English Channel – he assumed command on D-Day, June 6, 1944. Randolph had served in the Officers Reserve Corps since 1926 and had been a high school math and science teacher in Birmingham, Alabama in civilian life. During the war he was the Chief of Tactics at the Fort Knox OCS (Office Candidate School) and then served in two Armored Divisions, the 3rd and the 6th, before coming to the 712th. He was forty-one years of age.

When he first arrived at the battalion he proceeded to the field kitchen where the men were preparing to eat. When the officers from HQ arrived and got in the mess line, he pulled them all to the side and told them that no officer should eat until everyone of his enlisted men were fed. Thus, in short order, he proved to the men of the 712th what kind of leader he was and won the respect and admiration of all who were under his command.

CHAPTER 3

The Sherman Tank

The best armor is staying out of gun-shot.

Italian proverb

There was nothing in the war movies of my youth that suggested that the American war machines in World War II were anything but invincible. One of the few facts Dad mentioned to me as a boy was that he was in a Sherman Tank during the war. I recall no portrayal of any deficiencies in American tank weaponry, consequently, my youthful inquisitiveness did not extend to question him on the intricacies of this military hardware. I never even bothered to ask why American tanks were called Sherman tanks.

The utilization of the tank by both sides caused it to be described as the decisive weapon in land warfare in World War II.[1] During the course of the war, the German Army had its Panzer tank series (Panzer II, III, and IV) culminating in its huge Panther Tank (Panzer V) and Tiger Tank (Panzer VI). In 1942 and 1943, as Dad was entering the service and was training at Fort Benning, the adoption of American tank warfare doctrines and the development of a tank with which to implement that doctrine fell under the direction and approval of the Army Ground Forces (AGF) and Gen. Lesley McNair. As author Steven Zaloga noted, "[it] came heavily to reflect on the opinions and biases of McNair, an artilleryman with prodigious administrative skills but no combat experience."[2] The principle tank selected by the US Army was the M-4 Sherman Tank.[3]

The American Poet, Edwin Markham, once said "choices are the hinges of destiny". As Dad and the other tank crews of the US Army completed final preparations before the Normandy invasion, few, if any, realized that the destinies that awaited them on the battlefields of Europe were hinged upon the choices made by Gen. McNair in 1942 and 1943. The Sherman tanks designed and built during those years and then stockpiled in England were being distributed to the tank units during the weeks and months before the invasion.

World War II was not the first conflict that employed tanks. The armored vehicle known as a "Tank" was introduced onto the modern battlefield by the

The Sherman Tank

M4 Sherman Tank.

British in World War I to break the stalemate that had developed in trench warfare. Early versions consisted of a cylindrical metal unit that looked like a water tank atop caterpillar tractor tracks. In order to maintain secrecy for this new weapon, non-essential personnel were told that a movable water tank was being fabricated. The name remained long after the military subterfuge was forgotten.

The use of armor on the battlefield dates back to antiquity beginning with protective garments and shields made of hides, leather, and bone, then evolving to protective gear made of bronze or steel. Armor was also used to protect war animals, such as war horses and war elephants, from battle wounds. Precursors of the twentieth century tank were the Egyptian chariots, the Roman legions' testudo, the medieval knights in armor and the horse cavalry which was the predominant military force from the middle ages through the nineteenth century.

Throughout the history of armor devices, there has always been a compromise between speed and mobility, striking power, and armored protection. Throughout history, mankind has had to reach a proportional balance between these three factors in the development of armored weaponry. Both the Allies and the Axis powers were faced with this proportional balance in the development of their respective tanks in World War II.

After the introduction of tanks into World War I by the British, the United States Army also developed a small tank corps when it entered the war; however, the American tank force was dismantled after World War I ended.

Germany started World War II with its invasion of Poland in September of 1939. Within weeks, the Nazis controlled almost all of western Europe. The

Germans called their new military tactic the *Blitzkrieg* ("Lightning War").[4] Germany was able to defeat its neighbors by concentrating its attack on one part of the enemy sector with fast-moving Panzer tanks and motorized infantry and artillery all supported by dive-bombers.[5] The Soviet Union was not drawn into the war at that time due to a non-aggression pact entered into between Adolf Hitler and Josef Stalin one month prior to the invasion of Poland. After the rapid collapse of France and the other western European countries, Great Britain became the only major country at war with Germany at the beginning of 1940.

As part of the Lend Lease Program, the United States moved quickly with the design and production of tanks for the British Army in order to counteract the German armored divisions facing British forces. Through use of these early tanks in combat by the British Army, some improvements and changes in American tanks were made when deficiencies in design were recognized. But the United States clearly lagged behind Germany in the technology of tank warfare.

The United States identified its various models of armored vehicles merely by alpha numeric designation. The British, however, affixed names to their weapons, and these early American tanks were named after famous American Civil War cavalry generals. The M-3 series of armored vehicles were the first utilized by the British in combat in 1941. The M-3 (and M-5) light tanks were named Stuarts, after Gen. J. E. B. Stuart. The M-2 and M-3 medium tanks were named after Ulysses S. Grant and Robert E. Lee. When the M-4 tanks went into full production in late 1942, they were immediately deployed to the British in Africa. The British named the M-4 tanks after Gen. William Tecumseh Sherman. The name "Sherman" stuck and even the Americans referred to these tanks by name rather than M-4.[6]

Ignoring his non-aggression agreement with Stalin, Hitler launched an invasion against the Soviet Union in June of 1941. Even though Russian tanks outnumbered German tanks two to one at the front and six to one overall, the Russian tanks were obsolete and generally in disrepair. As a result, Germany enjoyed the advantage during the first stages of the conflict. The Russians quickly recovered from these setbacks and introduced their medium T-34 and KV-l heavy tanks into the fighting, which were able to neutralize the German advantage. The Germans then discovered their tanks were not invincible. This led to the bigger and heavier tanks being designed by the Germans and swiftly introduced into battle.[7]

Meanwhile, in accordance with US Army doctrine that the tank would function as an infantry support weapon, the Sherman tank was specifically designed to favor speed, mobility and mechanical reliability over firepower and protection. McNair felt that tanks had no business jousting with other tanks, and that this task should be left to his pet service, the Tank Destroyers (TDs).

Sherman Tanks were regarded as infantry support weapons, in the case of those belonging to independent tank battalions, or as tools for rapid 'cavalry' exploitation of breakthroughs, in the case of armored divisions. McNair believed that any breakthroughs would be accomplished by the infantry divisions with local support from the independent tank battalions. Once a gap was made in an enemy line, the plan was then for armored divisions to pour through and wreak havoc in the enemy rear, destroying reinforcements, disrupting the command structure and forcing the enemy infantry to flee or be destroyed. This American approach was in distinct contrast to German doctrine, which viewed the Panzer divisions as a vital mass of mobile firepower, central to the securing of the breakout against both armored and unarmored opposition, as well as to the rapid exploitation of success. McNair may have been the architect of the American doctrine, but it was widely supported by the Army general staff, including Gen. George Marshall.[8]

"The basic fallacy of this American doctrine was the inability of the tank destroyers to deal completely with enemy tanks. [...] Tank destroyers were essentially under-armored tanks with slightly bigger guns [...] they were open-topped and were very vulnerable to overhead airbursts, mortar fire and even dedicated infantry attack. They were adequate weapons for ambush or fire support." But McNair's reliance on the TDs as the exclusive answer to German tanks was misplaced.[9]

The Sherman held its own or was better than Germany's Panzer III and early model Panzer IV, encountered in North Africa and Sicily in 1942 and 1943. The Sherman's armor had been designed to resist the 37-mm PAK 36, the truck drawn anti-tank gun used by German infantry at the start of the war. The Germans, however, started to replace the PAK 36 in 1940 after the fall of France. By the time of the Normandy campaign in 1944, the Sherman was badly outclassed by German medium and heavy tanks of that day, the Panther and the Tiger, as well as the improved models of the Panzer IV.[9] The armor of a Sherman could be penetrated at most ordinary combat ranges by any of the tanks and self-propelled guns commonly in German service in 1944. More protection through heavier armor plating was neither implemented nor even seriously considered because the chassis of the Sherman, then in mass production, could not accept the additional weight without sacrificing mechanical reliability.

The meager resources for tank research and development in the US Army forced hard choices that often degraded the ultimate combat capabilities of the tank. The Sherman's low-velocity 75-millimeter gun was chosen because the Army's artillery branch wanted a cheap, reliable weapon for fire support. Lloyd Sparks, one of Dad's 712th tank mates, described firing the short-barreled 75-millimeter guns. "The muzzle velocity was so slow that projectiles in flight were visible from a position standing directly behind the tank."

In another cost-cutting move, many Shermans were equipped with a radial engine originally designed for aircraft. On the battlefield, this engine produced a loud backfire when starting, instantly drawing enemy fire.[10]

Other design deficiencies of the Sherman were the storage compartments for ammunition. The ammunition bins within the crew compartment were located along the outer shell of the tank. When enemy shells penetrated the tank, more often than not, it also exploded this stored ammunition. The resulting fire and explosion had a disastrous effects on the crew and, in many cases, the tank was completely destroyed.

With the Sherman in full mass production by American industry and the Army's doctrinal thinking stuck in a pre-war mode, innovations in tank technology were stymied. Even though a prototype for a heavier American Tank had been developed, in 1943 the AGF nevertheless opposed the production of the M26 (Pershing). "Part of the resistance within the US Army to a heavy tank like the M26 to supplement the Sherman was a legitimate concern over logistics. American tanks had to be shipped thousands of miles to distant battlefields in Europe and the Pacific, and every extra ton of tank was a ton less of other vital supplies. The T26 (M26 Pershing) weighed nearly fifty percent more than the Sherman and would require elaborate new training, new spare parts and new ammunition."[11] Experiments showed that two Sherman tanks could fit into the space required by a larger tank on an LST.[12]

As Germany introduced its larger and heavier Panther, Tiger and King Tiger tanks, it was emphasizing firepower and armor at the expense of speed and mobility. The Sherman tank, M4 series, which was the mainstay of armored weapons of the US Army throughout World War II, fell behind the advances in German tank technology, during the period of stockpiling weapons in England.

The interior of the tank was noisy and confining, all of the crew had to fit in tight quarters. Dad said, "I don't know how we all didn't have prostate trouble. (We had a chair) but it wasn't comfortable, you couldn't stretch out like a lounge chair. It was more like a stool than a chair."

During training in 1943, the American tank crews were told that the Sherman was the best tank in the world.[13] Soon after D-Day, however, the tank crews quickly learned of more deficiencies in the Sherman. American tanks were easily knocked out by German tanks and 88-mm anti-aircraft guns which German troops regularly used as an anti-tank weapon, while the shells from their own 75-mm guns bounced harmlessly off the heavier armor of the Panthers and Tigers.[14] "The Sherman was universally denounced by anyone who had to fight in one against a Panther or Tiger."[15] Stephen Ambrose noted this major failure in the US Army to appreciate this growing shift within the German Army towards heavier and better armed tanks by citing historian

Max Hastings to wonder how "could American and British industries produce a host of superb aircraft, an astonishing variety of radar equipment, the proximity fuse … (not to mention the atomic bomb) yet still ask its armies to join battle against the Wehrmacht equipped with a range of tanks utterly inferior in armor and killing power?"[16]

Additionally, Sherman tanks were vulnerable to being crippled by a single soldier with a very simple weapon, the panzerfaust, which means tank fist. Stephen Ambrose described it as an ideal anti-tank weapon for the Germans in the hedgerow country. It was a one shot anti-tank rocket launcher, the German equivalent of the American bazooka but with a shorter range (up to 350 feet), which didn't matter in hedgerow country. "In some respects it was superior to the bazooka. It was operated by a single soldier and was so simple no special training was required, while the bazooka required a trained two man team. The panzerfaust launched a grenade type bomb that was bigger and better designed than the bazooka's."[17] The panzerfaust had greater penetrating capabilities than the bazooka. The hollow-charge head of the panzerfaust grenade contained enough high explosive to penetrate even the thickest tank armor, up to 200 millimeters. The explosive charge was shaped and when exploded caused the entire force of the explosion forward. The explosive force when striking the exterior of the tank was of such magnitude and intensity that when piercing the armor plate it caused the metal being pierced to become molten metal.

But the Sherman tank did have some advantages over the German tanks, the greatest being its sheer numbers.[18] At the height of production, one Sherman rolled off the production line every thirty minutes. The fact that the 75-mm gun could not penetrate the front of a German tank meant that Allied tank crews had to employ a different tactic than a one on one frontal attack. The Sherman crews would often defeat superior enemy tanks by outmaneuvering and "ganging up" on the Nazi tank. With a number of Shermans engaging a German tank, some of the Shermans could surround the enemy and get a shot at the thinner and weaker armor on the side or rear of the German tank, thereby disabling it. Although this tactic worked, it was costly. It has been estimated that four Shermans were lost for every Panther or Tiger destroyed.[19] Another tactic was to have a Sherman remain hidden. Once the German tank got close enough, a shell from the hidden Sherman, could penetrate into the side of the advancing German tank and knockout the enemy.

One of the Sherman's main strengths was the speed with which the turret could be traversed. The turret was powered by a hydraulic and electric system that enabled it to make a full revolution in only 10-12 seconds, compared with 25 or more seconds required by German tanks which were frequently turned by a hand crank. The Sherman's quick-turning turret often allowed it to get off a crucial first one or two shots in a tank duel.[20]

Other strong points over its German counterparts was the Sherman's higher rate of fire, and its higher degree of mobility. It was quicker and more maneuverable. The Sherman tank also exhibited high mechanical reliability — unlike the German Tiger and Panther tanks, which experienced frequent breakdowns. A minor breakdown in battle could be disastrous, exposing it to enemy fire resulting in the complete loss of a tank. The simplicity of the Sherman tank design lent itself to not only ease of production in great quantities but also relatively easy maintenance and repair in the field. In this respect the Sherman had a decided advantage over the German tanks.

The 712th Tank Battalion had the same organizational structure as other tank battalions in the US Army: Headquarters Company, a Service Company and four combat companies. Headquarters Company, and Companies "A", "B", and "C" were equipped with the Sherman M4 tanks; "D" Company was a light tank company equipped with M5A1 Stuart light tanks.

Each company consisted of three platoons containing five tanks each. The Sherman tanks were operated by a five man crew: a commander, a gunner, a loader, a driver, and an assistant driver/bow gunner. The priority of the crew positions were in the following order: tank commander, gunner, driver, loader, assistant driver/bow gunner.

The commander of the platoon, usually a 1st or 2nd lieutenant, was the commander of one of the tanks. Platoon sergeants were commanders of the remaining tanks in the platoon.

The tank commander sat behind the gunner and slightly above him when the turret hatch was closed. The commander's seat, like the driver and assistant driver, could be raised when the hatch was open. In this position, the commander's head and upper torso was exposed when the tank was not in combat. The commander also had direct control over the turret's traverse and could set the main gun in the direction of the target himself, but leaving the more precise aiming to the gunner. The commander also operated the radio, through which he communicated with other tanks and headquarters.[21]

Second in seniority was the gunner, usually a corporal. The gunner aimed and fired the 75-mm gun onto the targets indicated by the commander. He sighted the target through a periscope and traversed the turret and elevated the gun in order to effect the fire. He also fired the co-axial machine gun. The gunner's position was on the right side of the turret, immediately in front of the commander and behind the assistant driver. The tasks of the gunner required considerable training and the fate of the crew could often depend on the gunner's skill.[22]

The driver was next in seniority and was located on the left front side of the tank. Driving the tank was accomplished by a clutch-and-brake steering system. In addition to possessing the skills necessary to drive the tank, the driver had to have a reasonably good appreciation of tactics and terrain.

Cpl Gruntz with helmet and throat microphone. (*Gruntz Sketch*)

During battle, the commander many times relied upon the driver to align the tank in the best position for the gunner to achieve the most effective firing as well as positioning the tank to avoid enemy fire.

The lowest in seniority were the loader and the assistant driver/bow gunner. The loader's primary function was to keep the main gun and the co-axial machine gun in working order and supplied with ammunition. Of all crew members, the loader had the most room because he was required to reach all around the central portions of the tank to the areas where the ammunition was stored.

The assistant driver, located in the right front of the hull of the tank. He was primarily responsible for operating the .30 caliber bow machine gun. He also assisted the loader by feeding him ammunition from the forward bins.

The driver and the assistant driver entered and exited through hatches directly over their positions in the forward hull compartment of the tank. Both were furnished with seats which could be raised, so that their heads emerged from the hatches. This was how they operated the tank when not in combat situations. When the hatches were closed during combat, both used a periscope on the hatch covers in order to drive the tank.

When the tank was in operation, the noise was deafening. One tanker described it as like being inside a cement mixer. Conversation was impossible and the crew communicated vital information to each other by a rudimentary intercom system. Dad explained, "You couldn't talk to anybody in the tank, it was too noisy. We had a little strap around our throat with a button on the end and a thing in our ear and when we talked you could hear like through the speaker thing."

Patton was cognizant of the deficiencies in the Sherman tank but was satisfied that it would suffice in the hands of the men under his command. He stated, "It's the unconquerable soul of man, not the nature of the weapon he uses, that insures victory."

CHAPTER 4

The Beaches of Normandy

There is many a boy here today who looks on war as all glory, but boys, it is all hell.

Gen. William Tecumseh Sherman

Dad and I landed in Paris late in the morning and by the time we went through customs, retrieved our luggage and obtained a rental car, it was mid-afternoon as we began navigating our way through Paris on our afternoon drive to the Normandy coast. We arrived in Caen about dusk and decided to find a hotel room for the night and begin our tour early the next morning.

That night I plotted our next day's itinerary. With cinematic memories still guiding my perceptions of combat, I was anxious to begin my European vacation by sightseeing some of the locations depicted in one of my favorite World War II films, *The Longest Day*. I was anxious to visit the Pegasus Bridge near Caen, Pointe du Hoc, and St Mère Eglise. I must admit that my curiosity in seeing these sites was prompted as much by their depiction in the movies as it was by the actual events that occurred on June 6, 1944.

Our first stop on our tour of the landing beaches of Operation Overlord was the area near the Pegasus Bridge, captured by the British on D-Day. After spending just a few minutes there, we next traveled west along the beach road to the Omaha and Utah Beaches.

Some of the events on D-Day in St Mère Eglise, involving paratroopers of the 82nd Airborne Division, form a good portion of the plot in *The Longest Day*. In the early morning hours, a house adjacent to the town square catches fire, ignited by an Allied bomb. The townspeople are awakened and alerted to the emergency by the church bell and quickly assemble to form a bucket brigade to fight the fire. The German garrison occupying the town is also awakened. Although intended to be silently dropped in the dark countryside, paratroopers, including Private John Steele, who was portrayed in the movie by actor Red Buttons, are dropped in error far from the intended drop zone and begin landing in the well-lit town square among the French townspeople and the German soldiers. Private Steele landed on the church roof and as he was sliding down his parachute gets caught on the church steeple. Although wounded, he limply hung from the church pretending to be dead for several hours, all the while watching the German troops on the ground firing upon and killing other paratroopers helplessly floating slowly through the air.

Steele, although deafened by the continuous ringing of the church bell, is eventually rescued as other paratroopers of the 82nd Airborne, led by Lt-Col. Benjamin Vandervoort, portrayed by John Wayne, move into the town to secure its capture.

The townspeople of St Mère Eglise continue to honor their liberators from the 82nd Airborne Division; a mannequin hanging by a parachute is attached to the church steeple. One stained-glass window at the rear of the church, destroyed during the invasion, has been replaced with a new stained glass depicting the Blessed Virgin Mary surrounded by American paratroopers floating through the air. The site upon which that burning house was located, now houses the Place du 6 Juin, a military museum full of artifacts from World War II.

I was unaware until Dad told me that day that he had traveled through St Mère Eglise during the war; after coming ashore on Utah Beach, the 712th rolled through town on its way to its bivouac area the battalion's first night ashore.

From St Mère Eglise, Dad and I traveled to Pointe du Hoc, a high cliff situated between Omaha Beach and Utah Beach. It was fortified with heavy concrete gun emplacements with an excellent position to overlook and defend both beaches. The job of the Army Rangers on D-Day was to land on the beaches at the foot of the cliff, scale the cliffs and destroy the artillery guns.

When we arrived at Pointe du Hoc, I was somewhat surprised to see that the site remains essentially in the same condition it did after the invasion and essentially as portrayed in *The Longest Day*. Many bunkers remain, with holes where shells exploded. The ground still has craters formed by the Allied shelling and bombing on D-Day.

From Pointe du Hoc it is a short trip to Omaha Beach, the landing site that had the most casualties on D-Day.

Omaha Beach

The topography of the French coastline at Colleville/St Laurent sur Mer, the site of Omaha Beach, consists of cliffs and bluffs overlooking the beach. At seventy-five years of age, Dad was not up to making the trek down to the shoreline, therefore, I made this journey alone. At the water's edge I looked up the steep incline I had just walked down.

One picture may be worth a thousand words, but personal observation is worth a thousand pictures. The crest of the cliff along this section of Omaha

Beach is much higher and steeper than it appears in all of the photographs and film that I had seen; likewise, the distance between the water's edge and the base of the cliff is farther than it appears in photographic images of D-Day. Today there is a broad expanse of vegetation-covered sand dunes from the back edge of the beach to the base of the cliff. During the war, the Germans had removed all of this vegetation in order to provide a clear line of fire. I began to imagine what the infantry must have thought when they first gazed upon these bluffs on June 6, 1944, and the large amount of flat terrain that they had to run across to reach cover. As an out of shape forty-seven year old, I was huffing and puffing as I made my way back up the steps to the top, and thinking of how the GIs traversed this area weighted down with all of the gear they had to carry. I began to understand why Omaha Beach had the highest casualty rate on D-Day.

Despite living through the Vietnam era, my deep-seated youthful concepts of war as a glorious adventure still lingered on. An old Latin proverb best described my perceptions: "Sweet is war to those who have never experienced it."

The Cemetery in Normandy

The maps of Normandy show the American Cemetery as being adjacent to the English Channel overlooking Omaha Beach. It is 172 acres in size, however, the maps and these statistics did not prepare me for what was in store.

When I entered the front gate, the main area of the cemetery was hidden from view. Whether, this landscaping feature was intentional or accidental, it certainly added to the visual impact when I first saw the main grounds. After a short walk along a footpath bordered on both sides with trees and shrubbery we arrived at the Memorial, the Wall of Missing, and the reflecting pool and I caught my first sight of the burial field containing over 9,386 graves with a panoramic view of the English Channel as a backdrop.

Thousands of white marble crosses and occasional Stars of David stand row after row in perfect symmetry regardless of the angle of sight. The weather that day was perfect without a single cloud in the sky. The rich dark green grass was perfectly manicured and the morning sun striking the headstones made each one brilliantly radiant; it was soul stirring. It is hard to describe the emotional impact when I first beheld this scene, it is a combination of patriotism, sadness, humility and gratitude all rolled up into one.

Abraham Lincoln referred to the Gettysburg battlefield as hallowed and consecrated ground. Such is an appropriate description of the Normandy Cemetery. Visitors speak in soft hushed tones and with the same reverence reserved for the interior of a church or synagogue. When standing amidst those white crosses, although I was in a foreign country thousands of miles from

Normandy Cemetery. (*Author's collection*)

America, I had a feeling of being home again, the feeling of being on American soil. I have been to Arlington Cemetery and the Tomb of the Unknown Soldier, outside of Washington DC, on two occasions, once while I was in high school and again as the chaperone for my sons' Boy Scout troop. I was awestruck with Arlington on both occasions perhaps because of the sheer size of that cemetery. Those experiences could not begin to compare with the emotional impact of Normandy. Perhaps my experience was more enhanced because I was in the company of my father, who personally knew some of the young men lying beneath those headstones.

Prior to entering the cemetery, we had stopped at the visitor's center, where Dad asked for the grave locations of three soldiers he knew from B Company of the 712th Tank Battalion, Nicholas Milczakowski, Frank Krusel and Tullio Micaloni. He also asked for a small pail of damp sand and a sponge. Dad wanted to take photographs of the headstones of Milczakowski, Krusel and Micaloni, but, the carvings in the white crosses are not readable in ordinary photographs. We placed the wet sand inside the chiseled inscriptions and wiped away the excess sand with the sponge. The contrast between the dark moist sand and the white cross makes the inscription readily visible and easily photographed. Within days, the wind and rain wash away this small amount of sand and the headstone is again solid white. Dad learned this little fete of photographic wizardry a dozen years earlier from his friend Henri Levaufre.

We first found the grave of Frank Krusel. In June of 1944, Dad was twenty-five years old, and was several years older than most of the men in B Company, but he was not the oldest. Frank was several years older than Dad. In civilian life Frank was a university professor, yet in the Army he was a Private First Class. Dad, a corporal, outranked Frank; he asked him once, "Frank, what are you doing being a Pfc.? With your education you could be an officer." Frank replied, "I don't want to go any higher than this. I have a better chance of surviving the war as a Pfc. than as an officer." Frank was killed less than one month after landing in Normandy. Dad spent a few moments in quiet conversation over Frank's grave and as we walked away he said, "I can still see him with his cigarette in a cigarette holder that he always had while smoking."

We next went to the graves of Nicholas Milczakowski and Tullio Micaloni, which are within one grave site of each other. Milczakowski, who was shorter than Dad, was known as "Little Nick" and played the bugle. He and Krusel were in the tank commanded by Sgt Tullio Micaloni.

Throughout training in the United States and in England, Dad went to church regularly. After landing in Normandy the opportunity to attend church services became rare. However, a couple of weeks after landing in Normandy, the town of St Jores was captured with the town church relatively undamaged. During the lull in battle, a Mass was being celebrated in the church for any soldier who could attend.

Dad said, "The day before Micaloni heard there was going to be a Mass, and he asked if he could come to Mass with me. So I said yes. We came to Mass and when we got to Mass, the Catholic Chaplain was there with the French priest and they said Mass. And the Chaplain said any of you soldiers who want to go to communion, say a good Act of Contrition and then go to communion. In those days to go to communion, you should go to confession first and fast from midnight. But the Priest dispensed that and he told us to go to communion and to go to confession the first chance we got.[1] Micaloni said, 'Louie, you think I can go to communion?' And I said, 'Sure you can go, just say an Act of Contrition.' So we said the Act of Contrition and went to communion. The next day he went out and his tank was destroyed and he and all the crew were killed." Dad spent another few minutes by himself over the graves of Micaloni and Milczakowski.

We next walked along the path and the stone wall overlooking Omaha Beach and the Atlantic Ocean. The view that day was spectacular and the silence of the cemetery was only broken by birds chirping in the nearby trees. I thought to myself that the serenity and sunlit beauty of that day was in sharp contrast to the overcast and brutal conditions on D-Day. There were certainly no birds chirping at that location on the morning of June 6, 1944.

Since every soldier had a dog tag, I asked Dad how could there be so many graves marked "Unknown". Dad said that many times the explosion of a

Beach obstacles. (*Author's collection*)

bomb or artillery shell would fall directly upon a soldier and the upper part of the body would be blown away; the only portion of the body recovered was the bottom half of a torso, or maybe just arms and legs and there would be no dog tag. I was embarrassed by how naive I had been to the realities of combat; the answer was so obvious to anyone who realized the full destructive capabilities of the weaponry utilized in World War II.

As we departed the American Cemetery, I realized that this trip with my father was not a European vacation – it was a pilgrimage.

Utah Beach

Dad and I departed the Omaha Beach area and proceeded to the beach at St Marie du Mont, which is now known by its military code name, Utah Beach. This is where Dad and the 712th Tank Battalion landed on June 28, 1944. B Company and part of Headquarters Company were the first to disembark late in the afternoon and early evening but then the tide went out and the rest of the battalion had to wait until the next morning to come ashore.[2]

Dad remembered the night of June 5, when the invasion began for the Allies, as they were embarking for the landings the next morning, June 6. "The night of the invasion (June 5) we were out on maneuvers in a field all night. The planes start going over and there were thousands of them. We knew something

The Battle Route in Normandy to Hill 122. (*The History of the 712th Tank Battalion*)

was up. As soon as it got daylight they called us in and said 'OK pack up we're moving out. We're going down to the coast to load on LSTs to go to France. The invasion is on.' So we got everything ready, we got the tanks gassed up and started down the road to Dartmouth. Man, we were flying, a couple of tanks had trouble and broke down because that was a long haul down there. We had to stop and fix them.

"And when we got down to the coast they said 'OK we're going to load up in three hours.'" But then the orders to load up were postponed; at the time Dad had heard that while they were not scheduled to be in the initial wave, they were scheduled to go in on one of the succeeding waves on either the first or second day after the invasion, but their debarkation had been delayed due to the experiences of the tank crews that were in the first wave on D-Day.

"We were supposed to come in… we had snorkels on the tank so we could go under water.[3] But the tide changed, they had two tides, at the beach, Utah Beach. And they had calculated only one tide so that when they (the initial tanks landing on D-Day) came in they went underwater and many of the tank crews drowned. So we couldn't go in, they told us to stay in England – 'We're going to wait awhile.' – and then when we were ready to come in the weather got bad. That's when the storm came up on the Channel." No doubt the change in command from Lt-Col. Miller to Lt-Col. Randolph on D-Day may also have played a part for the delay in the 712th moving across the Channel.

The landscape of Utah Beach is in no way similar to Omaha Beach. There are no cliffs or bluffs; the land abutting the beach is flat and easy to traverse. The landing site at Utah Beach now houses a military museum. Dad and I spent about an hour reviewing the artifacts and film. Utah Beach is also the site of several war monuments, one of which is dedicated to the 90th Infantry Division and its supporting units, including the 712th Tank Battalion.

Also on Utah Beach is the first Borne de la voie de la Liberté, a small marker, designating the "Way of Liberty". These milestones of liberty are dotted along and mark out the route of the liberating US Army from Utah Beach and St Mère Église to Bastogne in Belgium.

From the site of the 90th Infantry Monument, we could see a house several hundred yards down the beach. Dad said that he remembers seeing a house at that same distance when he landed in 1944 and it perhaps was the same house.

After landing early in the evening of June 28, 1944, the 712th Tank Battalion removed all of the waterproofing material and moved to an assembly area in Picauville, where the entire battalion bivouacked after coming ashore.

Louis Gruntz Sr. and Louis Gruntz Jr. (*Author's collection*)

90th Infantry Division Monument at Utah Beach. (*Author's collection*)

Before Dad and I left Utah Beach on our way to Picauville, about 9 miles inland. I asked what the beach was like in 1944. Dad replied, "They had equipment and everything all over. It was just about dark and they had balloons up in the air to keep the German planes from diving. We were the first tank battalion to land intact."

Dad also said that when he landed he remembers the strong sickening smell of death, the odor of dead and rotting flesh. I said that I would have thought that the bodies of American soldiers would have been buried by then. He said that Americans had been buried. "Grave Registration would come along and pick up the bodies and take one dog tag off. That's how they knew who got killed. And then they took them back and put them in areas where they were ready to bury them. They identified them and the other dog tag stayed with the body so they would know who they would bury." But Dad was uncertain if all the Germans had been buried by that date. He also said that the smell that hung in air when he landed was probably from the dead livestock that were lying all around that had not yet been disposed of or buried.

Dad's first entry onto the European Continent was clearly memorable, just not pleasant.

CHAPTER 5

The Hedgerows

The best tank terrain is that without anti-tank weapons.

Russian military adage

"We are now in hedgerow country," Dad explained as we left the Utah Beach area and headed inland. The terrain of the Normandy countryside is generally level farmland separated into patterns of small fields. For centuries each small field was bounded by an earthen mound or wall 8 to 10 feet in width and 4 to 6 feet in height, which served as fences for the enclosed fields. The hedgerows are covered with brush and other undergrowth; along the top of the wall there is a row of trees and along the base of the hedgerow runs a small ditch.

"Notice they run about 100 or 200 feet deep and they have hedges all around and mud piled up in bunkers like. Now we had to fight through those hedgerows. On the other side the Germans were dug-in in foxholes. When we got a hole in the hedgerow, we ran the tank through to get the next one. Then they (the Germans) fell back and we had to do the same thing all over again. They had machine guns and infantry men in there. A few years ago, Henri (Levaufre) told me they found a skeleton in one of the hedgerows, an American soldier. He crawled up in there (during the battle) and he died up in there. He wasn't discovered until over forty years after the war."

Father Murphy, a Chaplain in the 90th Infantry Division, wrote a similar description in his diary and added that the hedgerows "…made a complete screen – something the enemy could use for cover. We were walking targets. Many of the fields were marked 'minen' (mines) signs probably put there by Germans to scare us […] The fields were not more than a hundred yards square, but the sad part of it was that each was bordered on four sides by these high fences of dirt and shrubs. In French we found the word for them – 'Bocage.'"[1]

Alongside the fields are narrow, winding, sunken roads, which run between the hedgerows. As Dad and I drove, we had to stop on one occasion as a

The Hedgerows

Hedgerow lined road. (*Author's collection*)

French farmer moved his cattle across the road from one hedgerow enclosed field to another.

The Allied forces had not made the expected advances into the French countryside that had been hoped for prior to D-Day due to the natural defenses that hedgerows provided the Germans. Stephen Ambrose called the failure of the Army to prepare the troops for fighting in hedgerows one of the greatest military intelligence failures of all times. The aerial photography of Normandy before D-Day revealed the hedges, but photo interpreters, looking only straight down at them, thought they were like the small hedges in England and had missed the sunken nature of the roads entirely.[2] Military intelligence personnel relied solely upon aerial reconnaissance in formulating battle plans; they overlooked other means of information, such as the writings of the nineteenth-century French novelist and playwright, Honoré de Balzac. In his writings, over one hundred years before D-Day, de Balzac described in graphic detail the hedgerows of the Normandy terrain:

> a raised bank of earth about each field, forming a flat topped ridge, two meters in height, with beeches, oaks, and chestnut trees growing up the summit. The ridge or mound, planted in this wise, is called a hedge; and the long branches

of the trees which grow upon it almost always project across the road, they make a great arbor overhead. The roads themselves, shut in by clay banks in this melancholy way, are not unlike the moats of a fortress.

Tanks were intended for use in open fields. Tank crews were not wild about the idea of running their tanks along these sunken roads because of insufficient room for the turret to traverse any more than a few degrees; furthermore, the hedgerows impaired visibility thereby making long range use of the 75-mm gun and the tank's machine guns ineffective. The hedgerows also gave the Germans a defensive advantage, if the tanks tried to enter a field through the gate on the hedgerow, it was easily knocked out by mortar fire and panzerfausts hidden a short distance away behind the next hedgerow which had zeroed in on the gate. If a tank tried to climb over the embankment, it exposed its unarmored belly to enemy fire and was soon disabled.

It was not until American ingenuity entered the picture that the problem of the hedgerows would be solved. Someone suggested making hedge-cutters and attaching them to the front of the tanks. They were simple in design, and made by pieces of steel angle and T-iron, sharpened on the front edge. There was steel in plentiful supply in Normandy left by the Germans. The landing craft obstacles that the Germans positioned on the beach were made of just the right size iron beams. Those cutters struck the earth hedgerows about two and a half feet above the surface of the ground. With one lunge a hole was cut in the hedgerow and the tank kept on going before the Germans could take aim upon it.[3]

When the hedge cutter was first being tested behind the lines, a group of officers were observing the demonstration. One of those officers was Gen. George S. Patton Jr., who would soon take command of the Third Army. Capt. Belton Y. Cooper of the 3rd Armored Division described the scene:

> A tall officer standing in the middle of the group could be identified immediately. [...] General Patton had come to witness the demonstration, but because his Third Army had not yet been activated, his presence in Normandy had been kept a secret.
>
> Patton was a fine-looking man with rugged features and piercing eyes. In his Eisenhower jacket, brightly polished riding boots, riding britches, and leather belt with a brass buckle and holding ivory-handled pistols, he looked every inch a soldier. Although some felt that he looked overdressed, this was part of his mystique. One could not help but stand in awe of him, and he dominated the conversation by his bearing and presence.
>
> [...]
>
> The test worked beautifully the first time; the tank went through the hedgerow without a problem. [...] When Patton nodded his approval, we knew it was a go situation.[4]

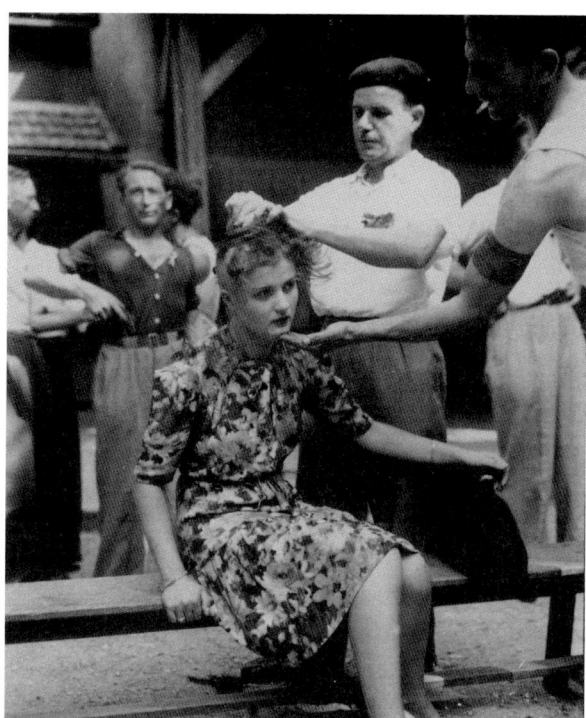

German collaborator. (*US National Archives*)

During those first few days in combat, Dad said almost everyone was a little jittery and trigger happy. One night they heard something outside of the tank, Dad yelled out for whoever was there to identify themselves but there was no response. The other members of the tank asked Dad, "' What are you going to do?' I said 'I'm going to throw a grenade out there.' I threw it out there." The tank crew heard no more noises around the tank the rest of the night, Dad said, "The next day there was a dead cow on the side of the tank." It seems that the many cows in Normandy did not fare well during the initial months after the invasion, as Father Murphy wrote: "There is fresh meat in many of the companies. 'The cows did not know the password.'"[5]

Further remembering an event that occurred in a hedgerow, Dad said, "We knew they (the Germans) were usually in the corner. One time, we fired a round from the big gun into that corner and all of a sudden I saw a pair of high heels fly up into the air. He (a German soldier) had his girlfriend in the foxhole with him."

"When we started going through these little towns, every time you saw a woman with a bandana on her head, that was a woman who was fooling with the German soldiers. As soon as they liberated a town, they (townspeople) grabbed them and shaved all their hair off. To let everybody know they were collaborators."

After the Allied forces successfully established beachheads on D-Day and consolidated their positions in the succeeding days, the Germans withdrew to fallback defensive positions away from the English Channel coast. One such defensive position the Germans occupied was Forêt de Mont Castre, designated on military maps as Hill 122 – its height above sea level measured in meters. The Romans had utilized this hill as a fortification during the Gallic Wars. This ancient fortification with its natural steep slopes is located in the middle of the Cotentin Peninsula; it was the most "commanding terrain feature of the entire peninsula, and the enemy used it to good advantage."[6] The Germans could see not only the Atlantic Ocean, about 8.5 miles to the west, but they also had a commanding view of the area between Forêt de Mont Castre and Utah Beach, about 17 miles to the northeast, the countryside occupied by the United States Army. From this position, the Germans were able to spot American forces and direct artillery fire upon American troops. Dad said, "So after that we came on in and at that time they (the Allies) only had a couple of miles (occupied). And the Germans had Hill 122, that was the military name. The Germans controlled that. We couldn't move there, they looked down on us. In fact I stayed in my tank for seven days without getting out. They would fire either artillery fire or mortar fire at us."

Although, the 712th did not officially enter combat until July 3, 1944, they were subject to enemy artillery fire beginning that first night ashore and remained subject to constant artillery barrages.

Tec 5 Fred Becker was an early casualty. He was killed on July 8, 1944 in Fortaire, France. Fred Becker was in the tank commanded by Sgt Orin Bourdo. Becker had gotten out of the tank to get some fresh air. As he was sitting on the front of the tank, a German artillery shell landed nearby and he was killed by a piece of shrapnel. The driver of the tank, Cpl Richard Gosselin, who was half out of the driver's hatch had an arm blown off. Gosselin was evacuated to a field hospital, the 76th Evac. Hospital, where he succumbed to those wounds on July 16. Orin Bourdo, who was standing in the top hatch and witnessed the unfolding tragedy, was unharmed.

In conformity with its status as an independent battalion, when the 712th entered combat, it was attached to the 90th Infantry Division, except for A Company, which was attached to the 82nd Airborne Division.[7] After these initial days in the Normandy campaign, the 712th was almost exclusively attached to the 90th for the remainder of the war. Although the 712th Tank Battalion was never made a part of the 90th Infantry Division, by war's end, the 90th considered the 712th as its own and the members of the 712th considered themselves as part of the 90th.

The 90th Infantry Division had been inactivated after World War I. The new 90th was reactivated in 1942 at Camp Barkeley in Texas. The 90th Infantry Division of World War II wore the olive drab patch with the red inscription that the 90th had worn in World War I. "To inquisitive strangers the 90th patiently explained that in past days the letters stood for Texas and Oklahoma, for the original (WWI) division was made up almost exclusively of men of those two states. Later, however, the division drew its men from every corner of every state in the nation and the T-O came to represent, by common consent 'Tough 'Ombres'."[8]

Part of the 90th Division came ashore at Utah Beach on D-Day, the remainder was scheduled for landing the next day. Its entrance into battle was marked by an event which one could say was a bad omen of things to come. The 90th crossed the English Channel on the transport ship, USS *Susan B. Anthony*. As the ship was moving to its landing position, it struck a mine and sank within two hours. The men of the 90th were beginning to move to the deck and load onto the landing crafts. They were loaded down with all their equipment – rifles, grenades, extra clips, BARs, tripods, mortar bases and tubes, gas masks – when a massive explosion midship knocked out communications and electricity. Soldiers still in the hold of the ship began to panic but the officers took charge and told the men to strip all unnecessary gear to abandon ship. Men discarded helmets, rifles and other equipment; some even took off their boots before scrambling to the deck. All personnel were safely removed from the Susan B. Anthony before she sank. The troops, having been transferred to Higgins landing crafts, went onto Utah Beach, but, many were barefoot, had no helmets, no rifles, no ammunition, and no food. They had to resort to re-supplying themselves with these basic items from the dead and wounded men on the beach and inland areas.

St Mère Eglise, the town so prominently chronicled in *The Longest Day* as being liberated by the 82nd Airborne Division, was also briefly occupied by the 90th. Father Murphy's diary entry for June 8, 1944, reads: "About midnight we hiked though the small village of Ste. Mère Eglise. There was no life visible. Doors of houses hung open; we passed the Church and the Church clock struck the hour of midnight. So we kept on going until we found our place in a field."[9] The 712th Tank Battalion's first bivouac area after coming ashore, Picauville, is not far from Ste. Mère Eglise. The 712th,[10] attached to the 90th Infantry Division, was committed to battle on July 3. After Picauville the 712th moved to Beuzeville La Bastile and then 500 yards south of the Chateau de Franqutot, where it bivouacked before entering battle on July 3, 1944.

"When we first came into contact with the 90th Division," explained Jim Cary,[11] "they were so amazed when we got the tanks where they were supposed to be on time; this had never happened to them before. They had worked with a different battalion. I thought, 'Why are they so surprised at this?' I mean, I would have caught hell if I hadn't gotten the tanks somewhere on time. We always got there on time."[12] On that first day, July 3rd, the town of St Jores was liberated en route to Hill 122. In the attack on St Jores that day, two tanks were lost to enemy action; Glen Halbert and John Mitchell were killed. Five others, Robert Naughton, Lt Otto Kreig, George Vernetti, Zygmund Kaminski, and Orval Williams, were wounded and evacuated to a field hospital.[13] Lee Sullivan was slightly wounded but did not require hospitalization. The first day of combat for the 712th was costly.

After leaving Picauville and passing by Franqutot, Dad and I stopped in St Jores to visit the church where he and Micaloni had attended Mass the day before Micaloni's death. St Jores is a small village about 13 miles inland from Utah Beach. Like many of the small towns that dot the French countryside, the church is located in the center of town, the church yard that surrounds the church contains the town cemetery. It being Saturday, the church was empty except for a man who was obviously the town drunk. He was laying against the side of the church and had urinated in his pants.

The church was unimposing, it was plain and obviously aged. As I looked around at the old stained glass windows, Dad knelt in one of the pews in quiet prayer. Dad seemed oblivious to my presence, in his mind's eye he was back in 1944 once again kneeling in the church surrounded by American GIs with Micaloni beside him. After several minutes of prayers, we departed and continued our trek along the battle route of the 712th.

Hill 122

The fortifications at Forêt de Mont Castre were part of the main German defense known as the Mahlman Line. This defensive position was meant to keep the Americans bottled up on the Cotentin Peninsula. "On the eastern side of the Cotentin peninsula was the city of Carentan; on the western side, the city of La Haye Du Puits, each located on the coast. In the center of the peninsula a large swampy area called Prairies Marecageuses de Georges virtually denied all military traffic through it and divided the peninsula into two sectors."[14] The Mahlman Line stretched from the Atlantic coast of the peninsula to Hill 122 and eastward to the swamp and flooded area east of the town of Le Plessis-Lastelle. B Company had engaged the enemy on the left flank at the ruins of an old castle which was marked on the military maps as Beau Coudray, near the town of Le Plessis-Lastelle.

The infantry would dig fox holes within which they would spend the night. With the constant shelling by artillery and mortars, the tank crews would park the tanks over the fox holes in order to protect the infantry from the incoming fire. Dad said, "We were stuck in the tank. We stayed in the tank for seven days. We couldn't get out, the mortars were coming in off the mountain. Leslie Vink was in a tank next to me. I saw him getting out of his tank and I said 'Where are you going Vink?' He said, 'I'm going to take a shit.' I said, 'If I were you I'd shit in my pants.' Just then and there a mortar came flying in and back into the tank he went and I never saw him (outside his tank) anymore (that day).

"After seven days, I had a beard so long that after I got out, after we pulled back and got away from the firing of the artillery, I went to shave and in those days you had a hand razor. It took me a pack of blades to shave."

When Dad finally got out of his tank after those seven days, he had a chance to go to the rear. He said, "The first body I ever saw… when I got onto land was German soldiers in the foxholes. We were out of the tank, and down the road and they had two German soldiers dead in foxholes. One was reaching over with a bottle of Cognac handing to the other one and all of his stomach was blown out, a shell hit him, a mortar, and blew all his stomach out. He was a nice looking fellow too, with red hair. I'll never forget it, red, red hair."

Hill 122 rises above the hedgerow laced fields of Normandy and in 1944 was covered with thick, tangled underbrush and scraggly trees. C Company of the 712th engaged the enemy at Hill 122 and sustained heavy losses. When Dad was training in the US, Jim Flowers was a lieutenant in B Company and Dad knew Jim well. But when the 712th came overseas, Flowers was reassigned to C Company.

In the fighting for Hill 122, Flowers and his tank platoon were assigned to the First Battalion of the 359th Regiment of the 90th Infantry Division. However, on July 10, Flowers volunteered four of C Company tanks to help out the Third Battalion of the 358th Regiment, also of the 90th. The infantry battalion had been encircled by the Germans near the summit of Hill 122.

Flowers' tanks reached the trapped Third Battalion, which was under the command of Col. Jacob Bealke. Although Flowers' platoon did not meet stiff resistance on its way to the encircled battalion, it did encounter mortar and small arms fire. Rather than have the infantryman withdraw from the hill via the path Flowers' tank took to reach them, Col. Bealke devised a plan for Flowers to punch a hole through the underbrush and the rear of the German line at a different location and continue the fight to obtain control of Hill 122. The 712th tanks successfully opened a path off of the hill, clearing underbrush and knocking down small trees and reached hedgerow lined fields on the side of the hill opposite the American forces. While attempting to bust through these fields to reach the American side, Flowers' unit encountered German 88 anti-tank guns.

Flowers' tank took a direct hit and the German shell ignited the ammunition in the tank, engulfing it in flames. Flowers pulled the gunner to safety and jumped from the tank only to realize when hitting the ground that his right foot had been shot off.

He used his belt for a tourniquet and assembled the survivors of the other three tanks that had also been hit. After fighting off German infantry soldiers,

Flowers ordered the survivors to withdraw but he, his gunner, and an infantry soldier were too badly wounded to go with the survivors. They stayed on the battlefield and requested that medics be sent with litters to pick them up.

Before medics could rescue the three Americans, Germans came through the field to their position. Upon seeing them and how badly they were wounded, the Germans ignored them with the exception of one German medic who bandaged their burns.

The next day, American artillery bombarded the area in preparation for another attack. One of the shells exploded between Flowers and the infantryman. A piece of the shell took off Flowers' left leg just below the knee. He placed a tourniquet on this leg and bandaged the infantryman with strips of cloth torn from his shirt. Flowers, the gunner, and the infantryman spent another night in the field that was still being shelled with American artillery. American infantry troops reached Flowers the next day but not before the infantryman died from his wounds. Flowers survived and was sent home. He was nominated for the Medal of Honor but was only awarded the Distinguished Service Cross because there were no corroborating witnesses to every segment of his heroic ordeal. Of the 712th's tanks twenty crew members that ascended Hill 122, nine were killed, several more were wounded and some were captured. The Third Battalion of the 358th Regiment suffered a similar fate. Early on July 10, the Battalion strength was nineteen officers and 563 men; by the end of the day their casualties, dead, wounded and captured, totaled eleven officers and 343 men, leaving only eight officers and 220 men to continue the battle. By the 12th of July, when Flowers was rescued, Hill 122 had been captured, and the Third Battalion now consisted of four officers and 126 men. The actions of the Third Battalion of the 358th and C Company of the 712th on July 10 were considered the major factor in the Americans breaking the Mahlman Line.

Dad and I visited the base of Hill 122, where a small stone monument with a marble plaque stands as a memorial to nine men from the 712th who were killed in action during that battle.

Not far from this monument, down the lane adjacent to it, is the spot where Flowers' tank was knocked out. The fire from its destruction was so hot that the soil underneath it was sterilized. To this day, the area where Flowers' tank burned is plainly visible from the remainder of the field – vegetation does grow on that spot.

B Company of the 712th and the 357th Regiment were on the left flank of Hill 122 near Beau Coudray. While Jim Flowers and his platoon from C Company were battling near Hill 122, B Company engaged the Germans and were also sustaining casualties. Sgt Gerald Thomas was killed; Wilbur Beneway, Edward Petke, Melvin Koehn, Bill Nick, and Leslie Arnold were wounded and evacuated.

The Hedgerows

Above: Hill 122 Monument. (*Author's collection*)

Right: Hill 122 Monument plaque. (*Author's collection*)

After the capture of Hill 122, Father Murphy entered in his diary, "July 12, 1944 – Wednesday. Moved to Beau Coudray. This is the place we were fighting for. [...] The whole town is shot. Many of the enemy dead are along the way."[15]

As Dad and I drove down one of the rolling Normandy roads, it reminded Dad of another event that occurred in 1944. While traveling on a similar road, Dad's tank came over the crest of a rise in the road and was facing the gun barrel of a Panzer Tank. Knowing that a Sherman Tank had little chance in a one on one frontal confrontation with a Panzer, instinct and adrenalin nevertheless caused them to prepare to fire a shot, but in the instant before firing and while the Panzer was getting its gun into position, an amazing thing happened. "Everyone thought we were finished when all of a sudden it (the Panzer) burst into flame. An American P-47 came flying over, saw the German tank heading toward us, and dropped a bomb on it. The P-47 made another pass over us and we cheered and waved to him in thanks."

With casualties mounting, B Company received its first set of replacement troops – twelve soldiers joined the company on July 14.[16] On July 18, another seven replacements arrived, including a new lieutenant, Robert Vutech.[17]

The Seves River and Périers

After the 90th and the 712th broke through the Mahlman Line and captured Hill 122 and Le Plessis-Lastelle, the Germans withdrew to the south side of the Seves River. Although called a river, it is no more than a stream that meanders through the fields of Normandy. The relatively flat fields and small hills on either banks of the river are only slightly higher in elevation than the river bed. Despite its bucolic and tranquil appearance today, in 1944 the Seves River and its surrounding terrain provided the Germans a formidable defensive stronghold. The Germans had dug in and fortified the hedgerows on the southern bank of the river.

Prior to the invasion, the Germans had expanded the natural swampy boundaries of the Prairies Marecageuses de Georges by flooding the low lying areas behind the coastline in order to drown any invading paratroopers and impede any advancement by invading land forces. This pre-invasion flooding of the Normandy countryside had made the terrain swampy on both sides of the Seves River and practically impossible for tanks to traverse.

On July 22 the 90th resumed its southerly attack toward Périers by attempting to cross the Seves River east of le Plessis-Lastelle, near the town of St Germain sur Seves. The area of the battle became known as Seves Island. Although not technically an island, the battlefield is, high open ground surrounded with the river on one side and the swampy area formed by the flooding on the other side making it appear as an island.

Seves River. (*Author's collection*)

On that day, Dad was in a tank with Albert Stewart, Wilburn Moody, Harold Slayton, and Lloyd Sparks. He stated, "When we went into this area, St Germain Sur Seves; that's where I lost the first tank. We attacked and we went through the marshland and my tank sunk up to the belly in the mud, you couldn't move it. The ground was too soft and we bogged down. And they (Germans) started throwing artillery fire and mortar fire, so we had to jump out of the tank and get back. We had to run through a little fence with a gate on it, and they said be careful coming through that fence, they've got that gate zeroed in. So we had to run out one at a time, so if they shelled, it wouldn't hit everyone at one time."

I asked Dad what happened when a situation like that occurred, where did he go? Dad answered, "Wherever you could, you'd try to get back to company headquarters. And that's where you'd wait until you get your next deal. Evidently, after that they (the service unit) were sent out there with a cable on it and pulled that tank out. Well, when you regroup at night, if anyone had casualties, they'd split us up and put us in another tank. And, they always had replacements coming up, then when the new tanks came in we might be placed in those. Also (the service units) would go get a disabled tank and tow it out."

With the Germans dug in and fortified on the southern side of the Seves River, the 90th proceeded with a daylight attack across the open area of Seves Island with disastrous results: one officer and sixty-eight men were killed, five officers and ninety-nine men wounded, and eleven officers and 254 men captured. With the dead and dying strewn across the field, three American chaplains brokered an eight hour truce with the German commanding officer in order to remove the dead and wounded.[18]

By all historical accounts, the senior officer corps who commanded the 90th in the early days of battle proved to be weak and ineffective combat leaders.[19]

After approximately two months of combat, they were eventually replaced because of the high casualties sustained by the 90th in those first few weeks after D-Day.

American Army tactical training manuals stressed the need for tank-infantry cooperation.[20] In Normandy this proved difficult for all infantry and tank units for practical reasons – communications. No one had foreseen the need for air to ground communications, or communications from pilot to tank commander, or even to infantry walking beside the tank to communicate with the tank crew when the hatch was down.[21] While these practical difficulties were quickly solved with modification of the tanks communication system, by allowing the infantry to plug in a field communication headset into a communication port at the rear of the tank, there were additional problems existing between the 712th and the 90th.

While the armored divisions had trained with their attached infantry personnel, the infantry divisions, such as the 90th, and the independent tank battalions that were to support them had no opportunity to train or work together prior to being thrown together in combat. This lack of training was self-evident in July of 1944 when the 90th and the 712th were put into combat together.

During those initial days of combat, the coordination between the lines of command for the 712th and the 90th were stretched to almost the breaking point. The infantry commanders had no knowledge on the capabilities and proper tactical deployment of tanks in the Normandy terrain.

During this early period, the senior infantry officers would pull rank on the junior tank officers and ordered the tanks to proceed into situations hazardous to the tank. Following the debacle on Seves Island, the 90th again tried to advance across the Seves River on July 26, as part of the beginning of Operation Cobra and the push to take the town of Périers.

The shortest distance from Le Plessis-Lastelle to Périers is along the road known as the Old Roman Road. It dates back to the time when the Forêt du Monte Castre was an outpost for the Roman legions. The bridge on the Roman Road across the Seves River had been destroyed by the Germans and like the area around Seves Island further east, the area on either side of the destroyed bridge was open swampy fields. Not to repeat the fiasco of July 22, the commanders of the 90th did not want the infantry advancing across this open swampy area. Several hundred yards east of the destroyed bridge, the river was shallow and there was a natural ford known as Hausley Quarry Ford. Although the open area of the ford was narrower than the expanse near the bridge, it was nevertheless heavily defended by German troops entrenched in the hedgerows on the south side The infantry commanders made the decision to advance across Hausley Quarry Ford with the 712th tanks leading the way.

Dad explained what happened to Micaloni and his crew on that day.

That's where Micaloni got killed, he was in our company, B Company. He went up and his tank got blown up. It was right on the Seves River. These guys should have gotten nothing less than the Silver Star because they didn't have to die. They were ordered to go and they went. They had to go through that river, the Seves River. The (infantry) colonel gave a direct order for them to take the tank up in there. Captain Galvin (712th B Company commander) didn't want them to go. Galvin was a big guy, kind of heavyset and boy he could drink some booze. He told Micaloni, "Don't Go." Micaloni told him, "I will go Captain." Galvin was right.

The terrain was not meant for tank warfare – the surrounding swampy fields could not be traversed by tanks and the northern approaches to the ford had been mined. "They hit a tank mine and it blew the tank completely up." All four of the 712th tank crew, Tullio Micaloni, Frank Krusel, Nicholas Milczakowski, and James Gaither were killed, due to the explosive device containing approximately 400 lbs of TNT.[22] We had visited the graves of Micaloni, Krusel, and Milczakowski at Omaha Beach, but I had asked about the other crew member, Gaither, and the fifth member of the tank crew. Gaither was from Alabama, after the war his remains were brought back to the US, at the request of his family.

"The fifth guy was sick. I understand that on the first day of combat he killed sixteen American soldiers. He shot in the woods (thinking them to be Germans). Now that was just hearsay, I don't know if that was true or not. It was probably true. But he was sick and Micaloni told him to get out. So he got out and they asked somebody to volunteer so an infantryman jumped in. Nobody knows who he was."

After Micaloni's tank was lost, "The captain went back to the generals at HQ and told them that area was not a place (the marsh around Seves River) for tanks to fight. All you could hear was the captain (yelling). Nobody else said anything. The general told the captain 'Ok you run your tanks,' and he told the infantry colonel, 'You take care of the infantry.'"

The end of the campaign in Normandy was at hand. Operation Cobra was designed to permit the US Army to breakout of the hedgerow country. It involved a massive bombing of the German defenses around St Lô followed by the Americans moving across the German defenses along the road between St Lô and Périers. Dad said that during the bombardment, they sat on the top of their tank and watched all of bombers dropping their bombs. The sky was dark with all of the planes that were flying on the bombing mission, about 3,000 planes.

Operation Cobra, however was not without mishap. On July 24, the weather was poor and the attack was postponed, some of the bombers however, did not get word of the one day delay in the attack. The pilots proceeded with the bomb run, but due to the poor weather, some of the bombs were dropped upon American GIs instead of the Germans, killing or wounding over 150 Americans. The next day, the attack proceeded again. Once more the weather was not ideal; it was difficult for the bombers to identify the front lines and once again some of the planes inadvertently dropped their bombs on American troops. Friendly fire killed over 150 Americans and wounded over 500 that day. Included in the fatalities was Lieutenant-General Lesley N. McNair, the architect of the Army's reorganization and tactical doctrine for armored forces. McNair had only just arrived in Europe three days earlier and was positioned on a hill to observe the attack. He was the highest ranking American General killed in World War II.[23] McNair is buried in the American Cemetery in Normandy.

As part of the breakout operation, B Company tanks of the 712th were engaged in indirect firing on the town of Périers. Indirect firing was essentially using the 70-mm tank cannon as an artillery piece.

Despite the initial heavy fighting, Périers was liberated by the 359th Regiment of the 90th with the help of D Company of the 712th along with one platoon from B Company. Dad was in that B Company platoon and explains, "I was in the first tank that entered Périers and we proceeded toward the train station. My tank commander, Sgt Warren Willinger, told us that whoever captures the train station in a town is credited with capturing the town. Ours was the first tank at the train station"

Dad and I passed by Henri Levaufre's home on the way into town. Henri, however, was in the United States attending a reunion of the 90th Infantry Division. We spent the night in the hotel in Périers. Being a Saturday, we attended the vigil Mass in the town's church, across the street from the hotel.

There were photos on the wall of the hotel taken in Périers during the war. The town had been virtually destroyed by the bombs and artillery shells of the US Army. In 1944, Cpl Albert O. Maranda, was in the 4th Armored Division that participated in Operation Cobra wrote in his diary, "29th July: Raining – moved out at 07:28 hours. Went down St Lô – Périers highway through Périers. All towns and villages in shambles. Périers almost flattened – people streaming back to their former homes if they can find them."[24]

After the battle front had moved on, the badly damaged church and the town hall were rebuilt to appear as they did before the destruction. Many of the ancient buildings in France are constructed of stone. Dad said that when these buildings were destroyed during the war, the citizens would reuse the same stones and reassemble the buildings piece by piece like a jigsaw puzzle. When Dad and I attended Mass in the church in Périers, I noticed that the structure itself was reassembled with no apparent visible difference. The statues and other ornamental decorations inside of church were also apparently the originals and reused but they were damaged and scarred. The main crucifix over the altar showed visible breaks and cracks. Henri Levaufre said that the repairs to the church in Périers were not completed until 1960.

At the same time of the breakout and the liberation of Périers, the United States Third Army was being activated under the command of Gen. George S. Patton. The 90th Infantry and the 712th Tank Battalion was transferred to the command of Patton. Under Patton's command the rapid pace across Europe began. Whereas in June and July, the army was fighting and measuring its advance in yards per day, now the advance was being measured in miles per day. The Battle for Normandy was over, but it was costly.

The 90th had the eighth highest battle casualty rate of all divisions in World War II. The weak leadership of the 90th at this early stage of combat led to it having this high rate; of the roughly 14,200 troops in the Division that landed June 6 and 7, approximately 6,000 were wounded and over 1,000 were KIA. The ineptitude of the 90th's leaders had an equally devastating effect upon the 712th Tank Battalion; of the KIA casualties suffered during the entire war, 35 percent of the 712th's KIAs occurred in the month of July 1944.

These dismal casualty statistics almost led to the 90th's death knell as a Division. On June 9, Gen. Omar Bradley had issued orders to Lieutenant-General Joseph L. Collins to cut off the Cotenin Peninsula at its neck before going to Cherbourg. The 82nd Airborne, the 4th, 9th and 90th Divisions were assigned the task.

For three days the 90th floundered in starting its attack. On the fourth day, Gen. Collins asked that the 90th commander Brig.-Gen. Jay W. MacLelvie be relieved. Shortly before leaving the United States, MacKelvie, the division's former artilleryman, was promoted to division commander, a job for which he was not adequately trained. His problems in combat were further compounded by too many inept subordinate commanders.

Gen. Omar Bradley wrote about the 90th after the war:

Our choice of the 90th turned out poorly. For three days the division floundered in its starting attack. [...]

For the first few days in combat most new divisions suffer a disorder resulting from acute mental shock. Until troops can acclimate themselves to the agony of the wounded and the finality of death, they herd by instinct in fear and confusion. They cannot be driven into attack but must be led, and sometimes coaxed, by their commanders. Within a few days this shock ordinarily wears off, the division overcomes its baptismal panic, and troops respond normally to assured and intelligent command.

Where possible we made an effort to relieve the severity of that shock by conditioning each new unit in a 'quiet' sector before committing it to attack. But when the 90th came ashore on the heels of the 4th Division across Utah Beach, there was no 'quiet' sectors. We had no choice but to fling it into an attack that would have tested the mettle of veterans. But this sudden immersion was not confined to the 90th alone. Other equally green divisions entered the line under even more appalling conditions and most of them weathered the ordeal with distinction. Almost from the moment of its starting attack, however, the 90th became a 'problem' division. So exasperating was its performance that at one point the First Army Staff gave up and recommended that we break it up for replacements.[25]

Maj.-Gen. Eugene M. Landrum, Gen. Collins' deputy at VII Corps, was chosen to replace MacKelvie, and cautioned to clean house throughout his new command. However, after three more weeks of poor performance by the 90th staff resulting in two companies surrendering to the enemy and a battalion position falling. Landrum had not made enough changes. The division's morale had been shaken and whatever confidence it had was gone. Landrum had not supplied the needed spark and was relieved from command of the 90th, although Gen. Bradley's staff strongly suggested that the division be cannibalized for replacements, Bradley was not convinced that the division could not be rescued by an outstanding commander.

With the Third Army about to be activated, Bradley decided to keep the division intact rather than cannibalize it for replacements as suggested. He transferred it to units that would soon comprise the Third Army that would be under the command of Gen. George S. Patton Jr.

Every war seems to have one or two generals whose names are indelibly associated with that conflict throughout history. Patton is one such general of World War II. He was not without his supporters and critics during and after the war but the successes of the Third Army under his command are indisputable and assure his place in military history.

Eisenhower said of Patton, "He was one of those men born to be a soldier, an ideal combat leader whose gallantry and dramatic personality inspired all he commanded to great deeds of valor. His presence gave me the certainty that the boldest plan would be even more daringly executed. It is no exaggeration to say that Patton's name struck terror at the hearts of the enemy."[26]

George Patton is largely known by my generation as a result of the 1970 movie, *Patton*. Surprisingly, George C. Scott's portrayal of the man, his public persona and the events that helped create it, is regarded as being highly accurate.

Patton's flashy uniforms, his polished helmet, and ivory-handled pistols resulted in some of his contemporary American and British generals considering him a showman. Patton's public image was for the most part, by design, of his own making to boost morale among his troops and the American public. Other generals of WWII era portrayed themselves as "just an ordinary Joe".

Patton deliberately chose another style – he was not trying to be perceived as "democratic general" or "a man of the people". He wanted his image to be one of a hard charging, aggressive general with a desire to win, but at a minimum cost in American lives. The opening seen of the movie *Patton*, where George C. Scott appears on a stage before a group of troops is an accurate portrayal of both the appearance and words of the speeches George Patton made to the troops in England in the spring of 1944. Much of the dialogue in the movie faithfully drew on the actual words of Patton.

Beneath the flashy and brash exterior, however, Patton was a thoughtful, intelligent and professional soldier. He was on the forefront of progressive leadership style which distinguished him from other Allied generals. In both strategy and leadership methods, Patton abandoned some of the old military ways and employed a new style. Patton abandoned the old command methods of the US Army – close supervision of subordinates and written specific orders, instead issuing detailed orders he preferred in "mission command": "Never tell people how to do things, tell them what to do and they will surprise you with their own ingenuity."

Patton utilized military intelligence to his advantage. The Germans encrypted their military messages with an Enigma machine, a keyboard device for enciphering and deciphering their messages; they believed the Allies were incapable of intercepting and deciphering their secret messages and orders. But in 1940 the British had recovered an Enigma machine from a sunken submarine and soon began intercepting most of Germany's top-secret messages. To preserve the secret that the cipher had been broken, Allied intelligence derived from enigma signals were a special security Ultra Secret Source, and referred to as ULTRA.

Instead of engaging in frontal attacks on an enemy's main defense, resulting in a large attrition of manpower, Patton believed in maneuver warfare. Patton's idea was to keep the enemy off balance – keeping his troops moving while the enemy's troops were in disorder. "My men don't dig foxholes. I don't want them to. Foxholes only slow up an offensive. Keep moving. And don't give the enemy time to dig one, either."

Patton used the military intelligence of ULTRA in formulating his tactical battle plans, picking the enemy's weakest points and then planning rapid attacks resulting in the fewest American casualties, whereas the Allied generals tended to determine the objective and then consult with military intelligence to assess the attack plan.

When Patton began to review the units that would be under his command, one of the first orders of business for the 90th was to fill the vacancy at the top position. When Patton was given a long list of possible replacements, he caught sight of two names on the list: Raymond S. McLain and Theodore Roosevelt Jr.

Patton is quoted as stating, "I recalled, however, in thinking of Roosevelt that Eisenhower and I had once agreed in Sicily that Ted's easy indifference to discipline would probably limit him to a single star. 'The men worship Ted,' I had explained to Ike, 'but he's too softhearted to take a division – too much like one of the boys.' But it was not a disciplinarian the 90th needed now. It called for a man with vitality and courage, a man who could pick up the division singlehandedly and give it confidence in itself. If anyone fitted that description, Ted Roosevelt was his name. With a thick-skinned disciplinarian as his second in command, Ted would have the 90th brawling with the Germans in a couple of weeks."[27]

Patton telephoned Eisenhower at SHAEF (Supreme Headquarters Allied Expeditionary Force) on July 13 to recommend Roosevelt for the job. But it was about midnight and Eisenhower had gone to bed. Patton told Gen. Bedell Smith of his choice. Smith said that he would pass it by Eisenhower in the morning. It was Eisenhower's decision to forward the recommendation to Washington for Roosevelt's promotion.

Patton relating the incident stated:

> Bedell called back early the next morning. I had not yet gone to breakfast. "I've got the answer for you on Roosevelt. Ike said O.K. It's the right thing to do."
>
> "It's too late, Bedell," I answered, "Ted died of a heart attack at midnight last night." The news had been telephoned me from the 4th Division where Ted had been assigned as a spare brigadier. The coronary attack had come unexpectedly and without warning; Ted died as no one could have believed he would, in the quiet of his tent.[28]

General Roosevelt is buried in the Normandy Cemetery above Omaha Beach.

As a result of Roosevelt's death, Patton had to make another choice for a replacement for the 90th. On July 30, Patton chose, Brig.-Gen. Raymond S. McLain who had served with him in Sicily. He informed Bradley of his choice. "As the discussion ended Bradley said: 'George, you haven't commented on any of these officers. This Division is going to belong to you; you had better speak up.' Patton replied, 'Hell, damn it, I told you McLain and that is what I meant.' McLain got the 90th. He had earned Patton's trust and that was good enough."[29]

McLain would take over the reins of the 90th as the Battle for Normandy was coming to an end and the Battle of Northern France beginning. McLain was told to replace any subordinate officer he wanted. Within two days McLain had a list of sixteen officers he deemed unsatisfactory in his command. They were quickly transferred out of the 90th.

CHAPTER 6

The Breakout

Death in battle is a function of time. The longer troops remain under fire, the more men get killed. Therefore, everything must be done to speed up movement.

General George S. Patton Jr.

Give George a headline, and he's good for thirty miles was Omar Bradley's assessment of Patton's motivation for his rapid advance. After slugging it out for seven weeks in the hedgerows, Eisenhower appreciated every mile gained by Patton's forces.

The month of August, 1944 has been chronicled as one of the most remarkable periods in military history.[1] The month began with the ultimate success of the D-Day invasion still in doubt. More than any other campaign of the war, it sealed the fate of the Axis powers. The coming of age of the American army as an outstanding military organization, the unprecedented movement of Allied forces, and the Allied military strategy in Western Europe during this month had a major impact on the outcome of the war. It tipped the scales between victory and defeat.

The US Third Army's rapid progress across France during the month of August began immediately after Patton assumed command. In the fifty-one days from June 6 to July 27, the US Army had progressed a mere 25 miles inland, the distance between Utah Beach and Périers. In contrast the distant from Périers to Avranches is approximately 34 miles and the Army traversed that territory within two days.

With our tour of Normandy at an end, Dad and I left Périers and headed south on the road to Coutances and beyond that Highway D-7 to Avranches, the very road where the 712th tanks traveled on August 2, 1944 as part of the Third Army.

As Operation Cobra was in progress, Gen. Omar Bradley told Patton on July 28, 1944 that the Third Army would be officially activated on the 1st of August. In the meantime Patton was given interim command of the VIII Corps, which included the 90th Infantry.

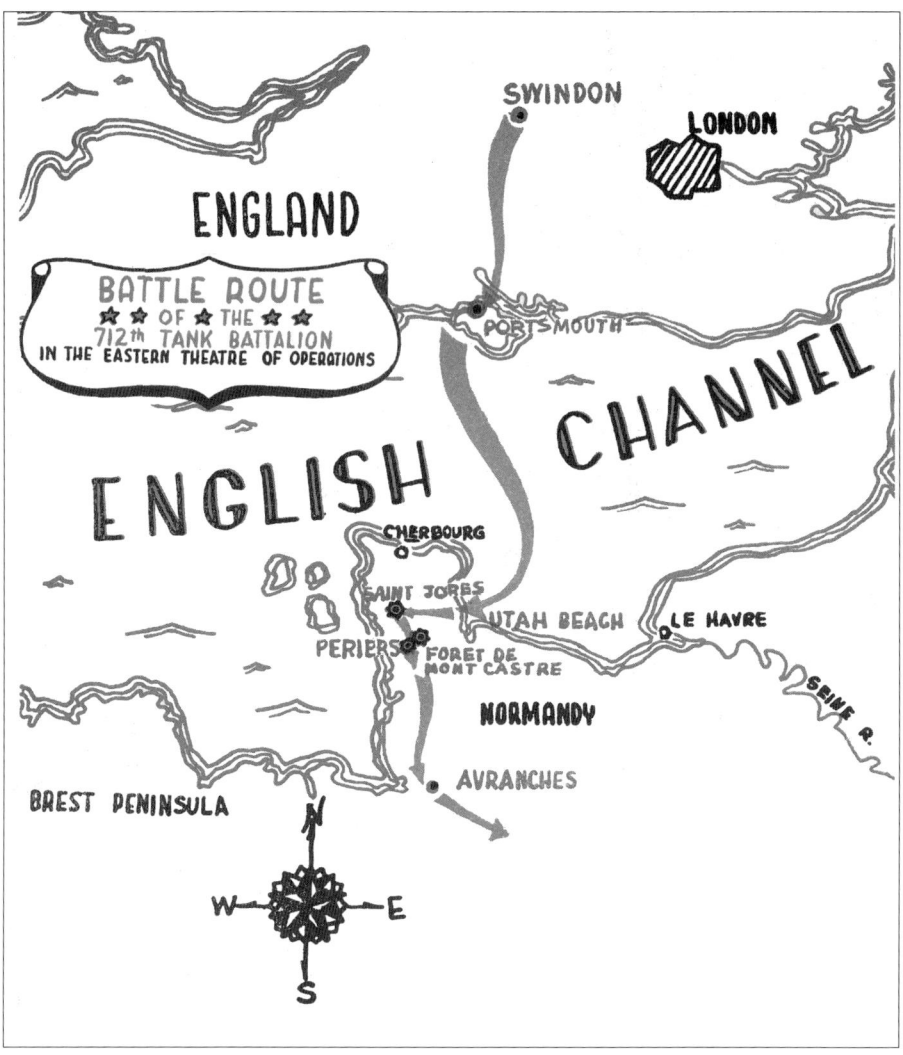

The 712th Battle Route – Normandy Campaign. (*The History of the 712th Tank Battalion*)

The original plans for the Battle of France called for the Allies to advance westward into Brittany after breaking out of Normandy. The ultimate goal was to seize two the deep water ports of Brest and Lorient. The Allied military planners wanted to use the ports along the Brittany coast for discharging the supplies that would be needed to move across France methodically and defeat the Germans. Patton, however had already realized that the bombings and breakout had the Germans in disarray and that the initial success of Operation Cobra also presented an opportunity to move eastward and encircle the bulk of the German forces in Normandy. But to do that there had to be a rapid movement of troops through the opening in the enemy lines.

The Third Army's attack in all directions. (*The History of the 712th Tank Battalion*)

On July 29, 1944, as troops began moving south, Patton found a battalion of the 90th Infantry digging foxholes. He chastised the troops to begin moving, by shouting to them, "It is stupid to be afraid of a beaten enemy."[2]

Mindful that his orders were to advance only westward in Brittany, Patton had his staff make contingency plans for an eastward movement as well. In order to convince both Bradley and Eisenhower to allow him to both move eastward as well as fulfilling the Third Army's initial mission for Brittany, a sufficiently large number of troops through the breakout corridor was essential.

On the afternoon of August 1st, Patton went to Avranches to do the impossible – move two armored divisions and two infantry divisions, more than 100,000 men and 20,000 vehicles, within a two day period, across a single bridge and along the one main north-south street through town. That afternoon, he took control by replacing an MP and began personally directing the traffic. By the end of the day, Patton had gotten the four divisions through the bottleneck and on their westward movement, he also succeeded in getting the 90th through and situated southeast of Avranches in anticipation of getting permission from SHAEF to move eastward in a looping drive to Paris.

Patton was now in a position to put his personal philosophy of tank warfare into practice in territory where he was no longer hampered by hedgerows.

> The question of whether infantry or tanks lead in attacking is determined by the character of the ground and of the enemy resistance. Whenever the ground permits tanks to advance rapidly, even with the certainty of a loss from mine fields, they should lead. Through dense woods or against prepared positions or unlocated anti-tank guns, infantry leads, followed closely by tanks, which act as close supporting artillery. But irrespective of the foregoing, some tanks must accompany the infantry when they reach the objective. These tanks are for the purpose of removing enemy weapons which emerge after the passage of the leading tanks.[3]

The tank column of the 712th was moving at a rapid pace (rapid being a relative term since the maximum speed of a Sherman Tank was 20-25 miles per hour), the 90th Infantry hopped on the sides and tops of the tanks for a ride. Dad explained, "This is the road into Avranches. The infantry rode on the tank. We went barreling down the street."

Father Murphy writes:

> We are going in our vehicles at top speed through dark roads, no lights, all on a long convoy. [...] We go through the towns of Countances and Avranches with its church on a high hill.
> [...]
> We saw Patton at one point standing on a jeep urging the troops to keep moving. [...] Tanks are coming up and preceding us all the time."[4]

The column reached Avranches at about midnight. In the History of the 712th Tank Battalion this event is recorded as:

> Suddenly the black night was pierced by flares dropped by an attacking squadron of Luftwaffe bombers. The tankers crouched in their tanks and experienced all the fearful perils of a bombing as the Boche dumped his load.

Dad continues his account, "We had a night bombing at Avranches. That's when they (the infantry) jumped off and got in the ditches to protect themselves from the bombing." Fortunately, in Dad's sector, the accuracy of the Lufwaffe's bombers was poor, only one truck was hit and the column detoured around it and continued their forward progress. As Dad told it, "When they were bombing us along in here, during the night, they'd drop flares to see what was on the ground. They dropped one and it hit an ammunition truck and it had gasoline on it. And it blew up and the ammunition started going off. We had to get it pushed on the side to keep on going. The pilot was diving so low you could see him in the cockpit with the flares out there."

An officer on the Third Army's staff described the bombing that night and Patton's reaction to it.

> General Patton had ordered our Headquarters set up in several adjoining fields in the center of this gap, so that he could be right on the ground to see that all of our divisions were pushed through the opening quickly. [...] Just after dark – almost midnight – [...] the bombers came over, by the hundreds it seemed, and they laid their eggs. You could hear them whistle and scream as they fell and the ground rocked with the explosions. The planes circled over for more than an hour, sounding like a great hive of angry hornets.

At the height of the bombing a secret message in a sealed envelope arrived for Patton. The messenger was directed towards Patton's trailer where he found him smoking a cigar and looking up into the sky watching the bombing. "The Gen. was cool as a cucumber. He just looked up into the sky and kept saying aloud: 'Those goddamn bastards, those rotten sons-of-bitches! We'll get them! We'll get them...'"[5]

As Dad and I drove though Avranches along the main highway, we came to a point on a cliff overlooking the Atlantic Ocean and in the distance we could see Mont St Michel. We took a little time to detour off the battle route and visit one of the most scenic spots in France.

This rocky islet, jutting above the sandbanks and waters of the Gulf of St Malo, has a walled village at its base and a Benedictine abbey, dedicated to the archangel St Michael, perched atop its highest point. With a history dating back to the year 708, the present abbey was built between the 11th and 16th centuries.

The geography of the Mont is what gives it its most unique characteristic. On this northwestern shore of France, the difference in the sea level between low tide and high tide is at times as much as forty feet. During low tide each day Mont St Michel is surrounded by land; and you can actually observe the sea rushing in to surround the Mont at high tide. The overall height of the of the island, including the church is well over five hundred feet and it is a spectacular sight to see it silhouetted against the western sky from the French shoreline.

Mont St Michel's awesome fortifications were attacked many times during the Hundred Years War, but never captured. During World War II, German soldiers barricaded themselves on Mont St Michel, but Dad said that the Third Army just bypassed it and eventually, when the Germans ran out of food, they surrendered. Among his many spiritual duties, St Michael is the patron saint of soldiers; how fitting it was that this shrine to St Michael went unscathed during World War II.

In August 1944 the troops did not have the luxury of stopping for a sightseeing tour. I doubt that the soldiers in 712th and the 90th even got a glimpse of Mont St Michel in the dark distance. After reaching Avranches, the Third Army split up and advanced in three different directions at the same time; several days later it was attacking in all four directions, north, south, east and west. The 90th Division and the 712th were part of Task Force Weaver heading eastward toward Paris.

On August 2, 1944, Patton wrote in his diary his thoughts regarding the 90th Infantry Division.

> East of Avranches we caught up with the 90th, which is moving along the road between the See and the Selune Rivers. The division is bad, the discipline poor, the men filthy, and the officers apathetic, many of them removing their insignia and covering the markings on their helmets. I saw one artillery lieutenant jump out of his jeep and hide in a ditch when one plane flew over at a high altitude firing a little. I corrected these acts on the spot. I got out and walked in the column for about 2 miles, talking to them. Some were getting rides on guns and others made no comment. I called them babies and they dismounted. They seemed normal but are not in hard condition.

Due to its performance record in Normandy, Eisenhower and Omar Bradley had the same assessment of the 90th Infantry Division. In Eisenhower's words, the 90th had not been "well brought up," – that is, not well trained in the United States and had had a particularly grueling initiation into combat in the Cotentin. But McLain and Weaver would soon turn it into a hard-hitting outfit.[6]

Regarding his decision not to disband the 90th, Bradley commented, "we stayed with the division and in the end the 90th became one of the most outstanding in the European Theater. In the metamorphosis, it demonstrated how swiftly a strong commander can transfuse his own strength into a command."[7] The disbanding of the 90th Infantry Division would not have affected the 712th's status as an independent battalion, it would merely have been assigned to a different infantry division. But, after that first month of on the job training, the 90th and the 712th began to gel as a team; if the 90th had been disbanded, that first month of combat – learning each other's strengths and weaknesses – would have been for naught. Attachment to another division may have caused the 712th to continue to experience a high casualty rate. Bradley's decision to "stay with" the 90th also benefitted the 712th.

Between the end of the war in May of 1945 and his premature death following an automobile accident in December of 1945, Patton wrote his wartime memoirs, compiling information from his diary and letters he had written. In his memoirs, Patton again writes about that meeting with the 90th on August 2. With the benefit of hindsight, he was a bit more reflective and wrote:

> On the second of August, Stiller and I joined the column of the 90th Division marching east from Avranches, and walked in their ranks for some hours. At that time the efficiency of this division was extremely dubious, but had just secured the services of General McLain and General Weaver. When we got to a point where the road turned south to St Hilaire, I met McLain and Haislip, and was informed that the fighting down the road was caused by Weaver, personally leading an assault over a bridge. This was the beginning of the making of one of the greatest divisions that ever fought, and was due largely to these two men. The division subsequently had a series of great commanders.
>
> Driving back to Army Headquarters with Haislip, I saw a young officer and his driver leap wildly out of a jeep and into a ditch. I went up to find out what was the matter and they said an enemy plane was overhead. That was true, but it was so high it was practically innocuous; just another instance of the nervousness of a first fight. They got back into the car even faster than they got out.[8]

To achieve the liberation of Paris, the Allies had to occupy the City of Mayenne and then Le Mans in successive order. The Third Army, more particularly, Task Force Weaver, was charged with this objective. When the 90th was in the town of St Hilaire-du-Harcouet, a small town near Avranches, Brig.-Gen. William Weaver, the Assistant Division Commander of the 90th, was given his orders to take LeMans, 82 miles behind enemy lines. Sub-Task Force Randolph (named after Lt-Col. George Randolph, the commanding officer of the 712th) was the point unit of this eastward attack. The Third Army was essentially moving parallel to the English Channel coastline, approximately 60 miles inland. The English and Canadian forces were still held up along the beaches of Normandy. Consequently, the German army was situated between the English and the Americans.

Since the Wehrmacht was in a state of disarray as a result of the breakout from St Lô, the plan called for the use of surprise and speed and with as little as contact with the Germans as possible. Weaver sent out his various reconnaissance units with the instructions, "Don't look for Germans. Just find out where they ain't."

Dad said of the 712th's involvement, "Task Force Randolph – that's when they told us to go and keep going as far as we could go." Dr William

M. McConahey, a medical officer in the 90th Division, described this mad dash after the breakout in much the same way, "Now the Germans were disorganized and our armored divisions were on the loose. Then the 90th got orders to take off: to strike out boldly to capture LeMans, far to the southeast. We were just to keep going, not worrying about enemy troops on the flanks and behind us. Just keep going!"[9]

It was en route to Mayenne that the newly liberated French greeted the American troops with flowers and wine. It was a happy day, flags were taken out of hiding and hung from windows. Signs were erected exclaiming "Vive la France, Vive L'Amériqué" and "Welcome to our Liberators". Dad explained how the people cheered and greeted the American troops.

> We are on the road to Ernee and on the road to Mayenne from Avranches. And all the people from these villages back here came out with flowers and apple cider and poured it into our canteens. They came out with pouches of apple cider and they filled up our canteens with cider. The infantry was riding on the back, we were traveling at a pretty good rate of speed and we were moving quite well. This is where they threw the roses on the tank. When we were training in the United States, I told the tank commander, Willinger "These things (Sherman Tanks) are only iron coffins." So when we got here I said, "You see I told you these were iron coffins, they're putting flowers on us already."

The Bridge at Mayenne

The 90th and the 712th were moving toward the Mayenne River when they received information that the 1st Infantry Division had been held up at Mortain and was unable to reach the highly important town of Mayenne. The 90th and the 712th undertook this mission, they cut through Ernee and reached the outskirts of Mayenne early in the evening of August 5, 1944.[10]

As Dad and I approached the outskirts of Mayenne, Dad began, "This is the area where we first hit resistance when we entered Mayenne. The GIs riding the back of the tank disembarked and we proceeded at a slower pace until we got (close) to the Mayenne River and the bridge."

The Mayenne River runs from northeast to southwest through the City of Mayenne. Buildings and homes of the city occupy both sides of the river and the adjoining terrain is a gradual slope from river's edge back several hundred yards inland. The Mayenne River itself is a steep-banked stream about one hundred feet wide and five feet deep. The narrow streets approaching the bridge, with buildings lining the narrow sidewalks on both sides, was reminiscent of the architecture and crowded city scape back home in the French Quarter in New Orleans.

The Breakout

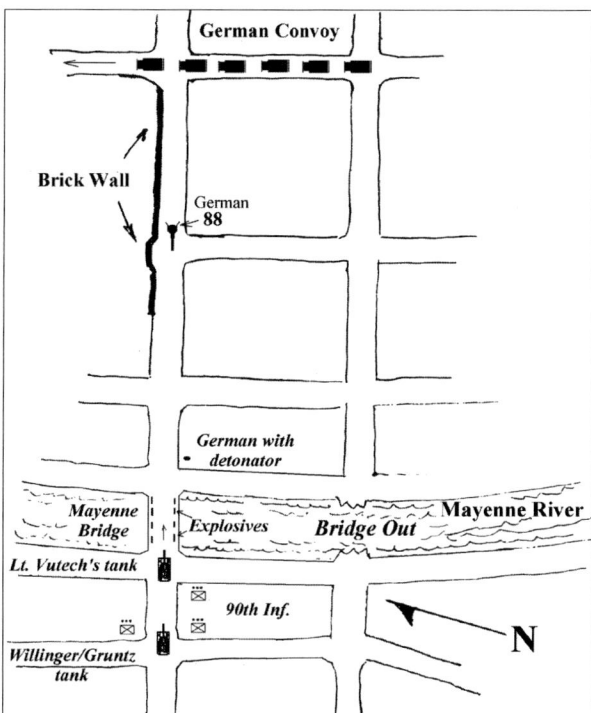

The capture of Mayenne, August 5, 1944. (*Gruntz Sketch*)

The 90th and the 712th advanced upon the river from the northwest. The main street was a straight shot to the bridge and on the other side the Germans had located an 88-mm gun and a 20-mm gun. The Operational Journal of the 712th Tank Battalion merely noted: "5 August 1944, Time: 19:00 – B Co has one plt across bridge into town other two plt along road SE into town. Germans are fleeing South."

This sparse entry belies the military significance of the events of that transpired that day.[11] The History of the 712th Tank Battalion written after the war provided a few more details:

> ...a platoon of B Company forged into town into the mouth of several 88s, crossed the bridge and seized important ground on the south side of the river. An enemy force had just reached the approaches to this bridge but B Company forced them to retire.

The tank officer heading the platoon was Lt Robert Vutech, who commanded one tank in the platoon of two.[12] The other tank in that platoon was commanded by Sgt Willinger; Dad was the gunner in the Willinger tank.[13]

The capture of the bridge over the Mayenne River was of utmost importance for the eastward movement of American troops and the ultimate objective of reaching Le Mans. The other bridges in Mayenne had been blown up by the Germans. This remaining bridge was rigged for demolition with eight 550 lbs bombs located on top of the bridge in plain view. And with the German guns looking down the throats of the Americans, the capture of this bridge looked to be a suicide mission and an impossible task. Vutech was both respected and well-liked by the soldiers in his command and he would not order them to do anything that he wouldn't be willing to do himself. Dad described what happened as the plans for the attack were made, " We stopped in a little area to have a recon to see what we were going to do to cross this bridge since it was the only bridge left in Mayenne to be crossed. The brass came up and looked at it to decide which way we were going to attack it. So they decided to send two tanks across. (Vutech and Willinger) drew straws to see which tank would go across first. (Vutech pulled the short straw) and went first and then we went after."

This reconnaissance by Vutech was typical of his style. Leslie Vink, describing Vutech in another action, stated, "Bob Vutech was very different. As soon as the tank stopped, he was out scouting to see what was around us."[14]

Vutech's tank began rolling down the hill toward the bridge firing its 75-mm cannon on the move. Dad's tank was buttoned up and as they proceeded he viewed the unfolding events through his gunner's periscope.

> When we crossed the bridge, Vutech's tank started firing. (The Germans) had torpedo bombs on the bridge, they were on the side. And when he started firing he (German with detonator) ran.
>
> When we crossed the bridge, there was an anti- tank gun at the first corner there – that building wasn't there then. He (the gunner in Vutech's tank) knocked out the anti-tank gun. I don't know what happened to him (German anti-tank gunner). I don't know whether we killed him or not. Then we went up the hill and there was a cross roads.

A German convoy was traveling on a road which ran parallel to the river several hundred yards from the bridge.

> There was a German truck right here (in the cross roads) loaded with soldiers and he (Vutech's gunner) blew it up; and (on that corner) there was a house, a lady came out right after that, after it stopped burning. She came out with a broom made out of like branches from a tree and she started sweeping the sidewalk to get the debris off the sidewalk. We set up an outpost (on the German side of the bridge).

Dad did not have the advantage of a panoramic view the infantry had of the unfolding events in taking the bridge. His view was constrained by his gunner's

Mayenne Bridge A. (*Author's collection*)

periscope which focused his attention on the targets and firing accuracy of the tank in front of him.

Major Ed Hamilton[15] of the 357th, details the infantry's perspective of the events as follows:

> The preparation commenced on time and very shortly succeeded in hitting the ammunition caisson of an 88-mm gun, which resulted in a terrific explosion and a pall of smoke blanketing a portion of the street leading to the bridge. I immediately told (Lieutenant) Stevens to go across and I would call off the artillery and mortar preparation. The leading tank was beckoned to wheel and it and the leading engineer squad headed for the bridge. All of us who saw this realized that we were witnessing a classical example of coordination.
>
> Stevens, with his fortitude and guts, led his men across in a hail of machine gun and small-arms fire. As the engineers and tanks headed for the bridge, two engineers were hit with what at first appeared to be a rifle grenade (later determined to be a 20-mm shell) and momentarily seemed to disappear. One of the men, Pvt. James McCracken, was killed and the other's leg was blown off just below the knee. This did not deter this fine squad in its mission. It proceeded to clear the bridge and the first tank rolled across belching cannon fire.
>
> As the leading tank moved up the street across the bridge, it blasted a Kraut gun and its crew, located on a side street [...] More credit should be given [...],

Mayenne Bridge C. (*Author's collection*)

(to) the tank commander. He unhesitatingly drove across the bridge and on up the hill through the town without infantry support.¹⁶

The army engineer, Private James McCracken, who was killed on the bridge has been remembered by the citizens of Mayenne. The bridge is affixed with a plaque stating "pour sauver ce pont James Mac Cracken du 315e Bon USA se sacrifia le 5 Aout 1944" which translated means that McCracken died saving the bridge on August 5, 1944.

After capturing the bridge at Mayenne the rest of the 712th Tank Battalion came across the bridge and bivouacked on the southeast side of town. The fact that the bridge had been captured intact and crossed by the Americans came as a surprise to some of Germans that night. Col. George B. Barth, the commanding officer of the 357th Regiment, stated:

> By the time the river crossing had been made and Mason (another 357th officer) was on high ground behind the town, the 1st Bn. had the complete town, and Gen. Weaver ordered a halt for the night with all-around defense. [...] As we were unloading our captured German CP truck, another German truck drove up and stopped. Out of it came 15 bewildered Krauts who were planning to

put up at this same place – they had no idea Americans were anywhere around. All night there was bedlam in the town of Mayenne. The Germans apparently had no idea where we were, and stray vehicles kept barging into town. Our CP platoon knocked out four and captured a number of prisoners right in front of our CP. Similarly blocking groups on other roads piled up quite a score – nothing got through.[17]

The next morning Tanks from A Company of the 712th thwarted a German counterattack.

Once in Mayenne, Gen. Weaver studied his map and speculated on a way to Le Mans that would offer the least resistance. Weaver decided to split his force along two parallel routes. One of those routes would take the tanks of the 712th through the small town of Sainte-Suzanne. Gen. Weaver's decision would be a fateful one for the crew members in Dad's tank.

Dad and I spent the night at the Grand Hotel in Mayenne, located next to the river at the northwest entrance to the bridge. The hotelier, Richard Van Marle, spoke fluent English and told us that the hotel had been in operation during the war. When Dad related the fact that he had been in Mayenne during the war, Van Marle became very interested in hearing details from an American veteran that helped liberate his town. He provided us a corner room on the second floor corner overlooking the bridge. I spent a long time that night peering out of the window at the bridge my father helped capture fifty years earlier.

CHAPTER 7

The Purple Heart – 7 August 1944

> So, as you go into battle, remember your ancestors but also remember your descendants.
>
> Tacitus (AD 54-117)

On August 7, 1782, Gen. George Washington issued an order establishing a military decoration for bravery in action; that decoration became known as the Purple Heart because of its design, purple cloth in the shape of a heart. A man who received the Purple Heart, regardless of his rank, would be granted privileges normally reserved to officers and any recipient of the award would be allowed to pass by guards and sentinels with the same courtesy enlisted men paid to officers. This is the treatment Gen. George Washington envisioned for the recipients when he established the award. Prior to Washington's order, acts of bravery during the Revolutionary War were rewarded by a promotion in rank; this practice was stymied after the Continental Congress informed him that it could not afford to pay the officers he promoted. Therefore, Washington established the Honorary Badge of Distinction/Badge of Military Merit for military merit specifically to honor lower-ranking soldiers. The philosophy of the European military establishment in the eighteenth century reserved military honors for officers and members of the nobility, thus, medals and decorations were unpopular in Colonial America because they were associated with Europe's upper classes.

On the 200th Anniversary of George Washington's birth, February 22, 1932, the War Department revived the Purple Heart military award by Order of the President. This revived Purple Heart is a combat decoration awarded to members of the armed forces of the US who are wounded by an instrument of war in the hands of the enemy and posthumously to the next of kin in the name of those who are killed in action. August 7 of each year is designated Purple Heart Day.

The Purple Heart – 7 August 1944

The 712th Battle Route – Northern France Campaign. (*The History of the 712th Tank Battalion*)

Sainte-Suzanne

On August 7, 1944, the one hundred sixty-second anniversary of the establishment of the Purple Heart, four members of B Company of the 712th Tank Battalion earned this badge of honor in the small French town of Sainte-Suzanne.

Sainte-Suzanne, located approximately 20 miles southeast of Mayenne, is a medieval town that sits on the top of a cliff overlooking the French countryside to its east and south. The terrain on the northern and western side of the town is low rolling hills. The American attack on Sainte-Suzanne came from the western and northern entrances into the town. The northern entrance

East Road into Sainte-Suzanne. (*Author's collection*)

to town, where Dad's tank advanced in 1944, has a fork in the road with a walled cemetery positioned in the middle of the fork. The road on the left of the fork leads directly to the old center part of town and the town church; this road dips in elevation a few feet below the elevation of the cemetery. The road on the right, although the same elevation of the cemetery, leads to the western edge of town.

Sgt Warren Willinger was tank commander, Dad was the gunner, Lloyd Sparks was the driver, Dee Johnson was the assistant driver, and a replacement private, William Land, who joined the Company on July 14 was the loader. Dad's tank had taken over the lead position in the advance when the other tank in the squad got stuck in the mud off the main road into town.

In war, the farther forward you are, the more you know about the immediate situation but the less you know about the overall situation; the farther rear you are, just the opposite is true.[1] As Dad explained, that truism was in effect on that day:

> We were at the top of the hill coming this way. We thought they were firing artillery at us, so what we did was we fired a shot at the steeple of the church and knocked half of the steeple off (to knock out any enemy artillery spotter).

Up until then the infantry was walking close to the tank; as the tank proceeded, the infantry stayed behind under cover.

Then we proceeded with the tank up this road here and we took the road on the left next to the wall of the cemetery. We were firing at Germans running across the street in Sainte-Suzanne (running from right to left perpendicular to the direction the tank was traveling). When we were firing we got radioed from the officer in charge in the back and said we were firing on friendly troops and we stopped firing. We got up to the wall – a few yards up that road to that cemetery way and we stopped.

We saw the Germans still running across the road going in toward the church, toward the center of town. We started firing again. They called back again and said you are firing on your own troops. So I told Willinger, 'You tell them if we are firing on our own troops then they had German uniforms on.' So we ceased firing. Willinger was sticking his head out (of the turret). He was afraid someone was in the cemetery and he grabbed a hand grenade. [...] He may have seen something in that graveyard. When we (stopped firing) the bazooka came out the cemetery and hit the tank.

The German soldier behind the stone wall in the cemetery was armed with a Panzerfaust and, at that close range, he hit the tank turret.

The turret top was up and it (the shell) hit the top of the turret and it melted and all the steel went all through the tank. Willinger was standing up (behind me) and he got hit in the head and it came over his shoulder and hit me in the back. He fell down. He fell on me, not on top of me, and fell down to the (bottom of the tank). A ball of fire went through the tank, the tank lit up you almost went blind with the light. I jumped out and I told everybody, "Get out, let's get out." We couldn't proceed any further and were afraid it (the tank) was going to blow up. Willinger was dead.

As the molten slag produced by the rocket's impact splattered around inside the tank, it set the tank ablaze and also welded the gun breech closed. Dad began exiting through the top hatch, the driver, Lloyd Sparks, opened the tank's main power switch then crawled onto the back deck and operated the fire extinguishing mechanism on the tank.

I asked Dad if they had attempted to get Willinger out of the tank. He said.

There was nothing we could do, we had to get away from the tank. He had a hand grenade in his hand and the pin was pulled. (He died instantly and he had a death grip on the grenade.) If we tried to grab him the grenade might have fallen out. And it would have blown up and killed everyone.

Also, we didn't know what the Germans were going to do. We ran back this road about two hundred yards to this hedge here. It was all open fields in there. Behind those hedges the American infantry was laying down. (There was a young lieutenant and he looked scared.) And I said to the lieutenant, "What the hell are you doing back here?" He said, "We are pinned down." I said, "God Damn it, you're pinned down my ass, we just got our tank knocked out and a man got killed in it because you're back here. I just came back this road and never had a shot fired at me. How the hell did I get back that road and nobody fired a shot at me?" He said, "Don't get mad at me, don't get mad at me it's not my fault." He might of been scared because he thought I was going to shoot him. That's when I got back to the jeep and they said, "What happened up there?" And I said, "You sons of a bitches know a tank can't take a town without infantry." That was the end of it.

When Dad exited the tank he realized he was wounded, but thought the other surviving tank crew members made it out of the tank as well. Sparks helped the assistant driver, Dee Johnson, get out of his front hatch and helped him back to the hedgerow where the 90th infantry had taken cover.

> When Sparks was running behind me down the road after jumping out of the tank. He said he saw so much blood on my back, he thought for sure I was going to die, that I was going to bleed to death.

When they reached the hedgerow, Sparks left Dee Johnson with the infantry and returned for the seriously wounded loader, William Land, who was still in the tank. The enemy fire, complained of by the infantry lieutenant, was silent, as Dad, Sparks, and Johnson retreated from the smoldering tank, thus leading Dad to believe it was non-existent. That enemy fire, however, resumed and began menacing Sparks as he ran back to the tank. Despite the machine gun fire directed at him, Sparks pulled William Land from the smoking turret and carried him back to the aid station. Dad said that Land's wounds were so serious that he believed he never returned to combat and shortly thereafter was shipped home to the States to recuperate.

After recovering Land, Dad explained how Sparks again returned to the tank started the engine, "But Sparky went back (into no man's land) and got the tank and backed it up (to where the 90th had dug in)."

In addition to recovering the tank and moving it off the road to allow the other tanks to proceed with the advance on Sainte-Suzanne, Sparks' run through no-man's land also lured the Germans into resuming fire and exposing their hidden machine gun position, which the American forces soon silenced.

"That's when he got the Silver Star for that." Lloyd Sparks was the only one in the tank who was not wounded, he was awarded the Silver Star for gallantry in action. The medal was personally pinned on Sparks by the 90th Division Commander, Gen. James Van Fleet.[2]

After the tank was retrieved from no-man's land, Willinger's body was removed from the tank and carried back to the rear wrapped in a blanket.

Dad continued, "I was bleeding, they took me in the back and the medics cut my jacket and put sulfur powder on me and helped me out a little, and told me to cross over through here (the field) and to go in where Headquarters was. And about an hour or so, an ambulance picked me up and brought me to a field hospital."

Dad later admitted that it was a mistake for the tank to proceed into town without infantry support. It was a mistake that cost Willinger his life. Dad remained puzzled for many years regarding the orders they received to stop firing. The officers back in the Headquarters of B Company kept telling him that he was firing upon American troops, but he could plainly see German uniforms. After fifty years, however, the mystery was unraveled as we read about the incidents on that morning in Sainte-Suzanne in the accounts from the 90th Infantry.

> In the morning we pushed on to aid the first battalion, which had been having serious trouble up ahead around Sainte-Suzanne. They had gone into and on past the town, but had been attacked from the rear by about five hundred fanatical, screaming paratroopers. They had fought a wild pitched battle in the darkness all night. In the streets of Sainte-Suzanne, American and German soldiers had fired each other from point-blank range. The battalion command post in the cellar of one of the buildings had been isolated and attacked by the enemy, so that everyone from the colonel on down fought madly to bear off the foe.[3]

Col. Barth had radioed Major Ed Hamilton, who was ahead of Barth's command post in Sainte-Suzanne, to double back and handle the Germans who had re-entered Sainte-Suzanne from the south. Before Hamilton's forces could recapture the town, Dad's tank was approaching from the north The German troops Dad had been firing upon were immediately around the building containing the cellar into which Col. Barth sought refuge until relief came. The shells were apparently hitting this building containing Barth and, thus, Dad was ordered to stop the shelling.

As the rescue of Col. Barth was unfolding, Dad was brought by ambulance to the field hospital further to the rear of the American lines.

> The field hospital was a big green tent. It had no floor and all of the beds (and other equipment) was just sitting on the ground underneath the tent.
>
> I had about fifty small pieces of shrapnel all over my back. They wanted to give me morphine at the scene. But I told them no. I did not want to get hooked on drugs and become a drug addict. The doctor came in and examined it and said that he thought he could pull them out without giving me anesthesia. I said OK.

I was laying on my stomach and he was pulling out the pieces in my back and a nurse came in. While he was pulling one of the larger pieces out, I said "Ouch." The nurse said, "You mean this man does not have anesthesia?" She had to leave the tent, (she couldn't bear to watch it).

They put some kind of paste on my back and I had to lay on my stomach for a couple of days. Later some of the wounds got infected and they had to re-treat those area and put small bandages there. After that I had a general recovery.

Dad spent about two weeks recuperating in the field hospital.

I subsequently asked my mother, how did she learn about Dad being wounded. Mom recounted that day.

I had moved back to my parents and was living with them. I was still sleeping because I worked the night before. When Maw-Maw [Gertrude Casteix, my maternal grandmother] opened the door, the (Western Union) girl said "Telegram!" and (seeing the telegram was from the War Department) said "I can't call my daughter (without preparing her for the news)." She (the Western Union girl) said, "You have to." Maw Maw said again "I can't." So the girl said, "I'd lose my job if they knew I was telling you this but your son-in-law is alive but he's not seriously hurt. But you do have to call your daughter."

My grandmother woke up my mother and she signed for the telegram and cried and cried.

Mom received the telegram two weeks after Dad was wounded. Ironically, this was about the same time Dad had completed his hospital recuperation and was released to be returned to his unit. It was the first word she received that Dad was wounded.

Dad was worried that Mom would not get any details of his injuries in the official telegram from the War Department and that she would agonize over not knowing how bad he was wounded. Among the letters from Dad that Mom received during the war are several on American Red Cross stationery. A week after being wounded, Dad knew that Mom had not yet been notified because his mail from home was still being directed to the Battalion instead of the hospital. Although he could not be specific because all the outgoing mail of soldiers was censored for security reasons, the first Red Cross letter begins:

Darling I haven't heard from you in over a week. And I don't guess I will hear from you for another couple of days. I guess you wonder why I say that. Well I will tell you if you promise not to worry. I have been slightly wounded. And I am in a convalescent hospital. But don't worry Love I am not hurt bad. I will be back in action in a couple of days. Darling I am sorry I can't tell you how or where I was hurt or what is wrong with me. I wish I could because then I would know you wouldn't worry. I intended to wait until I got back (to action) Darling and then tell you I was wounded and in the hospital for a while. But I was afraid you would get a telegram from Washington and it would worry you to death. So that is why I am telling you. But please don't worry Darling because I am alright.

Although this letter was postmarked August 18, 1944, she did not receive it until a day or two after the telegram arrived.

Dad and I left the cemetery on the outskirts of Sainte-Suzanne and headed toward the church and the center of town. Next to the main entrance door to the church there is a plaque. The inscription on the plaque states that the original church structure was built before 1125. Dad hadn't known that fact during the war. He clearly had remorse during the war for firing directly upon a house of God. Now, fifty years later he was again remorseful upon learning the antiquity of the structure. We entered the interior of the church and stopped to say a prayer. Dad made a cash gift in the collection box at the rear of church. It was his way of making a small token to cover present day repairs for the church that he had damaged fifty years earlier.

St James Cemetery

Dad had known for many years that Micaloni, Krusel and Milczakowski were buried in the Normandy cemetery; it was only shortly before our trip that Dad had learned that Willinger was buried in the American Cemetery in St James. The cemetery at St James is about a quarter the size of the Normandy cemetery. It is located off the beaten path in rolling farm country outside of the town of St James. It does not have the same awe inspiring panoramic surroundings as the Normandy Cemetery, and although it is smaller size, it is nonetheless a beautiful and serene final resting place for over 4,400 American heroes and is another patch of hallowed ground.

While heading toward the cemetery we were driving through a heavy rainstorm and it appeared the rain would interfere with our visit. As we stopped at the cemetery gate, however, the rain subsided and the sun began to shine. We proceeded to find Willinger's grave site. Like the Normandy cemetery, it was quiet and peaceful. As we walked down the main walkway on the side of the cemetery, the silence was occasionally broken by the faint bleating of sheep on the other side of the cemetery's stone wall fence.

We located Willinger's burial site and just as in Normandy, Dad spent a few moments in quiet conversation to his friend. Willinger was a Staff Sergeant. He was from California and had entered the army in 1939, when he was nineteen years old. He was in the unit when it was part of the 11th Cavalry and stationed in California.

Willinger Cross. (*Author's collection*)

The American Cemetery in Normandy receives a larger number of American visitors than St James. This fact was evident during our visit – there were no other visitors at St James when Dad and I were there. Consequently, the young American sexton enthusiastically received us. Happy to hold a conversation in English with some fellow Americans, he gave us a special tour which included a visit to the top of the chapel steeple, which is normally closed to the public. There we were treated to a spectacular view of the surrounding countryside; on the distant mist shrouded western horizon we could see the silhouette of Mont St Michel.

The grounds of both the Normandy and St James cemeteries were beautifully manicured and meticulously kept. Knowing that these European cemeteries would be kept in such conditions perpetually by the American government, Dad expressed the belief that many American families may have done their loved ones a disservice by having their bodies relocated back to the United States after the war. He felt certain that many of the cemeteries back in the States, where American soldiers were finally laid to rest, were not as well kept as these American monuments to our war dead in Europe.

As we were walking back to the car, Dad was reflecting on the ultimate sacrifice these soldiers made. The vast majority were between eighteen and twenty-five years of age, not married or like Dad, at that time, had no children.

Dad said, "You know, under almost every cross and Star of David here, lies the head of an American family that never existed, a family that never was and never will be. If I would have gotten killed, you would never have existed."

I had heard the words "ultimate sacrifice" and "supreme sacrifice" used before to described the deaths of soldiers killed in action. Until then I thought it was just a superlative description for being killed in action. Dad's comments made me think about the loss of a soldier. Not only was his life lost, but also his lineage; his parents were as much a casualty of war as he was, they had lost not only a son but also they lost hopes of grandchildren and great-grandchildren. The toll on a soldier's family is also an ultimate and supreme loss.

It was also a sobering thought to realize that if the Panzerfaust shell had hit a few inches lower and to the right, neither I nor my children would have ever existed.

As we left the cemetery, the sun slipped behind the clouds. We had no more rain but the rest of the day was gray and gloomy. After getting back on the highway and heading east, we noticed a road sign indicating the direction of Falaise, Argentan, and Alencon.

The Falaise Gap

While Dad was in the hospital recuperating from his back wounds, the fortunes of war took a dramatic turn. The battle of Falaise Gap was taking place. Sainte-Suzanne is approximately 60 miles due south of Caen and approximately 50 miles east south east of Avranches. In six days, the 90th Infantry and the 712th, under Patton, had traveled over 70 miles from Périers to Sainte-Suzanne. The Germans that had trapped Col. Barth in Sainte-Suzanne were moving through the town from south to north and were apparently trying to join the main forces of the German 7th Army that were positioned between Caen and Sainte-Suzanne. On the morning that Dad was wounded, August 7, 1944, the German 7th Army began a westward counterattack against the American forces. The Americans identified this action as the Mortain Counter Attack, the Germans called it Operation Lüttich. This action was planned by Adolf Hitler himself; he planned on attacking the left flank of the American supply lines at the town of Mortain and advancing westward to Avranches and the Atlantic Ocean, thereby cutting off Patton's Third Army. American intelligence had learned of the counterattack in advance and the American forces were prepared; they stopped the German attack in Mortain.

The lead elements of Patton's Third Army had reached its objective, the city of Le Mans. When the German attack started, Patton's forces were ordered to stop their eastward advance, make a sharp 90 degree turn and move north to meet the British forces, under the command of Field Marshal Montgomery, moving south from Caen. Gen. Omar Bradley declared this was "an opportunity that comes to a commander not more than once in a century. We're about to destroy an entire hostile army. We'll go all the way from here to the German border."[4]

When Patton turned his forces northward, Hitler's forces in Normandy became trapped in a pocket surrounded on three sides by Allied forces. The only route of retreat for the Germans was to the east on a road through a 12 mile wide valley between the towns of Falaise and Argentan and Chambois. The high ground on either side of this valley provided the Allies with excellent observation of all enemy actions and movements.

It was planned for Montgomery's forces to capture the town of Falaise and meet Patton's forces. Montgomery did not reach his objective on schedule. Patton's forces, including the 90th and the 712th, reached Argentan and surrounding areas before the German Army could begin its eastward retreat. Patton could have advanced to Falaise in a matter of hours, thereby trapping the entire German army. Instead, for what is purported to be political reasons, he was ordered to stop his advance at Argentan, in order to allow the British to take Falaise. All historical accounts record that there was a longstanding rivalry between Patton and Montgomery; both wanted all the glory of victory. This order to halt did not sit well with Patton.

Patton's forces reached its stopping point on August 15, seventy days after D-Day, after moving over 250 miles. During that same period, Montgomery's forces were still 10 miles from Falaise. In that same seventy day period, Montgomery had only moved his forces 20 miles. Montgomery did not reach Falaise until August 19 thereby allowing approximately 240,000 German forces to fight their way out of the pocket and escape the trap that Patton could have closed four days earlier.

Upon reaching Chambois and the Falaise Gap, A and B Companies of the 712th, the 773rd Tank Destroyer Battalion, and other elements of the 90th Infantry Division were deployed across the bottom flatland area of the valley to stop the German escape. C Company of the 712th was on a ridge along the side of the valley. The remainder of Task Force Weaver occupied the surrounding high ground.

Lt-Col. (Ret.) Edward S. Hamilton of the 90th stated that "In war one can expect only the unexpected". He went on to comment that he observed this truism firsthand in the startling developments that unfolded at Falaise – the death of an entire army.[5] The awesome scene of annihilation was difficult to imagine, let alone witness first hand, yet this was the fate that befell the German 7th Army.[6] Even though many Germans escaped because of Montgomery's delay in closing the pocket, many more were killed or captured trying to escape through the narrow gap. The Allied forces had not only the

The 712th Battle Route – the Falaise Gap. (*The History of the 712th Tank Battalion*)

advantage of the high ground but also air supremacy over the field of escape. That route became a killing field and the battle of Falaise Gap was marked as a stunning Allied victory. Over 200,000 Germans were taken prisoner and over 50,000 were killed, even the Germans who escaped had to do it on foot and most of their vehicles and heavy equipment were left behind and destroyed by the Allies. Of these, the 90th Infantry Division took more than 13,000 prisoners, and killed or wounded approximately 8,000. More than three hundred enemy tanks were destroyed along with 3,270 other types of vehicles and 164 artillery pieces.

Lt Jim Gifford of C Company described the events of that day:[7]

It was just daylight, I took out my field glasses and I went back up the hill so I could see out over this valley. I'm looking down in this valley in the early sun and I see all these little sparkles, little sparks all over the valley, what the hell is that? ... I couldn't believe the sight I saw. It was thousands of bayonets flashing in the early morning sun. They had hundreds of horse drawn artillery. These infantry guys are walking toward us, they're about three miles away up the valley, and they're dispersed among hundreds of tanks. Holy shit this was coming toward us, this is it. So I ran down, I got on the radio and I started hollering over the radio what's coming.

About 20 minutes after Gifford's radio call, P-47 Thunderbolts began flying over unloading on the German column.

Well those poor bastards ... were catching bloody hell. We were firing at them from a mile or two away. We weren't waiting till they got to us, we were blasting away at them.... And this monolith, whatever you want to call it, was slowly rolling, with all the destruction that was going on, it was slowly coming along right by us – and Jesus, it wasn't stopping – and we were hitting everything.... A and B Company and the 773rd were catching hell because the Germans started rolling through them. And when they hit these two companies plus the 773rd, they started piling up, and the next thing they turned and started to go back and started running into themselves.

By 2 o'clock in the afternoon Piper Cubs were flying over dropping leaflets on the Germans telling them to surrender.

Dad said that Capt. Galvin of B Company had personally accepted the surrender of over 1,200 German troops. The incident surrounding the capture of these enemy troops was described in detail by Sgt Leslie Vink:[8]

We'd cut the last highway through Falaise, and the Germans tried to counterattack. We held the high ground, and our planes were strafing and bombing the area that the Germans had. This went on for several hours. Finally our medics cleared it with the corps to go down and pick up the wounded and bring them out. They came back and said to Captain (Jack) Galvin, "There's a whole bunch of Germans who want to surrender."

Galvin said to Lieutenant Vutech, "Cut the artillery, I'm going down in there." He got in his jeep and went down and accepted the surrender of what was left of the garrison. He said at the time he was a bit ashamed, we had been in combat for several days, we were unshaven, unbathed, and he said the German officer came up in a fresh uniform, presented him with a sword, and surrendered soldiers, but it seemed like a column of four for a mile and a half at least. I think it was over 1,200 that surrendered at that time.

Galvin brought them out, and as they were coming past us, we were sitting on the high ground there, and one of them looked at Vutech and said, "I've seen you before."

He had probably seen him over a hedgerow, or through a peepsight someplace.[9]

Probably while Vutech was out of his tank scouting around during the fighting before the breakout.

Lt Gifford recalled the carnage and the line of POW's:

Their equipment was burning all over the place, as far as you could see, burning equipment ... these guys were coming out waving flags and waving papers, there were hundreds of them ... all dusty, dirty, filthy and tired. They were a bedraggled army, it was a defeated army. They were so goddamn glad to just be alive.

By the evening of August 21, the decisive Allied victory achieved at the Battle of Falaise was over. Two days later Paris was liberated, and by August 30, the last German remnants had retreated across the Seine River.

The victory at Falaise Gap, however, was not without a price to the 712th. Dad's friends, Robert Gerald, William Hogue, and Bob Hodges were killed in action. Dad was saddened to hear the news of these casualties. Bob Hodges was married and had an infant son back home in Oklahoma. Robert Gerald and William Hogue were both from Kentucky. Hogue was an only son raised by his single mother in Bowling Green. Following the war, Hogue's mother requested his body be returned home. He was laid to final rest in the Davis-Hoffman Cemetery in Bowling Green.

CHAPTER 8

Return to Action – Fortress Metz

Courage is resistance to fear, mastery of fear, not absence of fear.

Mark Twain

After the Allied victory at the Falaise Gap, the Germans were in a state of shock and were struggling to prepare their defenses between the Seine and Loire Rivers. Patton was convinced that the Breakout from Normandy and the envelopment at Falaise had to be exploited by a push deep into France to prevent the Germans from developing a defensive front between the Seine and the Loire. When Bradley and Eisenhower gave Patton the green light, the Third Army sped across France. Patton's advance was described as "rolling like a juggernaut and slashing toward the Saar" by one newsreel commentator. The march across France and the liberation of Paris occurred while Dad was in the hospital. When it was time for him to return to the 712th, the battalion had advanced east of Paris.

Dad told me that as he was about to be discharged from the hospital and sent back to his unit, his near death experience had shaken his courage and he sought the counsel of a priest. He told the priest that he didn't believe he could go back to the combat, he didn't believe that he could hold up to that stress. The priest told Dad to advise an officer how he felt. After considering the priest's advice, Dad decided not to follow it.

The more Dad thought about the situation, the more he was overcome by his sense of duty; many of his buddies were still back on the front undergoing all of the same hardships that he had endured before he was wounded. Dad said that he didn't want to let down his buddies. He believed he had a duty to go back, a duty to his country and a duty to his buddies and a duty to himself.

One of Patton's favorite expressions was "Do not take counsel of your fears." He would say this to himself whenever he would get nervous prior to implementing a battle plan.[1] In his memoirs, Patton commented on the aspects of bravery and courage.

> If we take the generally accepted definition of bravery as a quality which knows not fear, I have never seen a brave man. All men are frightened. The more intelligent they are, the more they are frightened. The courageous man is the man who forces himself, in spite of his fear, to carry on. Discipline, pride, self-respect, self-confidence [...] are attributes which will make a man courageous even when he is afraid.[2]

When I was a boy bragging to my friends about my father, I believed him to have all the heroic qualities of the soldiers in the movies. That day in 1994, my boyhood beliefs that my father was a brave and courageous soldier were confirmed.

Dad was released from the hospital and authorized to go back to the front. Bill Nick, also from B Company, was released from the hospital at the same time as Dad and they returned to the 712th together. Getting back, however, was easier said than done, it took several more weeks before they finally transported back to their unit. They were first transported to a replacement troop depot somewhere in Belgium.

As Dad and I continued driving eastward toward Metz, Dad related several stories.

> I went to a Frenchman and he had chickens running all around his yard and we had nothing to eat but K-rations or C-rations out the can and we had some stew, hash we used to call it in those days, in cans, so I went to the Frenchman, and I said "How about making a deal. I'll trade you these cans of stew for a chicken." He said "No." I said "Yeah come on, I want a chicken." He said "No, No," and I said "Yeah, Yeah take the stew." He said "No, No." But I grabbed the chicken anyway.
>
> I took the chicken and wrung his neck. I skinned him and fried him. We never had any cooking oil, I just put him in my skillet. And I cooked some potatoes. I had chicken and french fries, right outside next to the tank.

Whenever Dad had the chance he always wanted something other than C-rations or K-rations.[3]

Bob Kellner was the mess sergeant for B Company. The kitchen was usually set up near the Company HQ where hot meals could be cooked. The men either rotated back to the kitchen from the front line or hot food was sent up to the front line in insulated cans.

During the time Dad was recuperating and being transported from the field hospital back to the 712th, the battalion had advanced east of Paris. While Dad and Bill Nick were being transported, the transport trucks had to travel along the Seine River. On one occasion when the transport trucks stop, Dad wanted to clean up.

I was outside of Paris and I hadn't had a bath in a long time. It was on the outskirts of Paris sometime in September and I hadn't had a bath in a long time, so I took me a bar of soap and a towel and I jumped into the Seine River and I got me a bath in about fifteen seconds. The water was so cold, I couldn't get out of it fast enough.

I had asked Dad about how soldiers changed into clean clothes while out in combat. He said occasionally they had showers set up when a Company HQ was established.

When I had a chance to take a shower, I went to the supply sergeant and said "I need a set of clothes." So he'd give me a whole set of clothes, I'd take a shower and put the new clothes on and bring the dirty clothes to him. He'd have them cleaned and give them to the next guy my size that came up.

When the question of what happened to damaged tanks arose, Dad said that they were taken to the rear and repaired if possible. If a tank was too badly damaged, sometimes they took parts off of it to repair other slightly damaged tanks. Dad's good friend after the war, John Ockenga was in charge of the minor repairs and maintenance of B Company tanks. Badly damaged tanks were handled by Service Company.

There was one other occasion when Dad didn't mince words with someone of higher rank, Dad explained:

One night we came to a town and we had an outpost to protect the town. And we had first contact with the Germans. This lieutenant (Lt Otto Kreig) jumped out the tank and said, "I'm going back to Battalion Headquarters to check on something, I'll be right back." So all night he was gone while we watched the town. So the next morning when he came back, I said, "Where have you been?" He said, "I slept back there." I said, "You had no business being back there, you should have been here with the tank to help pull guard at the outpost of the town." Well he didn't like that. I said, "You are supposed to stay here, we've got five men in the tank and five men are supposed to pull guard." He said, "I would have known about it if anything happened." And I said, "Yeah, if I would have called back there on the radio and told you. You're not supposed to leave this tank." He wouldn't talk to me for about three days. After the third day, he said, "You know, you are right." I said, "OK."

Dad and Kreig got along fine after that.

I asked Dad if he ever saw Gen. Patton up close. He said no but that once Patton passed right by his tank, he had come up to the front to assess the situation.

I was inside the tank and someone outside says, "Hey, there goes the Old Man."

We had stopped on a hill overlooking a valley with a platoon of infantry and had dug in. A tank column from an armored division had stopped on a road at the entrance of the valley. When Patton asked the commander of the column what was the hold up, the commander replied that the valley was under enemy observation and subject to shelling.

Patton was furious and pointed to my tank on the hilltop in the distance. He told the armored division commander to get his tanks moving, that if one tank and a platoon of infantry can hold that hill, the armored division could go through the valley. The armored division immediately rolled through the valley.

That's what one of the officers told us later.

Patton regularly went to the front and wanted all commanding officers under him to do likewise. One of his sayings was, "If you want an army to fight and risk death, you've got to get up there and lead it. An army is like spaghetti. You can't push a piece of spaghetti, you've got to pull it."[4]

I asked about how the tanks were re-supplied. Dad answered, "At night the supply truck and the gas truck would come up. They had to bring it to us because we were going into enemy territory." Depending on how far the unit traveled dictated how often the tanks needed fuel. "It depends on how we were running. Like when we started moving through France we had to get gas pretty often. About every one or two days they would come up with ammunition."

Dad said that the American supply trucks became known as the Red Ball Express. The drivers of these trucks rarely got involved in combat actions and sometimes the delivery of supplies became humorous.

> We got about 3 miles out of Mayenne and we stopped to outpost the town. The supply trucks came up. The infantry said you can't go there, this is the front line. Boy, when they said that, they turned those trucks around and went flying back.

It is said that during the war, of the millions of American soldiers in the military, only about one out of six actually was involved in combat. The rear echelon troops, supply troops, etc. did not experience the constant threat of death like the front line soldiers did every day. Dad commented, "Every soldier had a job in the army. Every soldier. But that man that was out in the front he was the man that was in danger at all times of being killed." The vast majority of the casualties were experienced by the front line troops.

Even though the supply drivers and the rear support troops were not in constant combat, their service was still just as vital to the war. As Gen. Patton once said:

An Army is a team. It lives, sleeps, eats, and fights as a team. This individual heroic stuff is pure horse shit. [...] All of the real heroes are not storybook combat fighters, either. Every single man in this Army plays a vital role. Don't ever let up. Don't ever think that your job is unimportant. Every man has a job to do and he must do it. Every man is a vital link in the great chain. [...] Every man does his job. Every man serves the whole. Every department, every unit, is important in the vast scheme of this war. The ordnance men are needed to supply the guns and machinery of war to keep us rolling. The Quartermaster is needed to bring up food and clothes because where we are going there isn't a hell of a lot to steal. Every last man on K.P. has a job to do, even the one who heats our water to keep us from getting the 'G.I. Shits.'

Dad mentioned that when there was fighting in or near a town, the civilians usually fled into the countryside. "We didn't want to stop inside a town we wanted to get past the town and get out of the town. (Usually) there was nobody around, you would never think anyone lived there it was like a ghost town."

Dad also shared his thoughts about being a corporal. "I was like poor (Frank) Krusel. I thought being a corporal improved my chances of surviving. I wasn't interested in promotions or winning medals. I only wanted to do the job, do my duty and go home. I never volunteered for anything and I never declined anything." The desire to do their duty, accomplish their job, and go home was a sentiment shared by most GIs.

I also asked Dad about the souvenirs he brought home. Did he get the pistol, the bayonet and the field glasses from the body of a German soldier? Dad said he didn't retrieve those items from a body. "Toward the end of the war, the battalion captured a German weapons warehouse. Someone from the battalion distributed items such as the P-38 automatic pistol, the bayonet and the field glasses to anyone who wanted them." Dad took them up on the offer, he said that during battles and the brief lulls afterwards, it was only the infantry soldiers that had opportunities to search for souvenirs among the bodies of the enemy, the tanks usually had to keep on moving.

I had also noticed that Dad's photographs taken during that time were either shot during the months of training or after the war during occupation. Did he take any photographs during battle? He said that the soldiers were under orders not to take photographs or have cameras in battle, neither were they supposed to keep a journal of where they had been. The reason being that if they were ever captured, the Army did not want the enemy to have this information to determine the American Army's troop movement. Even his letters home to Mom could not reveal any information on his specific location in the event the mail trucks would be captured by the enemy. I had noticed that many of Dad's letters home began with the date and the words "Somewhere in France". Even though they were under orders not to have them, some of the rearguard troops in the battalion had cameras and took pictures. After Joe Roush was wounded at the Falaise Gap, he returned to the battalion as a cook; he acquired a camera when he became a cook and took quite a few pictures after that.

Dad found a German camera at the end of the war. During occupation, he was able to get film and took a few pictures in and around Susice Czechoslovakia and Amberg Germany. Dad said besides the orders against taking pictures during combat, he never had the time to stop and take pictures, he and the other members of the tank crew were too busy with the duties of operating the tank and firing upon the enemy. The last thing on their minds was to take pictures. And, as I learned, combat soldiers would not need photographs to remind them of battle; those pictures would be indelibly burned into their minds for the rest of their lives.

Fortress Metz

Dad was hospitalized for approximately two weeks until the third week in August, all the while the 712th along with the rest of the Third Army were rolling across France with the Germans in retreat. After Dad's discharge from the hospital he was temporarily assigned to a replacement battalion and traveled with it for approximately another two weeks until the exact location of the ever moving 712th could be determined.

September 7, 1944, Mom was back home "celebrating" her 22nd birthday, not knowing too many details of Dad's wounds, worrying about his condition and whether he had returned to combat. Meanwhile Dad was still traveling in a troop truck with the replacement battalion and trying to catchup with the 712th.

By the 7th of September the battalion had passed through the World War I sites of Verdun and the Argonne Forest and had reached a bivouac area near the small crossroads town of Mairy. A German scout plane flew over the 712th at approximately 3:00 p.m. By nightfall, all of the battalion's companies were in the wooded areas on both sides of the road and within 1000 yards of each other. At 3:00 a.m. on the morning of September 8, the Germans launched a surprise counter attack against the combined 90th and 712th. A full column of the enemy struck toward a 90th Infantry Division Command Post situated near the area of the 712th A Company tanks. Five Mark V tanks, one half-track and a German reconnaissance car broke through and came down the road that ran between the tanks of A Company and B Company. Both companies were unable to immediately fire on the enemy for fear of hitting each other with friendly fire, but C Company tanks quickly moved into position to defend the 90th Command Post.

Normally full tank-on-tank battles occurred between armored divisions. This battle between the 712th and the 106 Panzer Brigade is the only recorded encounter between an entire panzer brigade and an independent tank battalion attached to an infantry division. German documents captured after the battle indicated that the Panzer brigade's mission was to "annihilate the armored spearhead of the 90th Infantry Division." By the end of the day, the German 106th Panzer Brigade was completely destroyed, through the combined efforts of the 90th infantry, its artillery and tank destroyers and all elements of the 712th. Thirty tanks, sixty half-tracks, and over one hundred miscellaneous vehicles were either captured or knocked out, and 764 prisoners were taken. From that date forward, the 712th was known as the "Armored Fist of the 90th". When Gen. McLain was later offered the use of a Combat Command of one of the Armored Divisions, he rejected the offer, jokingly boasting, "No thank you. I have the 712th Armored Division."

Dad finally arrived back at the 712th Battalion HQ shortly after the battle at Mairy. He was not disappointed in having missed the action.

Dad had not yet been reassigned to a tank, he related the following incident.

> I don't know how in the hell I got mixed up with the 1st Sgt (James L. Bennett) because he wasn't in a tank, but I was with him in a cellar. I believe it was right after I got back from the hospital … and caught up with the company. They (the battalion) were moving kind of fast then.
>
> It was about 12 o'clock at night. He wanted the kitchen crew to come up there by him because he didn't like being alone. He was scared, but everybody was scared. So he said to me, "Corporal," – that's how he talked – "Corporal, go tell Kellner to come on up here with the kitchen crew. They're down the street." So, I said, "OK" and I started down the street and I hear Germans speaking on both sides of the street. I turned around and walked back and I said, "Sergeant, if you want Kellner to come down here you go down there and get him yourself, they've got Germans out there, I ain't going out there."

When Dad had returned, Capt. Jim Cary was commanding B Company. Capt. Galvin had been wounded. Jim Cary had commanded C Company when the battalion landed in Normandy but he was wounded during the first few days. Following his recovery, he was assigned to B Company to replace Galvin. After the war, Jim was an Associated Press reporter and for a time was a member of the White House Press Corp. He is a distinguished and refined gentleman and by all accounts was an excellent officer.

By the beginning of September the rapid advance was slowed and eventually stopped; not so much by German resistance but by an increasing shortage of gasoline and supplies. Since June 6, all gasoline and supplies were shipped across the English Channel and loaded on trucks and sent to the forward positions. When the forces were in Normandy, the distance between the landing points on the coast and the front lines were relatively short distances. In the eastern part of France, supplying the front line troops was a logistics nightmare. Supply lines were stretched to the limits.

The Germans were routed and fleeing back to Germany but to Patton's dismay he could not advance because of the lack of fuel. To his further dismay, most of the fuel and supplies landing in Normandy were being directed to Gen. Montgomery for use in his offensive plan named Operation Market Garden. Montgomery's plan was to take bridges over the main rivers of the German-occupied Netherlands, thereby enabling the Allies to advance into Germany and end the war. Patton argued unsuccessfully to Eisenhower that if he was given the fuel, the Third Army could advance on Berlin in a matter of weeks and the war would end before Thanksgiving of 1944. Montgomery countered that his plan would end the war by the end of October.

The task of opening of the port of Antwerp, Belgium fell to Gen. Montgomery. The British troops liberated Antwerp but the port could not be used for unloading supplies because the channels to the coast were still subject to attack by isolated pockets of German resistance. If the port of Antwerp were in use, the shortages of supplies coming through Normandy would have been resolved and both Patton and Montgomery could have advanced.

Gen. Eisenhower decided to temporarily forego eliminating the resistance near Antwerp and to allot most of the fuel and supplies to Gen. Montgomery and to allow his troops to concentrate on Operation Market Garden. The territory that Montgomery's plan would capture contained the launching sites of the German V-2 rockets that were bombarding London.

Operation Market Garden failed and the Allied forces suffered sizable casualties. 1,400 British soldiers were dead and over 6,000 were taken prisoners of war.

Before the supplies to Patton were diverted, advance scouting parties had entered Metz, and gone through the Maginot Line and the Siegfried Line. They were empty, the Germans had retreated back into Germany. Patton's forces could have punched through these defenses if he only had the gasoline. In a letter to his wife on August 30, Patton wrote, "If I could only steal some gas, I could win this war."[5] US troops first entered Germany on September 11, 1944 – the Operation Overlord plans did not anticipate Allied forces to reach the German border until May 2, 1945. Patton had reached this point 233 days ahead of schedule.[6]

Because of Operation Market Garden and because the fuel for the Third Army had to be landed in Normandy, rather than Antwerp, Eisenhower called for a pause in the Allied advance in order to regroup. When Patton was given a minimal amount of fuel in mid-October, it was, unfortunately, too late. The

Germans also had regrouped and re-manned the network of fortifications that comprised the Maginot Line in and around the City of Metz.

Metz is an ancient walled city with narrow streets that today has expanded beyond its walls and become a modern bustling urban area. Although Dad never came within the city during the war, he and I drove to the Place d'Armes in the center of town for a brief visit.

Fortifications around Metz began in medieval times, the first set of modern fortifications began in the seventeenth century. Over a dozen forts were built around the city. One such fort on the outskirts of town is open for tourists. Dad and I visited this area as well. This fort reminded me of the fort I visited as a boy back home, Fort Pike.

In the Franco-Prussian War of 1870, Metz and the entire Alsace-Lorraine region were ceded to Germany at the end of hostilities. The Germans increased these fortifications between that time and World War I. After WWI, France regained control of the territory, and the French government built a series of new fortifications along the French/German border in order to prevent a German invasion. These fortifications were mainly underground and connected by a series of tunnels.

During that period between World War I and World War II, when Germany was no longer in control of the Alsace and Lorraine regions and the French controlled the fortifications within the Maginot Line, the Germans constructed another defensive belt of fortifications east of the Saar River on German soil, which became known as the Siegfried line.

The French were firmly in control of the Maginot Line at the outset of World War II in 1939. Unfortunately for the French, the Germans bypassed the fixed fortifications of the Maginot Line and invaded France through Belgium. The original fortifications, completed before 1870, consisted of an inner ring of fifteen forts and an outer perimeter of twenty-eight steel and concrete bastions built by the Germans in 1912. In 1941, the Germans improved and modernized the installations.

The Third Army had attempted to take Metz by frontal assault in September but was unsuccessful. Metz could not be captured by a normal assault; Patton's ultimate plan of attack, encirclement, could not be immediately implemented due to lack of supplies. Consequently, Patton's Third Army was stopped at Metz from mid-September through the beginning of November.

During this halt, the 712th was engaged in indirect firing on the various fortifications situated in the countryside surrounding Metz. There were no smart bombs or laser guided bombs in World War II, but Dad seemed to have acquired a certain degree of accuracy and proficiency in hitting targets. Dad told me about one incident when the 75-mm gun on his tank was being used for artillery fire.

We couldn't go any further. We were out of gas and short on ammunition anyway.

We were doing indirect firing into Metz. The forward (infantry artillery) spotter told me the settings for firing. I set my gun, and he told me what coordinates to set it. After the first shot he radioed back and said, "Up 400." After that shell he said, "OK, down 200." (After that shell hit) he said "Boy that one went right through the window." It went into a mess hall, the Germans had a hell of a meal that night.

Although Dad received no credit by name for his accomplishment, his feat nevertheless received a certain degree of notoriety. The History of the 712th Tank Battalion records the event as follows:

> October was a month of nibbling – at the Metz bastion – and waiting – for more gas, for more ammo, for warmer clothing. Fall weather had set in and with it incessant rain. The roads became mucky; the fields in which the tankers did their indirect firing became big seas of mud. Firing used up 24 hours a day and all crew members became experts with the Azimuth Indicators and Gunner's Quadrants which though inexact did not prevent one gunner from putting a shell through a window when the forward observer called for it."[7]

The 90th Infantry Division Newspaper, *The Sniper*, gives the following account of the incident.

> Citadel Metz became the target of the 712th guns when for a period of three weeks the Battalion assumed its secondary role as reinforcing artillery; this artillery group hurled 2400 rounds daily into enemy defenses. Jokingly a forward observer requested a shell lobbed into a window at 4,000 yards; the gunner complied and hit the window.

Dad recounted another incident that he remembered from the time spent around Metz.

> When we were close to Metz, the population, the children would come out with pots and pans and cans and take the leavings off of the American soldiers' mess kits to get something to eat. They never had anything to eat at that time. I gave a little girl an orange, she didn't know what to do with it. They never had oranges in France then. Everything was imported from Spain. That's where the oranges grew and they couldn't get anything from Spain because Spain was not in the Axis powers. So she didn't know what to do with it. So I showed her what to do with it, and she ran home with it to her family.
>
> That same little girl, a blonde headed little girl, was about six when we got there and she couldn't speak a word of English and by the time we left she could talk in English.

In a letter home to Mom, dated October 17, 1944, Dad writes about this little girl.

> ...there is a little girl around here and we were talking to her. Darling don't worry she is only 6 years old. Anyway she speaks French and German, mostly German ... we were talking to her that is a few things we could pick out and a few things she could say in English. Anyway she was telling us how they made the little kids dance for Hitler and how they had to give the Hitler salute until their arms were sore. She said they had to do that in the snow and after Hitler passed they would pick up snow and throw it. I guess after he was out of sight. Isn't that a shame to make a little child do that? She said she did that since she was about four.

In a letter dated October 27, 1944, Dad again writes about the plight of small children during war.

> Darling I just came back from chow. We had a pretty good meal. We had Spam, potatoes, gravy, relish, pears, bread, butter and jam and coffee. Doesn't that sound pretty good, Love?
>
> [...]
>
> I hope and pray this war ends soon, so we can be together and maybe the rest of the world can live in peace. Darling I saw something today when I was coming from chow that really made my heart ache. There was a bunch of little kids with cans asking for the food we had left over in our mess kit. So you can imagine how hard food is to get over here. When the Germans left, they took everything with them. So now the poor people over here have to go without.
>
> Darling I may be way over here fighting. But there is still plenty to thank God for and we can be plenty thankful to be Americans. Darling maybe some of those people at home that are always crying about things being rationed should read this.

Patton's troops would again be on the move in November, but not before November 8. Meanwhile, November 7, 1944, was Election Day in the United States. Franklin Roosevelt was running for an unprecedented fourth term as President. I asked Dad if the members of the armed forces were allowed to vote in the election during war. He said that he didn't know if any of the soldiers in the rear were allowed to vote but neither he nor anyone else he knew on the front line voted, they were all too busy preparing for battle. On that election day, bullets, not ballots, were distributed to the front line troops of the 712th Tank Battalion.

CHAPTER 9

The Mud of Lorraine

It's not the size of the man in the fight, it's the size of the fight in the man.

President Theodore Roosevelt

Patton was ready to have another try at Metz after the port of Antwerp had finally been secured and the flow of supplies to the Third Army began to increase. Despite continuous heavy rain and no air support because of the weather, the Third Army began its offensive on November 8, 1944. The assault plan called for an attack south of Metz by the 5th Infantry Division and a simultaneous attack north of Metz by the 90th Infantry Division,[1] including the 712th Tank Battalion.

The plan of attack on Metz was a pincer movement around the city with the two divisions linking up on the east side of Metz, thereby encircling it. Meanwhile the 95th Division would by-pass the outer ring of forts and destroy or capture the main garrison of German troops within the City of Metz.

The First Moselle Crossing

In order to accomplish this military maneuver, the 90th and the 712th had to cross the Moselle River. Being from New Orleans, and living a block away from the Mississippi River levee, my visions of what constitutes a river is somewhat skewed. When Dad and I crossed the Moselle River, it appeared to me to be no wider than a canal; it was well within its banks of no more than 350 feet in width. However, this was not the situation in November, 1944. The incessant rain in 1944 had caused the river to overflow its banks and at spots it was over 800 yards wide. The rain made even the preparations rough, the going was slow because of deep mud everywhere. "Day after day the rain poured down. Trucks, bringing vital supplies into the assembly area by night were sunk to the axles in a clutching sea of mud."[2]

Red Ball Express Truck in the mud. (*US National Archives*)

The 712th Tank Battalion had moved into its staging positions in the village of Evange. B Company tanks, attached to the 359th Regiment, had the left flank of the attack with the planned crossing at Malling. C Company, assigned to the 358th Regiment, had the right flank of the attack with a crossing at Cattenom. The tanks assisted in the preparatory artillery barrage prior to the attack.

The main obstacle on the east side of the Moselle River was Fort Koenigsmacher, one of the fortifications within the Fortress Metz complex, which was approximately 5 miles northeast of the City of Thionville.

The infantry crossed in boats on November 8, while the 712th waited for the engineers to complete construction of the bridges on the overrun banks of the river. The Germans on the east side of the river was the enemy, but the swollen river was more of an enemy for the engineers. It was estimated that it would take several more days to install the bridge.

The subsequent 5 days were anxious and frustrating ones for the tankers. Already the 712th-90th team had become 'blood-brothers' and yet one half of that team

Rafts ferrying 5 Company B tanks across swollen Mosselle River. (*90th photograph*)

was fighting to the very utmost while the other half – the tanks – was unable to assist. [...] The situation on the other side finally reached such a critical stage that supporting armor became essential if it were to be retained and exploited. So on 13 Nov. at 1400 a B Co. platoon pulled down to the river bank and under an elaborate smoke screen ferried across on rafts, with shells plopping in the waters all around them. The fire power of these 5 Shermans could not begin to compete in value to the morale boost they gave to the exhausted doughs. Both this platoon and C Co. tanks which came over shortly afterwards were greeted with cheers and tears. All armor fanned out to support all forward troops and in a short time the atmosphere was changed from overall feeling of last ditch retention of position to aggressive offense. Meanwhile work on the bridge continued despite adversities and success at last came to the dogged engineers. By evening of 14 Nov. the entire Battalion was across the pontoon bridge, along with great quantities of supplies.[3]

Dad was in one of those first five B Company tanks that made the crossing on the raft. The crossing by the 90th and the 712th was such an arduous task that both Patton and Brigadier Gen. James Van Fleet commended the troops.

Copies of Gen. Van Fleet's congratulatory remarks and Patton's commendation were later distributed to the troops. Patton stated that Moselle crossing by the 90th Div was one that "will ever rank as one of the epic river crossings of history."

The Oudrennes Mine Field

Later on the afternoon of November 13, just before dusk, one platoon of three tanks, including Dad's, made an advance with infantry from the 359th Regiment on the left into a wooded area called Reitholtz Woods in order to close a gap that had been created between the 359th and the 357th in the vicinity of the village of Oudrennes. Dad described what happened.

> We were advancing and we entered a mine field. My tank struck a mine and blew off one of the tracks. The infantry was walking along beside us. One of the infantry stepped on a mine and had his leg blown off. I could not get out to help him because we were under orders not to get out of the tank because it was too dangerous; if we tried to get out and help him we would probably step on a mine also. It was night and I could hear him crying. I yelled at him to put a tourniquet on his leg. We were ordered to stay put until the engineers could clear the mine field at daylight.

Dad listened to the infantryman most of the night and yelled words of encouragement to him telling him everything would be alright. When daylight came Dad no longer heard the infantryman. His tank was pulled out of the mine field but Dad never discovered whether the infantryman was rescued or whether he died in that field.

The 359th had been given the mission of clearing the woods between Oudrenne and Kerling but shortly after the attack began, the regiment was stopped by mine fields on all sides. Capt. Colby of the 90th described that evening and night.

> (Companies) E and F attacked southeast into the woods, but soon lost three tanks in an extension of the same mine field. The companies continued into the woods without the tanks, but just at dark became involved in an anti-personnel mine field containing 16,000 of the vicious little wooden Schu mines [...] The battalion tried to pick its way through the mine field, but soon had too many casualties. Every time a man stepped on one of the mines, his foot was blown off above the ankle.
>
> The battalion medical section performed especially bravely [...] every litter man in the battalion squad became a casualty. In two separate instances, two-man litter teams carrying a wounded soldier stepped on a Schu mine, seriously injuring both litter bearers and killing the soldier on the litter.[4]

By November 15, the 90th Infantry Division and the 712th had cleared this obstacle. On this date all previously assigned objectives had been scrapped and B Company and the 359th Regiment of the 90th were ordered to proceed, from Oudrennes/Kerling area, with utmost speed south toward the towns of Conde-Northen and Les Estang. The purpose of the rapid advance was to close the pincer and link up with the 5th Infantry Division, thus, cutting off all German escape routes from Metz.

Mussy L'Eveque

As the 90th and the 712th raced southward toward their rendezvous with the 5th Division in order to close the jaws of the pincers, "one after another of the escape highways leading out of the doomed city of Metz were cut. Enemy convoys, desperately attempting to squeeze through the ever narrowing gamut were met with concentrated artillery fire, small arms and mortar."[5]

Two and one-half miles north of the town of Conde-Northen lies the village of Mussy L'Eveque. On November 18, 1944, just outside of that village, Dad again displayed his accuracy and proficiency as a tank gunner. He received the Bronze Star for his heroic achievement on that day. Dad's Bronze Star commendation letter states:

> For heroic achievement on 18 November 1944 in the vicinity of Mussy L'Eveque, France. During an attack on the town, a platoon of tanks in support of infantry troops encountered a convoy of five enemy vehicles. Corporal Gruntz, Gunner, from his exposed position in the lead tank, fired his tank gun so effectively and accurately upon the convoy that all five vehicles were immobilized and 17 enemy were taken prisoner. The courageous and efficient action of Corporal Gruntz in disrupting the enemy column enabled the infantry to advance and accomplish its mission.

Dad and I drove in and around Mussy L'Eveque as he explained the events that day in 1944.

> We came over the top of the rise, right back there on top of the hill over there, we came from another town back there that we occupied the day before that was deserted when we went through there. It was in the afternoon, getting kind of late.
>
> We were in a field. We were out in the open just like right here. We came over a hill and the infantry had penetrated down to the road here. The Germans were coming down this road here. They were going in this direction (pointing northeast). The lieutenant said there are some vehicles going down the road. My

The little man who killed seven with one blow didn't have much on Cpl. Louis G. Gruntz, 3600 Beauvais St., Metairie. During an attack on a French town a platoon of tanks in support of infantry encountered a convoy of five enemy vehicles. The corporal, a gunner, from his exposed position in the lead tank, "fired his tank gun so effectively and accurately upon the convoy that all five vehicles were immobilized and 17 enemies were taken prisoner."

The corporal was given the Bronze Star Medal for his action with the tank battalion. He also has the Purple Heart for wounds received in action in France in August.

Cpl. Gruntz

Gruntz awarded Bronze Star.

tank was exposed and that's when I fired and knocked them out. I fired over the infantry's head, that's why it (the Bronze Star commendation) said I had accurate firing. I hit the first vehicle, then I hit the last one than I hit the other three. I knocked them out and we captured seventeen prisoners.

I did see one of the German soldiers; he had his hand shot off, his right hand was off right above the wrist. I still remember that.

Dad said he felt a little pity and sorrow for that wounded German.

The poor bastards were just trying to get home.

(The vehicles were) supply vehicles, some of them were horse drawn. Somebody told me they had a gang of wrist watches and all the loot they were taking back to Germany. But I never got any of that. It was just something that had to be done. We just kept on going, because we couldn't stop so we went over the road and on to the next town.

The records of the 712th Tank Battalion noted the rapid advance of B Company tanks from Oudrennes, stating.

B Company rolled forward so quickly and with such effectiveness that the (Germans) had no time to blow prepared demolitions on bridges and overpasses.

[...] they crossed the Nied River and took position at Conde-Northen squarely athwart the major escape route. Here they intercepted a fleeing column and annihilated it.[6]

The next day, the 712th and the 90th Division made contact with the 735th Tank Battalion and the 5th Infantry Division and the operation was over. Metz had not been conquered by assault since the year 471. In previous wars, armies laid siege to Metz and occupied it only after it capitulated. The United States Third Army did what no army had done in over 1,500 years.

Dad was unaware his actions on that November day had merited a Bronze Star. "I never knew anybody paid any attention to it. That wasn't the first time things like that happened." His actions were noticed by an infantry officer and reported up the line, Dad's commendation was issued almost two months later, on January 6, 1945. Dad indicated there were plenty of other actions by members of the 712th that were worthy of commendation but went unnoticed.

The 712th seemed to always be on the move and its After Action Reports were always sparse. This fact was recognized many years after the war when an Armor Memorial Park honoring the armored units of World War II was dedicated outside of the Patton Museum in Fort Knox, Kentucky. Among the memorial obelisks is one for the 712th Tank Battalion. In addition to listing all of the members of the 712th killed in action there is a plaque which lists all of the 712th Battle Honors and Awards. The individual awards of the battalion include two Distinguished Service Crosses, fifty-six Silver Stars, 362 Bronze Stars and 498 Purple Hearts. But this memorial goes further and states:

> This plaque also honors those men whose acts of bravery under fire were not officially recorded and rewarded in combat, valor was commonplace among soldiers who asked only to serve in trust and honor with honorable men, doing all that was asked of them at any price. Often they were numbered among our casualties and details of their heroic deeds, obscured by subsequent fighting were lost to after action reports. Their exemplary acts of courage and devotion to duty are forever enshrined in this monument. We accord them their rightful place among the honored in battle.

The Lorraine Cemetery

The Lorraine American Cemetery is located in St Avold, France, between Metz and the German border. With 10,489 graves, it contains the largest number of American dead from World War II interred in Europe. There are several 712th members buried here but only one from B Company, who was a replacement that Dad did not know particularly well, Alfred McLaughlin from the Bronx. I took particular note of the fact that he was killed in action on March 9, 1945, while the 712th was cutting through Germany, and long after it had left the area near Metz. I was curious as to how McLaughlin came to be buried in eastern France; I later learned that when the US Government established the permanent American Cemeteries in Europe there was a policy not to leave any soldier buried on enemy soil, therefore, those killed in Germany were eventually transferred to the cemeteries in France, Belgium, Luxembourg and the Netherlands. I would also later learn that there is at least one American WWII soldier who was laid to his final rest on Germain soil, TEC5 Henry Bockhorn of Company D of the 712th Tank Battalion, who was killed in action in France on August 8, 1944. Bockhorn's mother emigrated to the United States from Germany before he was born; following WWII, she requested that her son be permanently interred in her family's tomb in the Uthlede Cemetery in Kreis Wesermuende, Germany.

After paying our respects in the Lorraine Cemetery, we headed toward the Saar River and the town of Dillingen.

Crossing the Saar River into Dillingen

A cold driving rain provided B Company with a brief and uncomfortable Thanksgiving meal in 1944. Two days later, the Battalion launched a series of attacks to clean out enemy resistance in the area west of the Saar between it and the French-German border. B Company crossed the border into Germany and occupied the German border towns of Biringen and Oberesch. The Germans retreated behind the natural barrier of the Saar River and the Siegfried Line which was built on the eastern side of the river. On December 3, 1944, after other units had moved through and on toward and across the Saar River, B Company moved south and back across the meandering border into the French border town of Neuenkirchen. The next two days were spent in performing maintenance on the company tanks.

Between November 25 and December 6, the 90th and the 712th moved closer to crossing the Saar. Father Murphy described the fighting, "Many big shells are coming in. We are in the vicinity of the Saar River and the shells sound like big locomotives coming in."[7]

By December 1, the tanks had reached the western banks of the river and could see the towns of Dillingen and Pachten located on the eastern bank. The 90th and the 712th were on the left or northern flank of the Third Army's push across the Saar. Other elements of the Third Army were attacking further south in Saarbrücken and Sarraguemines.

The Siegfried line, Germany's western defensive wall, consisted of hundreds of mutually-supporting pillboxes, observation and command posts and bunkers. In the area around Dillingen, this line of fortifications came down to the river's edge.

"Dillingen itself was a fortress, studded with many camouflaged pillboxes. An innocent-appearing jewelry store, a hardware store, a railway ticket office and many other such buildings scattered through the town turned out to be steel and concrete pillboxes."[8]

The Siegfried line fortifications varied in depth depending on the terrain and population density of the locale. It had fairly well dispersed strong points from the heavily wooded hills in the Saar region northward. Many small cottages looked like innocent farm dwellings but were actually fortified pillboxes with twelve to eighteen inch thick concrete walls.[9]

Like the Moselle River which was crossed a month earlier, the Saar River in 1944 was overflowing its normal banks due to the incessant rainfall throughout that November and December. The hilly terrain on the west side of the river provided only a few spots for vehicular access to the short flat river banks. These access points meant there were only a few sites that could be chosen for bridge sites. In addition to this, the troops had to battle the rain and the thick mud.

When Dad and I arrived in Dillingen, the day was bright and sunny and the river was within its normal banks, unlike like the weather and conditions in 1944.

That winter in 1944, the hills on the northern side of Dillingen were occupied by the German observation posts. This allowed the Germans to observe all activity on the river and to direct their artillery fire accordingly. The swollen river and the commanding position of the German artillery, prevented the engineers from constructing a bridge across the Saar. The attack on Dillingen was even more arduous because the Prims River, a small tributary of the Saar, bisects the town of Dillingen.

Again the infantry had to establish a bridgehead on the east bank by mounting an assault in boats, with the tanks remaining on the west bank, where they provided supporting fire upon enemy positions on the east bank. As Dad explained, "The Germans were up on a mountain and we were down by the river trying to cross. They bombed the bridge so we couldn't get across on the bridge, so we put pontoons in. And they were looking at us and every time we got the pontoon bridge built to go across, they would get the artillery and blow it. Then we put a smoke screen out on that whole mountain for about a week it was covered with smoke so they couldn't see what we were doing." The smoke screen was aided by the burning buildings in Pachen and Dillingen

Finally on December 9, five tanks from A Company were ferried across the river. The river suddenly dropped and the ferrying operation was temporarily grounded. To make matters worse, the smoke screen dissipated. On December

12, another smokescreen was laid and the remainder of A Company was ferried across with a platoon from C Company. "One time the hawser that was guiding the ferry broke with the tank on it. The tank was stranded on its ferry for a whole day."[10] By December 14, the remainder of the battalion was ferried across.

B Company was the last portion of the 712th to cross the river. Dad explained his experience upon crossing the river, "When we got into Dillingen, we went straight through the town and outposted the town. There were three American soldiers killed, their bodies were lying right there where we were outposted."

Dad and I parked our car in the public parking lot near the river. We walked through the shopping district area to a small park area near the town church. When we reached the approximate spot where he was first outposted, Dad told me, "When we were going through town, the people obviously stayed in town until the last minute and then left and hid somewhere. They had a market and sausage hanging up on a hook, so I went in there and grabbed a big hunk of sausage and I had sausage for lunch that day."

Prior to the tanks arriving, the infantry was fighting house to house and sustaining heavy casualties. Dillingen was later to be called the hottest spot on the Saar. The 90th Infantry Division established a record by capturing or destroying two hundred pillboxes in one day.[11]

Dad described the destruction of one such pillbox.

Three or four American soldiers (infantry) were dead, they had just gotten shot in front of the pillbox. And we got to it, we fired at it to stop it from shooting the machine gun, you couldn't get nothing into it because they had steel in front." Dad was in a tank with a new replacement lieutenant, Lt Thermon Mesker. "(Mesker) started to run the tank up to the pillbox. So I said, "You can't, you shouldn't do that, they usually have mines in front of those pillboxes." We just came out from being blown up by a mine. I was leery about it.

Mesker ignored Dad's concerns.

So he pulled up into it and they (the Germans) quit firing. ... (The infantry) figured out what to do and they told him (Mesker) to come back up because they had other pillboxes firing. So an engineer got on the tank, in the back of the turret where they couldn't shoot him, so when we pulled up to the pillbox again, he got off and put a dynamite charge in the window and blew it out.

A colonel from the 90th Infantry witnessed this attack on the pillbox. Lt Bob Vutech and the colonel came up to Dad afterwards. Dad was angry at Mesker for not considering the possibility of the presence of mines, thereby taking such a foolish risk in bringing the tank directly up to the front of the pillbox.

Lt Bob Vutech. (*Company B photograph*)

That's when the (infantry) Colonel came up to me and said, "Corporal, who is that lieutenant?"

I said, "Aw, he is new, colonel." He said, "I thought so, he doesn't have any sense, but he's got plenty guts."

Vutech said "Louie you don't like this lieutenant, do you?" I said, "No, it's not that, but if that son of a bitch wants to get himself killed, I don't want him to get me killed with him.

Mesker was a new replacement. Dad didn't know if Mesker wanted to make the Army a career and was trying to win medals or be noticed for his action in order to be promoted. But Dad believed that he was being too reckless.

Vutech and the colonel both knew that Dad was right, Mesker should not have run the tank up to the front of the pillbox. Knowing Dad's concerns over Mesker's reckless tactics, Vutech later transferred Dad out of Mesker's tank and put him in another tank.

When the Americans were crossing the river, the Germans wanted to wipe out the bridgehead and in the ensuing battle they threw everything they had at the Americans. Jim Cary described the Dillingen operation as follows:

> They were attacking one flank, and the only way that the Americans could stop it was to turn all the artillery they had in the area loose on the German attack. [...] I saw what happened afterward and that was the most horrible sight I ever saw

in the entire war, and is something that I still visualize at times. [...] this extreme intense artillery came down right in the middle of that concentration of troops, both the German and American.

It was very shortly after that that we got our tanks across. [...] There were bodies absolutely stacked one on top of the other. There must have been eight or nine hundred bodies in that area with parts of their heads blown off; I remember in one case, a German had fallen face down in the road and it was muddy, and cars were driving back and forth over him, and I kept asking myself, "Why doesn't this bother me more than it does?" You get so immune to it.[12]

During our visit in 1994, it was obvious that most of the buildings had been destroyed during the war. The town looked like a blue collar factory town in America. The only structure that appeared to me to have any sense of antiquity was the church on the northern side of the town. Most of the stores in the shopping district did not seem to be European, the architectural style of full plate glass windows in aluminum frames covering the entire store front was reminiscent of American suburban shopping malls built in the 1950s and 1960s. I was struck with the sense that Dillingen had lost its unique pre-war character.

When the German counter attack had begun in the Ardennes, in what was to become known as the Battle of the Bulge, Patton had to withdraw his forces from the east side of the Saar River and move north through Luxembourg on order to breakthrough to the surrounded town of Bastogne. The units of the Third Army that were the southern or right flank of the push across the Saar were the first to withdraw and were the lead elements of the relief column headed toward Bastogne. Patton made a strategic move in designating the 90th and the 712th to be the last to withdraw. The 90th and 712th rearguard action was meant to protect the right flank of the relief column as it moved north on the western side of the Saar.

The Dillingen withdrawal began on December 19th and continued twenty-four hours a day until completed. At the time the enlisted men were not told the reason for the withdrawal. Since B Company was the last unit to cross the river into Dillingen, it was the last 712th unit to be pulled back to the west side of the river. With no bridge the armor had to be taken back by ferry – tank by tank. Roads on the German side of the river "became impassable and each vehicle required winching through the mud and over the steep banks. Enemy artillery destroyed the ferry, and with only a few hours remaining in which to complete the withdrawal, 25 armored vehicles remained on the wrong side of the river. In the darkness and in freezing waters, under continuous shelling the men at the river slaved through the night to salvage what they could."[13]

The last of the B Company tanks made it back to the west side of the river at 2:30 a.m. on the morning of December 23. Jim Cary described the 712th's withdrawal as follows:

Withdrawing from Dillingen. (*The History of the 712th Battalion*)

Then we got the orders to pull back, and we got into this very slow, very poorly done operation in ferrying these tanks back across the Saar. It's a good thing the Germans didn't have anything to throw at us or if they did they didn't want to waste ammunition, because we were sitting ducks. The infantry pulled out and we were left with our tanks strung out along the Saar River, and I finally got Colonel Randolph on the radio and asked him to do whatever he could to put a smokescreen down. We did get some smoke, and we slowly got the tanks back across the river.[14]

The few buildings in town, not destroyed in battle, were destroyed by a demolition squad before abandoning the town to the Germans; one such building contained a stock of C-2 explosives which also had to be eliminated. Cary described this event:

And then we did get back across, and I was standing on the other side of the Saar River when they blew that. The whole skyline lit up, it was one of those scenes like, do you remember what the burning of Atlanta looked like in "Gone With the Wind"? Very much like that. The buildings were silhouetted against the sky, and behind the sky there were all these flames, and the sky was red.[15]

Not all of B Company's tanks got back across the river. Dad told me that, "Lee Miller's tank got bogged down and they couldn't get back (across the river) because the pontoons and the ferries were knocked out. So he had to blow it (his tank) up. He put in some kind of explosive that melted the barrel of the tank, so they (the Germans) couldn't shoot it. And he had to swim back across the river, and it was cold too." For this heroic action, Miller was awarded the Silver Star.

Once back on the western side of the Saar, the 90th and the 712th assumed a position of aggressive defense. In Belgium, English-speaking German soldiers, wearing uniforms of captured Americans roamed behind the American lines sabotaging and destroying American equipment, killing officers, and spreading confusion. All units had been alerted to be aware of such tactics. The 90th and the 712th were alerted to the possibility of German paratroopers being dropped behind their position. Check points were established.

Dad explained:

> When the Germans attacked in the Battle of the Bulge, they sent men who could speak English and they came through the lines. They were killing American soldiers and taking their uniforms and taking their Jeeps.
>
> And we had checkpoints set up, everywhere you went you had to ask what was the password. And they (the Germans) got so good, we had to change the password more than once a day. Like if the word might have been red beans and rice, it might have been beef stew or leg of lamb, it could have been anything but if the whole Army got the word, that was it. Well, plenty of them were captured.

Soldiers on guard duty were reluctant to shoot what appeared to be another American. Dad explained that guards would ask additional questions to those who did not know the password.

> One of the questions they asked a guy, "Where are you from in the United States?" And the answer would be, like say New York and then he would give him a little fictitious question. Then he said "Where did you take your training?" And he (the German) said "I took it at Fort Hood." Then he said "Have you ever been in Tennessee?" And the guy (German) would say, "Yeah," and the guard would say, "Have you ever been in Texas?" And the German said, "No, I never did go to Texas." The guard knew he was a German since Fort Hood is in Texas.

When Dad was on guard duty, he stopped an American GI and was about ready to shoot him. He didn't know the password and didn't answer some of the questions. Fortunately for that GI, by questioning him further, Dad became convinced that he truly was an American and he let him pass through the checkpoint.

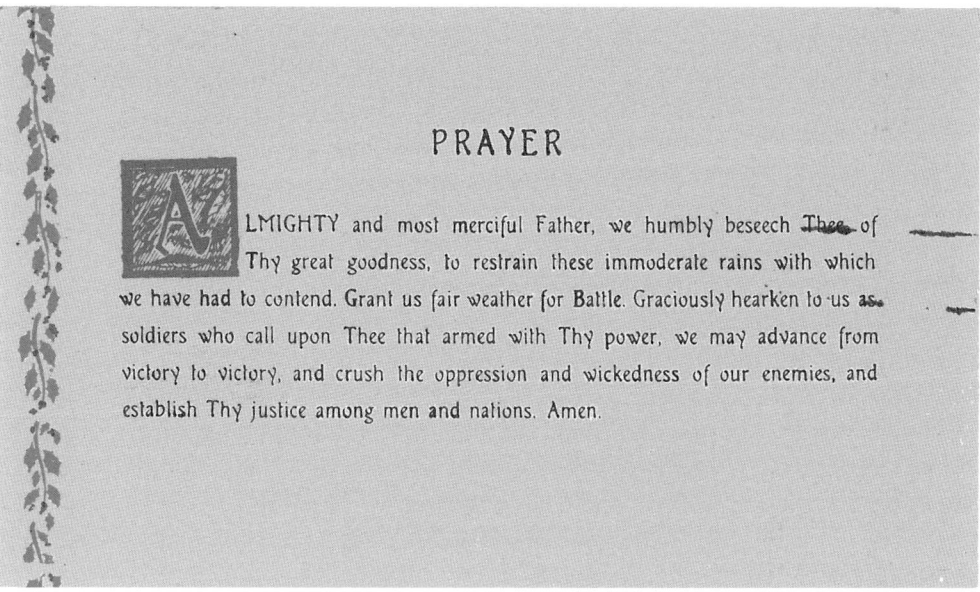

These pages: Cpl Gruntz's copy of Patton's Prayer. (*Author's collection*)

It was also around this period that Brig.-Gen. Edward T. Williams, the artillery officer for the Third Army, gave Gen. Patton a demonstration of a new innovation for artillery shells, a radar operated proximity fuse. Standard artillery shells either exploded on contact with the ground or were detonated by a time device. This new fuse, however, installed in the nose of the projectile, exploded the shell by use of a radar beam which traveled from the fuse to the earth. The shell exploded when the returning ray marked the designated height above the ground. The full blast of the shell showered shrapnel on all ground troops within the blast perimeter. Patton was reportedly pleased, after learning of this new device. Aware of the developing situation in the Ardennes, he ordered that it not be used immediately. He wanted to maintain an element of surprise with the introduction of this new device and use it when battle conditions were most critical. Within weeks, such situations would present itself during the height of the Battle of the Bulge.[16]

Patton's Prayer

One of the most memorable quotes from the movie *Patton*, was when a clergyman asked Gen. Patton, "I was interested to see a Bible by your bed. You actually find time to read it?" Patton replied, "I sure do. Every goddamn day."

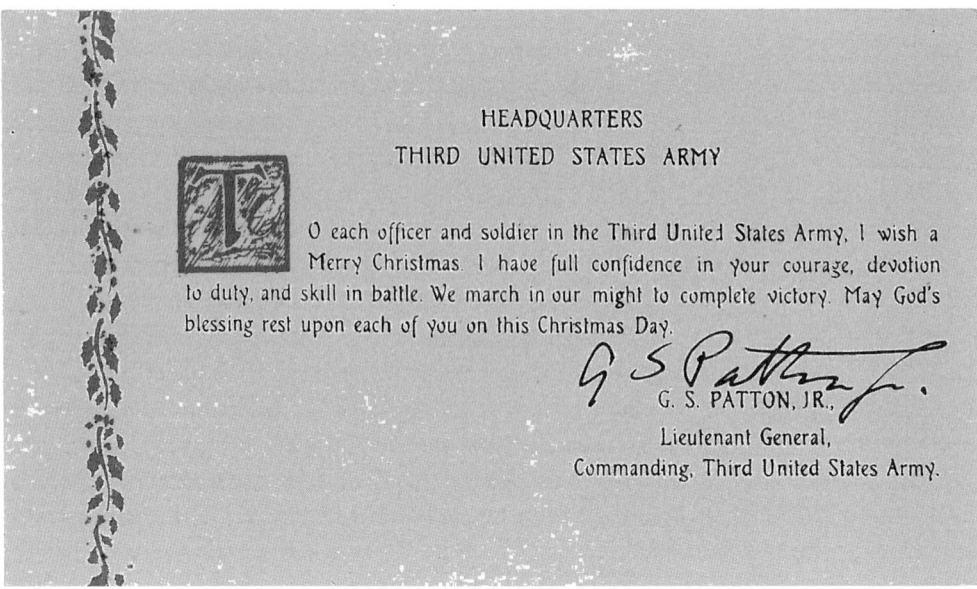

Patton's flare for using profanity to punctuate his messages made his request for a prayer to be written seem somewhat paradoxical for his persona.

I recall Dad saying the prayer actually existed when he saw the movie in 1970 and I became intrigued by the true facts surrounding the Patton's request of the Third Army's Chaplain.

In the movie, the producers engaged in a little cinematic license and portrayed Patton as requesting his chaplain to write a prayer for the snow to end, in order that his troops could make the breakthrough to Bastogne. But the movie's portrayal of the events are not entirely accurate. Actually, the prayer was offered in order to bring clear weather for the planned Third Army break-through to the Rhine in the Saarguemines area, then scheduled for December 21. The Battle of the Bulge changed these plans. As it happened, the Third Army was moving north to attack the south flank of the German Bulge in the Ardennes when the prayer was actually issued.

Fall is normally wet season in Lorraine, with an average monthly rainfall of three inches in September, October, and November. In November 1944, 6.95 inches of rain fell during the month.

Patton's efforts to take Metz and the rest of Lorraine, had been hampered by sheets of cold rain, mud clinging to boots and tank treads and the Moselle at flood stage, he was truly disgusted with the weather.[17]

In letters home, Patton continually complained about the rain and how it was hampering the Third Army's ability to advance against the Germans.

In a letter to the Secretary of War, Henry L. Stimson, he jokingly asked that "in the final settlement of the war, you insist that the Germans retain Lorraine, because I can imagine no greater burden than to be the owner of this nasty country where it rains every day…"

With respect to his prayer, Gen. Patton wrote, in his memoirs, "The weather was so bad that I directed all Army chaplains to pray for dry weather. I also published a prayer with a Christmas greeting on the back and sent it to all members of the Command. The prayer was for dry weather for battle."[18]

According to Patton's staff, the dialogue in the movie where Patton requested the prayer is accurate if not complete.[19]

By the time the prayer was distributed to the troops, the weather that had plagued the Third Army during November and most of December, when the prayer was requested, was no longer rain and mud, it was now snow and ice. The morning the prayer was being read by men of the Third Army, they were in a driving snow storm headed for the Ardennes. Gen. Gay, had reminded Patton that the prayer had been printed for an attack over the Saar and toward the Rhine.

"Oh, the Lord won't mind," was Patton's answer. "He knows we're too busy right now killing Germans to print another prayer."[20]

On December 23, it was a cold bright dawn all over the Ardennes. For the first time since the great offensive had begun, flying weather was perfect. Ceiling and visibility were unlimited.[21] When Patton looked out of his window and saw the sun, he was jubilant. "Hot dog!" he said. "I guess I'll have another 100,000 of those prayers printed. The Lord is on our side and we've got to keep him informed of what we need."

He called for his deputy chief of staff, Col. Harkins. He wore a smile from ear to ear. "God damn, Paul, look at that weather! O'Neill sure did some potent praying. Get him up here. I want to pin a medal on him."[22]

The next day, the weather was still clear when the Chaplain came to Patton's office. The Gen. rose, came from behind his desk with hand outstretched and said, "Chaplain, you're the most popular man in this Headquarters. You sure stand in good with the Lord and soldiers." The General then pinned a Bronze Star Medal on Chaplain O'Neil.[23]

In 1950, Monsignor James O'Neill wrote an article attempting to set the record straight on the true facts surrounding the now famous prayer that he authored. The former Chaplain wrote the story to not only enhance Patton's memory as great military leader, but as a person who had a genuine trust in God, and was true to the principles of his religion, being an Episcopalian.[24]

Monsignor O'Neill stated that Patton had called him on December 8, 1944 requesting a "weather prayer". When he presented the prayer to Patton, Patton questioned the Chaplain on how much praying was being done not only by the chaplains, but the soldiers as well.

When the chaplain admitted that not much praying was going on, Patton stated:

> Chaplain, I am a strong believer in Prayer. There are three ways that men get what they want; by planning, by working, and by Praying. Any great military operation takes careful planning, or thinking. Then you must have well-trained troops to carry it out: that's working. But between the plan and the operation there is always an unknown. That unknown spells defeat or victory, success or failure.... Up to now, in the Third Army, God has been very good to us. We have never retreated; we have suffered no defeats, no famine, no epidemics. This is because a lot of people back home are praying for us.... But we have to pray for ourselves, too. A good soldier is not made merely by making him think and work. There is something in every soldier that goes deeper than thinking or working--it's his 'guts.' It is something that he has built in there: it is a world of truth and power that is higher than himself. Great living is not all output of thought and work. A man has to have intake as well. I don't know what you call it, but I call it Religion, Prayer, or God....
>
> [...]
>
> We must ask God to stop these rains. These rains are that margin that hold defeat or victory. If we all pray, it will be ... one of the most powerful forms of energy man can generate, it will be like plugging in on a current whose source is in Heaven. I believe that prayer completes that circuit. It is power.

Patton requested a Training Letter on this subject of prayer to all the chaplains to get not only the chaplains but every man in the Third Army to pray. On December 14, 1944, Training Letter No. 5, was issued to the Third Army.[25]

Patton obviously believed in the power of prayer and that such a power could produce miracles, even during a war.

At the Christmas Day briefing, it was announced that the weathermen were now predicting clear weather for another seven days, which brought a general laugh from the staff, because there hadn't been that many clear days all winter and it just seemed impossible that such a miracle could continue. But it was explained that through a freak of nature, two high-pressure areas from opposite directions came together directly over the Ardennes, that they were approximately of equal force, and that the clear weather would continue until one or the other weakened and gave way.[26]

The weather in the Ardennes remained perfect for another six days, enough to allow the Allied planes to parachute supplies into Bastogne and to bomb German tank positions and troop concentrations around Bastogne and the rest of the Bulge. At the same time American troops on the ground were administering a pounding.

On December 26 the Third Army opened a narrow corridor to the besieged town of Bastogne.

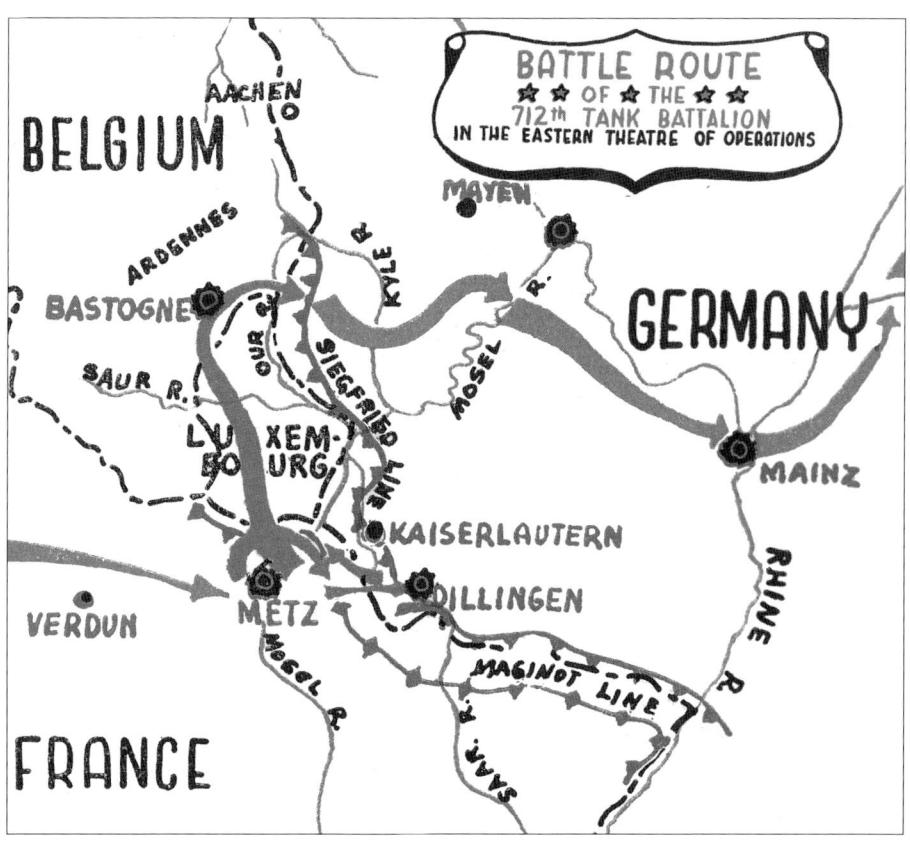

The Battle Route for the Ardennes and Rhineland Campaigns. (*The History of the 712th Tank Battalion*)

CHAPTER 10

The Battle of the Bulge

Under a good general, there are no bad soldiers.

Chinese proverb

On January 10, 1945, Dad's best friend, Sgt John Richard Williams, was killed in action during the Battle of the Bulge. Almost a year had lapsed since the married men of the 712th told their wives goodbye at Fort Jackson. Unfortunately for Richard and Opal Williams, their goodbye occurred during a period of marital discord. Dad had written Mom in November of 1944 and told her that he had asked Richard if he ever heard from Opal; Richard's reply was that he had not written anything in the past seven months. Dad stated: "A day or two before he (Richard) got killed he came to me, and said, 'Louie, I wrote Opal and made up with her and I told her we are going to try in make it together, so when I get back we are going to go back together.' He wrote her a letter and said that when he came home things were going to be different but he never did come home, he got killed two days after that."

More than a million men fought in the Battle of the Bulge.[1] It was the bloodiest of the battles that US forces experienced in World War II with 81,000 casualties 19,000 of whom were killed.[2]

As part of the Third Army's move into the Ardennes, the 90th and the 712th were moved north to protect the right flank and widen the relief corridor that the 4th Armored Division opened to Bastogne. From Dillingen the 90th and the 712th moved west to Cattenom which brought them once again on the west side of the Mosselle River; fortunately, this return trip across the river was via a bridge. From Cattenom, the 90th and the 712th moved north through Luxembourg City, the capital of the tiny Duchy of Luxembourg, and then over mountainous roads to an area southeast of Bastogne.

RECENT CASUALTY

SGT. JOHN R. WILLIAMS
Sgt. John R. Williams, 21, son of Mr. and Mrs. Omer Williams, and husband of Mrs. Opal Rodgers Williams, was killed in action in Luxembourg on Jan. 10. Sgt. Williims volunteered July 10, 1940 at 17 years of age. He was thought to have been with the 90th Division as he sent his father a history of that division which was received Monday of this week. He held the Good Conduct ribbon and a Defense Bar. He went to Europe during the invasion with a tank unit.

Richard Williams' obituary..

Luxembourg Cemetery

When Dad and I left Dillingen, we headed north toward Bastogne. Just outside of Luxembourg City, we stopped at the American Cemetery. We began looking for soldiers from B Company of the 712th buried there. The first grave we visited was that of Richard Williams. Dad spent a few moments in quiet prayer and reflection over Richard's grave.

Dad and I next located the graves of Giacomo Caruso, Buck Lee and Lee Miller. Lee Miller was the tank commander who received the Silver Star in Dillingen. He was killed on February 27, 1945, as the battalion was entering Germany. Dad had trained with Lee Miller; Caruso and Buck Lee were replacements. Caruso was killed on February 19, 1945, when his tank was knocked out by a panzerfaust in the town of Kesfeld, Germany.

We next found the grave of Lt-Col. George B. Randolph. Randolph was from Birmingham, Alabama. He was forty-two years old at the time of his death and was survived by his wife and two sons. For his actions in combat he was awarded the Distinguished Service Cross, Silver Star with Oak Leaf Cluster, Bronze Star, Purple Heart with Cluster, Legion of Honneur Chevalier, Croix De Guerre with Bronze Palm. He was killed on January 9, 1945, the first day of action by the 712th in the Battle of the Bulge.

Above left: Lt-Col. George B. Randolph. (*Company B photograph*)

Above right: Randolph Cross. (*Author's collection*)

In the opinion of those who served under him, he was one of our finest combat leaders. Religious, with great faith in his men, he was a man of integrity, honor, and courage. Tall, with a slow gait, he talked slowly and easily. Not given to small talk, but when he spoke he said a lot. He complimented his men for a job well done but was silent when it did not meet his expectations.

Each day he was out early to visit and check with commanders of the supported infantry units; he and his tanks were always welcome (by the 90th). He also visited his widely dispersed tank companies and platoons, encouraging them and orienting them on the combat picture. Among his men, he was especially renowned for his inspirational talk to them after the 712th's excellent performance in the Falaise Gap.

On 9 Jan. '45, Col. Randolph was, as usual, at the front coordinating with others on an attack plan. The explosion of an incoming shell killed him. His men say that the saddest words ever heard on their radios were:

'Randolph – killed – arty fire.'[3]

Dad said, "He probably would have been promoted to General before the war was over."

Dad and I also stopped at the grave of Gen. George S. Patton Jr. Patton did not die during the war, he died as a result of injuries sustained in an automobile accident in Germany in December of 1945. Patton always enjoyed being among his troops, his widow believed that it was only fitting that his final resting place be among those who died while under his command, hence he was buried in the Luxembourg Cemetery.

The Battle for Bastogne

After leaving the cemetery, we stopped for some refreshments and a brief tour of the City of Luxembourg before heading on our trek north. This city was quite beautiful and we would have liked to have spent a few more hours visiting the sites, but we were trying to reach Bastogne by nightfall, therefore, we were soon back on the road again.

It was a clear and sunny afternoon, the day Dad and I drove on the winding mountain road in Luxembourg with steep grades most of the way. Our traveling conditions were in stark contrast to the conditions in 1944 when the 712th was on this road. Dad explained that the tanks had to travel these roads in winter conditions at close to top speed, it was snowing and freezing conditions all of the way. When the tanks were traveling at night, they couldn't see the road or where they were going. There were no headlight on tanks, there was no lighting of any kind to illuminate the roadway ahead. A lead vehicle, such as a jeep led the column of tanks. Each tank had to follow closely to the tank in front of it by watching a small two red lights mounted on the rear of the preceding tank. The trailing tank had to stay close enough to the tank in front in order to see the red light, otherwise, it would go off the side of the road.

Jim Cary had described the operation.

> I remember a long, narrow road with trees closing over the top, it's one of those things that just gets imprinted on your mind.
>
> I thought we were going a little too slow. We knew there was going to be an operation on January 9th, and here it was January 8th, about the middle of the afternoon, and the way I remember it, the road was winding back and forth through a chain of hills and mountains. I went out ahead of the company, and I noticed a road outside of the mountains that looked like a very good road. So I went down there in my jeep and ran all the way up and then over it; it was a much shorter, more direct route. I thought, "Gee, that's great. I'll bring the tanks down here." So I took them out of the mountains down on this road and by the time we started down the road it started snowing, and the road was completely obliterated; you couldn't see anything. The only thing we had to guide us was a fence that ran parallel to it, and that pretty well kept us on the road. But the second we came out into open country – I didn't realize we were

under German observation – they started shelling us, pretty heavy too. We kept moving, deploying to scatter the tanks and then moving some more. We finally got through there.[4]

Dad and I arrived in Bastogne late in the afternoon. Our first visit was the Bastogne Memorial, which is located on the Mardasson Hill, just on the outskirts of town. The memorial is two stories high, in the shape of a five pointed star, with a circle in the center. It was started in 1950 as a memorial by the Belgium people to the USA. to thank them for having taken part in the Battle of the Bulge and the liberation of Belgium. The name of each of state in the Union is written along the top ring of the monument, and on the vertical columns forming the points of the stars are the names and insignias of the various Allied military units which participated in the Battle of the Bulge. We soon found and photographed the insignias of the Third Army and the 90th Infantry Division.

I climbed the steps to the top of the circle. From atop the memorial, one has a commanding view of the area, surrounding Bastogne, where the battles were fought. At the entrance to the Memorial Park stands the last Borne de la voie de la Liberté, Boundary of the Way of Liberty.

When we returned to the center of town, we found vacancy at the Hotel Le Brun. The hotel had served as the command post of Col. William Roberts of the 10th Armored Division during the war and had sustained damage when the Germans began shelling and bombing Bastogne. It was still daylight, therefore after renting the room, we walked the half block to the town square to find a restaurant for dinner. The town square has two monuments, a bust of Gen. McAuliffe and a Sherman Tank. The square has been renamed McAuliffe Square in honor of the commanding general of the 101st Airborne who was in Bastogne during the German attack.

"There he is – Gen. McAuliffe," Dad said, pointing to statue. "'Nuts,' that's what he told the Germans when they sent a note about surrendering. They (Germans) surrounded the town and they sent a note to him to surrender. And he sent them a note back with 'Nuts' on it. So he wouldn't surrender so they fought on."

With respect to the tank in McAuliffe Square, Dad pointed out the weakness of the Sherman's armor. The Bastogne tank has a hole in its side approximately four inches in diameter. Dad said, "An 88 went through here and out the other side it was so strong. Those things went through the our tanks like a hot knife through butter."

On the various roads entering Bastogne, I noticed the turrets of Sherman Tanks mounted on stone pedestals. It looked as if they were some form of memorial, but were oddly located in various spots on the outskirts of town. I later learned that these turrets are indeed memorials and they mark the

Dad examines a hole caused by an 88 in the side of a tank at Bastogne. (*Author's collection*)

Tank turret outside Bastogne. (*Author's collection*)

location of the outer defense ring of the American forces that were protecting Bastogne.

Dad and I drove across the Belgium/Luxembourg border to the area near villages of Bavigne, Mecher (Mecher-Dunkrodt) and Nothum, all of which are in Luxembourg, just a short distance from the border, a few miles southeast of Bastogne. We had driven through the town of Bohoey, situated on a hill and then to the village of Doncols, at the base of the hill. We stopped our car next to the side of the road and Dad pointed out the field where the major battle took place. From the base of the hill stretching southeast was a broad expansive meadow or field several hundred yards deep and at the far end of this field was a hill and wooded area. At the time of our visit the grass and foliage was just turning to autumn colors. When Dad first saw this field in 1945, the color was much different, it was white with snow. Dad explained how this was where the 712th entered the Battle of the Bulge, "We never went through Bastogne we came out in this area here and we had to get the high ground that's when we made the night march."

Dad commented that while the Germans had new and modern tanks, not all of their vehicles were new. "When they (the Germans) came to a place, or even in the city, a person who had an automobile or a truck or anything, or a tractor or a mule, they took it away from them and they'd use it for transportation. They used the same equipment as in WWI, they used plenty of it in WWII. They had mules pulling big guns. They never had plenty of equipment, soldiers were riding in cars just like this here. If they went to a place and saw a car they'd take it. But they still produced enough equipment that when they were sent into the Battle of the Bulge, the soldiers had the best equipment, all the best clothes and everything else."

On the night of January 5, 1945, the 712th and the 90th received orders to move to the Ardennes. Their rear guard mission was over. On the morning of January 6 they began the journey toward the Bulge.

On December 26, the German westward advance had been stopped short of the Meuse River. Although units in Patton's Third Army had punched a relief column through to Bastogne on December 26, 1944, the enemy still occupied the large amount of territory it had recaptured with its offensive. "The Germans were either pulling back or were stalled. For the moment it was a static struggle. Although the tide had not yet turned, the great offensive had been temporarily checked."[5]

The Allied plan to eliminate the German Bulge called for an attack force from the north and one from the south with both meeting at the town of Houffalize, which was in the center of the Bulge. Patton's forces were also to attack north between Bastogne on the west and Wiltz on the east in order to reach St Vith. However, Patton's plans had been stalled by snow, ice, and fierce resistance by the Germans.

The Battle of the Bulge

Monument at Café Schumann. (*Author's collection*)

In the period between New Year's Day and January 4, 1945, the 26th Division and the Germans had been involved in a succession of bitter attacks and counter-attacks in the area around Nothum, southwest of Wiltz. The crossroads, one kilometer north of Nothum, is known as Mon(t) Schumann; it was adjacent to a farmstead of several small buildings, the largest structure being an inn called Café Schumann. This crossroads, also identified by some as Café Schumann, was a main point on the road from Bastogne to Wiltz, and had been called the most important crossroads in the Ardennes.[6]

A small area of high ground, just north of the village of Berle, was located between the Café Schumann crossroads and Hill 490. "Although this thickly wooded hill was only several hundred feet higher than the surrounding terrain, it commanded the entire area from Café Schumann to Wiltz. Besides its obvious strategic importance, Hill 490 was also an invaluable observation point. It had to be taken."[7]

On January 2nd the 26th Infantry Division attacked to secure Café Schumann and Hill 490 beyond. Although the 26th, the Yankee Division, had been able to capture Café Schumann, their attempts at Hill 490 were not successful. Despite several attacks to capture this high ground, counter-thrusts by the enemy forced the 26th to withdraw each time to its original positions.

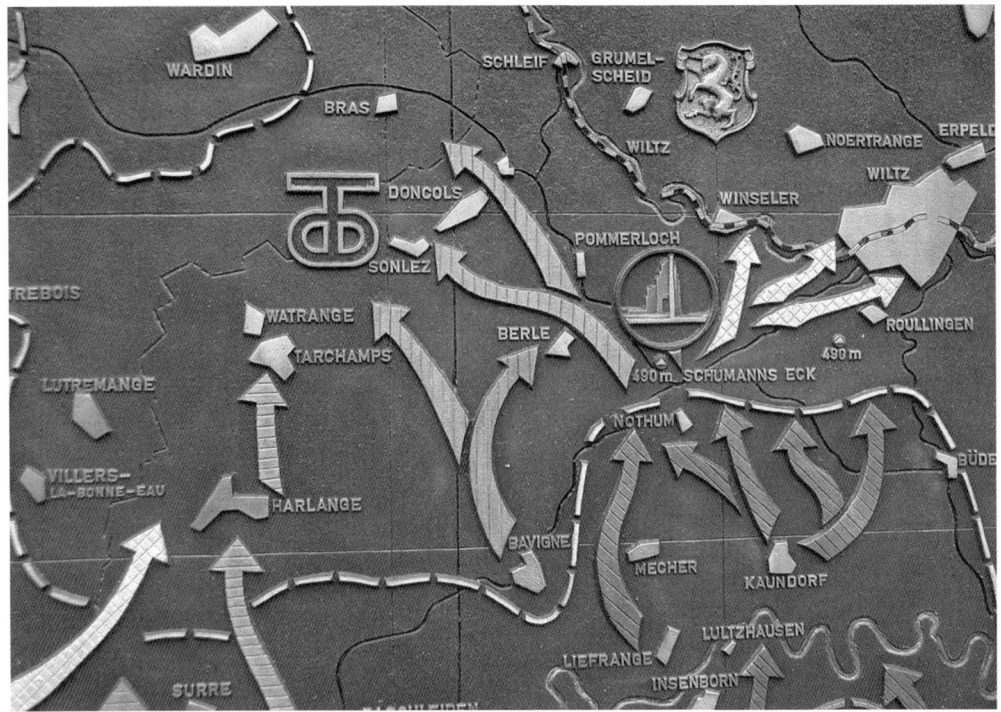

Plaque on Café Schumann. (*Author's collection*)

The Germans were well entrenched in the village of Doncols at the base of Hill 490. The battle for this real estate was a stalemate.

The Germans were not only offering fierce resistance to Patton's attacks, but were continually attacking Bastogne. With each stalled attack toward Houffalize and St Vith there was accompanying loss of men. This did not sit well with Patton, and he pessimistically wrote in his diary, "We can still lose this war".[8]

During the period January 5 to 8, the 26th Division maintained defensive positions in preparation for the arrival of 90th Infantry Division and the 712th Tank Battalion. Historian, John Toland, wrote:

> In the Ardennes not far from the battle-torn hills west of Wiltz an open jeep marked with three stars was slowly pushing through a seemingly endless column of trucks heading north. The trucks held doughs of the 90th Division, chilled to the bone, on their way to spearhead an attack through the tired Yankee Division (26th Infantry Division) to take Hill 490.
>
> In the jeep was Patton. The next day, January 9, he was to begin another general all-out attack…[9]

It was reported that when the men of the 90th had recognized Patton and were leaning out of their trucks, cheering as he passed by.[10] He waved, with confidence but realized that tomorrow many of these men, now cheering him, would be dead as a result of his orders to begin the attack.[11]

On January 9, 1945, the 90th and the 712th launched an attack to the northwest against the southern flank of the German salient, the jump off area was from the line running northeast from Bavigne to the crossroads north of Nothum.

The scene that awaited the 712th and the 90th was described in the History of the 712th Tank Battalion:

> Ahead lay steep, unrelated and snow covered hill masses, rising in instances to 2000 feet and manned by a well-equipped enemy with a better than average training and a fairly high state of morale. Successive defense lines were dug-in foxholes along the high ground and in the dense forests. [...] The cold was numbing and pierced to the very marrow of the bones. Snow was everywhere, its whiteness setting off the large, green silhouettes of the Shermans (a whitewash preparation was not used until the middle of the month)....[12]

Dad described the cold and unbearable weather conditions during January 1945:

> In the Battle of the Bulge, it was so cold plenty of them (soldiers) died from freezing, they froze to death, they couldn't move and they'd freeze to death. It doesn't take but a couple of minutes to kill you, especially if you are bleeding. I saw bodies stacked up like cord wood to be carried off to be buried.

Dad also said it was so cold that the body heat of the crew and the engine heat caused condensation to form inside the tank. This condensation froze and eventually a layer of ice developed on the interior metal walls of the tank.[13]

When the 90th and the 712th entered the Bulge, they were under constant artillery barrages and rocket barrages from German nebelwerfers, an artillery type weapon that fires explosive rockets (mortar shells) from a six-barreled mobile launcher in a 12 second period. The nebelwerfers were called "screaming meemies" by the Americans because the incoming rounds made a deafening high pitched screaming noise.

That day, January 9, was a bleak day for the 712th Tank Battalion. Cpl Walter Hahn, Randolph's driver recalls:

> We reached Nothum on January 9, 1945 about 4.00 AM. The drive to Nothum was long and very dangerous due to icy roads [...] By that time Northum was already subject to heavy artillery fire. I parked our Jeep between two tanks who

712th tankers in the Bulge. (*Company B photograph*)

offered some cover from the shelling. Lt-Col. Randolph told me that he had a meeting with General Van Fleet and his staff in the house across the road.

After this meeting Lt-Col. Randolph went to a Tank Destroyer and observed the surrounding area at Café Schumann for a planned attack that morning. After that he was crossing the road, to direct a company of tanks into Trentlehof, in the direction of Pommerlach north of Nothum when suddenly another heavy barrage of screaming meemies (Nebelwerfer) started. Hahn continued:

> At first I looked for cover under one of the tanks and I noticed that Lt-Col. Randolph took cover on the side of a Tank Destroyer. After the barrage was over [...] I found Lt-Col. Randolph lying on the ground next to the Tank Destroyer [...] He had been hit in his head by a piece of shrapnel...

Randolph died instantly.

Jim Cary, the commander of B Company, recalled, "Then we got into this wild march up to the Bulge, over roads that were icy [...] It took us two days to get up there."

Cary continued:

> The next morning (January 9) we were coming out, I was leading the company, and the line of tanks was supposed to go up this road. The road curved, and as

you curved around there was a road junction up ahead. [...]

Just as we were coming up this road, Col. Randolph was waiting, and I stopped and talked to him briefly. He expressed his pleasure that we had done so well in getting the tanks up there and said he was real happy about that. And that was the last time I saw him.[14]

Col. Ken Reimers, Commanding Officer of the 343rd Field Artillery Battalion of the 90th, wrote:

Becker-Dunrot (sic), 9 Jan.: [...] The Division lost a courageous and skillful officer at Trentchof (sic) while the 359th was clearing out the town. Lt-Col. Randolph was commander of the 712th Tank Bn., attached to the Division. He was killed by a mortar barrage while directing a company of tanks into Trentchof (sic). He has been with us ever since Normandy and received the Silver Star the same time I did. I believe he was one of the bravest men I have ever known.[15]

Major Kedrovsky, assumed command of the 712th and continued with the planned operations. Kedrovsky was later officially assigned the command and promoted to the rank of Lt-Col.

On that first day, tanks from B and C Company of the 712th made a flanking squeeze on the town of Berle and the neighboring village of Pommerloch. B Company on the right, or east flank attacked from the town of Nothum. Despite the German shells raining down upon the attack force, Berle was seized by the 90th and the 712th. Dad was in one of the B Company tanks that was moving out of Nothum toward Berle.

Dr McConahey described the 90th Infantry Division's entrance into the fighting at the Battle of the Bulge on January 9:

We moved into position between the 6th Armored Division on the left and the 26th Infantry Division on our right, and got set for a surprise attack at dawn on January 9. For many days the 26th had been battering against crack enemy troops on the southern flank of the salient without progress. They assured us that the 90th would be lucky to advance 100 yards.

At dawn our boys jumped off, and by dark they had driven the Germans back 2½ miles. We caught them by surprise, for so successful had been our secret move that the enemy did not know a fresh division had come into the line.[16]

Jack the Russian

Dad's first encounter with a panzerfaust in Sainte-Suzanne proved to be disastrous, resulting in the death of Sgt Willinger and the wounding of three

Lt-Col. Vladimir Kedrovsky. (*Company B photograph*)

others including Dad. Dad knew it was only a question of time before he had another encounter with a German anti-tank weapon. That encounter came during the Battle of the Bulge and with a most unlikely tank mate, a Russian.

When the 90th and the 712th was engaged in defensive action at the rear of the Bastogne relief column, Lt-Col. Vladimir Kedrovsky of the 712th had gone either to Paris or some other location in the far rear. During that trip to the rear he met a Russian boy, about sixteen or seventeen years of age, who had been liberated from a Nazi slave camp in France.

"He was a refugee. In other words they took him away from home when he was a kid. When they (Germans) went through these little towns they took them off to work and do things in Germany. The Germans were ruthless, they took mother and fathers and shot them. When we liberated the town in France where he was working, he wanted to go fight the Germans, he hated them," Dad explained.

Kedrovsky was of Russian descent; his grandparents emigrated from Russia to America. The Russian kid was from the same village as Kedrovsky's grandparents. Kedrovsky took this Russian kid under his wings and let him travel back to the unit with him. At first he stayed with the kitchen staff but he wanted to fight with the Americans and he wanted to kill Germans.

Kedrovsky let him ride in one of the B Company tanks. That tank happened to be Dad's. "We were short of men, so he got in the tank with us, his name was

Among the standing: Bob Kellner, Les Vink, John Essenburg, Francis James, Bob Vutech. *Crouching:* Floyd McBride. *Behind the Nazi Flag:* Jack the Russian, John Cavalieri. (*Company B photograph*)

Jack." He became known to the members of the 712th as "Jack the Russian".

As Dad and I overlooked the terrain north of Berle, Dad continued his explanation of what occurred on January 9, 1944.

> In the battle out here, we were running toward a gang of woods and the Germans tried to surrender. The Germans were desperate to get out, they were trapped and they came out. The Russian refugee was in the tank with me.

He was riding in the assistant driver's seat, located directly in front of Dad's gunner seat. The assistant driver's position is also equipped with a 30 caliber machine gun. Dad continued:

> (Jack) started shooting them because he hated them. They ran back and they wouldn't surrender. So I pulled him off the machine gun.
> And then I had to fire a shot into the woods, because we were told they had big stuff… big guns in the woods. We were right out in the field close to the woods.

And just as I fired, a (German) was firing a bazooka at me. And when I fired, I hit him first. The German bazooka shell went up in the air… it went straight up in the air. I would have gotten hit by another bazooka.

The battle had raged most of the day. As the tanks from B and C Company of the 712th captured Berle and Pommerloch, a platoon of tanks from B Company positioned itself on the small hill north of Berle. The enemy that had stymied the 26th Division fell to the 90th and the 712th.

Doncols, Luxembourg

Dad was in one of the platoon of tanks that took positions on a hill just north of Berle. Their position was just on the edge of wooded area that looked out on the open field that had to be traversed to capture the town of Doncols. Lieutenant Mesker, the new replacement lieutenant, was commanding that platoon and was in the tank next to Dad; also in Mesker's tank was a another replacement a young corporal that Dad befriended. "He wasn't there that long, a nice little guy his name was (Charles) Cragg. He was in a tank with the new lieutenant (Mesker) that just came in as a replacement."

The original members of the 712th rarely became acquainted with the new replacements in other tank crews. The men of the 712th that had trained together at Fort Benning, Camp Gordon, and Fort Jackson knew each other, but when they arrived on the battlefields in France, they were dispersed to various spots, sometimes miles apart. Once in battle, only on occasions were various platoons congregated in one spot long enough for the various crews to talk to their friends assigned to other crews. But, Dad did get to know new replacements assigned to his platoon. Cpl Charles Cragg was one such replacement. He was a gunner, like Dad.

Mesker was a youthful, brash replacement lieutenant that had come to the battalion just before it entered Dillingen. Mesker was the lieutenant that the infantry colonel referred to as not having any sense, but plenty of guts after he rolled his tank up to the front of the pillbox. Jim Cary, later told me that he remembered Mesker quite well.[17] Cary said that when a replacement officer was needed, he normally would have recommended one of the company sergeants for a battlefield commission in order to fill the empty slot. But he had only just returned to the battalion himself and was now in a command of a different company.[18] Being unfamiliar with the sergeants in B Company, Cary selected Mesker from the replacement officer corps. During the time Mesker was in B Company, Cary said that he often warned Mesker against standing too high in the turret, as he was often apt to do.

When Dad's tank was outside of Nothum, the flanking units had not kept pace with B Company's advance on Berle and the Germans attacked the flanks of Berle in an attempt to recapture it and also recapture Nothum. Lieutenant Mesker was standing in the turret of his tank while Cragg and the other tank crew members were inside the tank. Dad continued, "We were surrounded. They (a German sniper) shot at him, the lieutenant." The shot was fired as Mesker was turning in the turret and hit him laterally across his stomach. Being wounded, he either dove or fell back into the tank. "He says to the kid, 'A sniper just shot at me, see if you can see him.' And that poor kid stuck his head up (out of the turret) and he got shot right between the eyes." The fate that Dad had feared being in Mesker's tank in Dillingen had now befallen Cpl Cragg. Dad was angered, as it was one of those deaths that did not have to happen. Even recounting this story fifty years later, Dad was upset with Cragg's needless death.

Jim Cary described other events that day.

> Meanwhile, we continued down the road and got maybe a mile out of town. My sense of distance is very poor because we were moving very slowly at times; I'd say we got at least three-quarters of a mile and the attack bogged down. They were very deeply entrenched in strong positions.

There were two platoons on the line, one commanded by Sgt Schmidt and the other by Lt Mesker; Lt Vutech's platoon was in reserve. At about 5:00 p.m., the company kitchen and the gasoline truck was set up in a shattered building. Cary told Sgt Schmidt to send his tanks back one at a time to get food and gasoline. He then gave Lt Mesker the same instructions.

As Cary was getting back in his tank he was wounded.

> The fragment didn't go all the way through and was hanging out of the flesh. At first I thought it took my foot off. That's what it felt like; it seemed to me that the whole shell hit my right foot and exploded. You had no time to think, and I just dived off the tank to the ground on the other side. I looked down, and I was very happy to see I still had a foot, and I was lying there, thinking about all this, when the heads started popping out of my tank looking around, wondering what happened to me.
>
> I knew I was finished, so I got in the bow gunner's place in the tank and started back. We ran into Lieutenant Vutech; he was bringing his platoon up, and I told him what the situation was and turned the company over to him. I went back to the aid station, and about two minutes later they brought Mesker in; he had been shot across the stomach. That was my last day in combat.[19]

Lt Vutech assumed command of B Company that afternoon.

The evening of January 9 was one of the few times that Dad did get to see other members of the Company that he had trained with. In accordance with

Cary's orders, Dad and other crews were rotated to the rear area for a hot meal and to be re-supplied with ammunition and gasoline. During the time that Dad's tank was rotated back to the rear kitchen Dad saw David Dickson Jr., whom he trained with back in the States.

"Dickson was a comedian. He was a bartender from Philadelphia." During basic training, Dad and Dickson had a running gag. "We used to kid one another, he'd say, 'When they bury you, I'm going to piss on your grave.' And I'd say, 'Yeah, well when they bury you they better bury you face down cause I don't want to piss on your face.'" That evening, there was no kidding because they both knew the battle that lay ahead. Dad related what Dickson said to him that evening. "He told me 'Louie, if I make it past tomorrow, I am going to come see you in New Orleans after the war is over.'" Dickson must have had a premonition. He was killed the next morning.

After dinner and refueling the tank, Dad's tank returned to the hill on the north side of Berle and Pommerloch to maintain that position during the night.

Joe Cavalieri was a gunner in one of the other tanks positioned near Dad that night. His tank was situated in some brush on the side of the road that ran between Berle and Pommerloch. In the middle of the night the Germans launched a counterattack to regain Berle and Pommerloch with four tanks. As the lead German Mark V Panzer headed along the road, the German commander was standing in the tank's hatch and apparently did not see Cavalieri's tank. When the Panzer was about twenty yards from Cavalieri's tank, the German commander fired a flare to light up the area, but the flare had a short fuse and only lit briefly. The duration of the flare's light, however, was long enough for the Panzer to become visible in Cavalieri's sights. When Cavalieri opened up at that point blank range, the Panzer erupted in flames.

Cavalieri's action thwarted the counter-attack, the other three Panzers and accompanying infantry quickly retreated. Unfortunately, the flames from the destroyed German tank illuminated the entire area and all the American positions became visible. Dad said that weapons were firing from all directions that entire night.

About an hour after Cavalieri knocked out the Panzer, two columns of infantry advanced toward the 712th, one column on each side of the road. T/Sgt Dale Albee of D Company opened fire on the advancing soldiers.[20] During the firing a voice was heard calling on one side, "Stop firing, for God's sake stop firing! We're Americans, we're GIs returning from a patrol! Please stop firing!"

After the firing had ceased, the voice was heard again, "We're Germans. We want to give up and be taken as prisoners of war." Twenty-seven prisoners were taken and an undetermined number of German soldiers had been killed.[21] The Journal of D Company reported that throughout the night the area was subjected to artillery and rocket fire.

Dad said, "At night when we couldn't see what was happening, we would pray for daylight. During the day when the fighting was the fiercest, we would pray for the darkness of night."

Gen. Patton wrote in his diary for that day's activities that despite the limited flying weather, all units along the lime attacked as plan. "The 90th Infantry Division, making the main effort, received heavy casualties from artillery and rocket fire just after jump-off, but advanced two kilometers."[22] With the exception of the 90th, the 101st Airborne and Fourth Armored Divisions, all the other units made very limited progress.

With Lt Mesker out with wounds, and Cragg dead, Dad's platoon was undermanned and was ordered to hold its position. Dad explained, "We had several men wounded and so we couldn't go any further, so they sent another platoon through us." The tanks that moved through Dad's position participated in a dawn attack on Doncols.

From Dad's vantage point at the edge of the woods, Doncols could be seen in the distance across the open snow covered field. The Germans occupied Doncols and the high area to its rear, including the nearby town of Bahoey (Bohey). The open area between the American line and Doncols was under enemy observation.

An infantryman involved in that action described the night of January 9 and the morning of 10 January.

> Between standing guard and strange noises, we didn't get much sleep. The Captain had patrols out in the snow all night… Often, a patrol would move out to look over the objective, then there would be a skirmish heard in the distance, a few blasts of opposing machine gun fire, and that was it for the patrol.
>
> In the unborn morning of Jan. 10, 1945 we moved through the shattered streets of Berle […] As we passed the last building, the columns to our front were becoming visible […]
>
> As we became visible to ourselves, we also became visible to the German rocket observers. It was horrible that we, without any type of white covering for our clothing, had to make ourselves obvious to the enemy.
>
> The first action to confront us was an enemy machine gun placed to our front during the night. This forced everybody to sprawl out in the snow. It was calculated murder. Once we stopped, the rocket (nebelwerfer) fire began. In flight, these rockets made a sound as ghastly as the sound of the explosion when they hit. We called them 'screaming meemies', which is what they gave us when they came in […]
>
> We were bogged down among the trees for a time while we were being redirected towards the town of Doncols. Traversing enemy fire was being sprinkled around and some of it hit us […]
>
> We had to halt our advance toward Doncols, where we wanted to spend the night, but it was not to be that night. We stayed where we were.[23]

Col. Raymond Bell, the 359th regimental commander, believed the daylight attack that was ordered was a serious mistake. His troops had to attack over an open and barren area near Pommerloch, in bitter cold with unobstructed visibility, moving through deep snow and without flank protection on the northeast side. The German Artillery forward observers were able to look directly down on the 90th from the commanding Grumelscheider Heights. In spite of this situation, the commanders of the III Corps insisted on ordering the attack advising that the crossroads adjacent to Doncols had to be captured as quickly as possible regardless of cost.

Bell's fears proved to be well founded. As soon as the Americans appeared on the open ground, they became 'sitting ducks' for the German artillery and mortars. The attack bogged down and Bell's infantry troops began to suffer heavy casualties. The men dug into snow, and had to take the brunt of the enemy fire.

Bell commented, "A continuation of the attack was clearly suicidal and I could not let that happen to my troops [...] I finally was able to extract what was left of the leading companies and I was a very unhappy commander. In fact, I asked General Van Fleet to relieve me, but he refused."[24]

The mortars and the artillery that rained down upon the 359th infantry also unmercifully pounded the tanks from B Company, which had also moved into the open field that morning several hundred yards ahead of the infantry. Dad described the fate of the tanks accompanied the 359th in the attack that morning. "When we (B Company) attacked them during the daylight we had four tanks knocked out. That's when Richard (John R. Williams), David Dickson, Buck Lee were killed. Harvey Fowler was wounded and died of his wounds two days later on January 12, and I believe Dee Johnson was hit and was in them tanks (Dee Johnson also died on January 12)."

Dee Johnson and Dad were in the same tank in Sainte-Suzanne, and, like Dad, he was wounded in Sainte-Suzanne. Lt Otto Krieg was wounded by shrapnel in the foot; eight other B Company tankers were also wounded. All in all there were fourteen casualties from B Company that fateful day.

The Night Attack on Hill 490

General Patton made an unexpected visit to the 90th Division HQ. A junior officer mistakenly told him that the 359th Regiment and the tanks from B Company had achieved its objective – the high ground around the towns of Doncols and Bahoey. Satisfied with this progress report, Patton left the HQ. Other officers quickly realized the mistaken information given to Patton and informed the 90th Commanding Officer, Gen. Van Fleet.

"When he returned to the CP that afternoon, the General (Van Fleet) decided two things: He was not going to misinform General Patton under any circumstances, and the 90th (359th) would seize the objective that night to keep the record straight."[25]

In accordance with Gen. Van Fleet's directive, an unusual plan was developed for an attack on that night of January 10. The Germans knew that the Americans customarily attacked at dawn and rarely engaged in fighting at night. With the weather as cold as it was that day and with deep snow on the ground, the Germans expected even less that the Americans would attack at night, especially after the Americans had been taking such a pounding that day and the day before. As Col. Bell stated, "If there was ever a time to surprise the Germans with a night attack, it was now."[26] After the pummeling the 359th received during the day, planning the night attack for midnight gave everyone enough time to make the necessary preparations.

Lt-Col. Talbott explained the plan of attack by the two battalions.[27] "The regimental zone extended down the top of a ridge line with a winding, paved road along the crest [...] The plan was to put each battalion in a single file, one on one shoulder and one on the opposite shoulder. The regimental front was two men wide! A couple of hundred yards behind the point men an M-10 self-propelled tank destroyer was to come along…"[28] Bringing up the rear of that column were the remaining tanks from B Company of the 712th and other supporting vehicles.

Although the fighting earlier that day and the previous day had decimated B Company, Vutech was able to find enough manpower to fully man the only four Sherman tanks that remained fully operational. Dad was in one of those tanks that participated in that night attack, he described that night.

> It was freezing cold, below zero. We never had the right equipment or boots. We were supposed to go to the high ground between Doncols and Bahoey.
>
> I was in a tank and the infantry marched; we had a few tanks and the infantry marched on each side of the road. There had been orders not to smoke or no lights whatsoever and no talking. They (infantry) marched and the tanks were in the center (of the road). We went all the way through the German lines.

Lt John H. Cochran Jr., in the 3rd Battalion of the 359th, described that night:

> Colonel Smith said something like this: "I have been ordered to be on that hill to our front at daylight, and I damn well don't intend to be there by myself."
>
> Since resistance had been so dogged and fierce during the day, we believed our end was at hand. How could anyone survive this night? We would be marching to our certain destruction!
>
> [...]
>
> We moved out in the prescribed plan. What happened to the Germans we never found out. As we moved through their positions we could hear them talking on

either side of the road. I don't know if they knew we were moving through them and didn't fire, mistook us for another German unit, or plain let their guard down and didn't see us. The road turned out to be a boundary line between their units, and that is always a weak point.[29]

Cochran continued:

It was difficult to believe what was happening. Were we so bold or were the Germans in shock? We kept moving, waiting for the inevitable to happen. These were the ones that had stopped us in the afternoon and inflicted severe casualties on us. They were now sitting on each side of the road and not firing a shot. I must say that our attack was one of audacity, to say the least.

Just at daylight both battalions were on their objectives. On the top of the hill, where Col. Smith "Didn't intend to be by himself." He not only had a lot of company, his tanks and TDs were in firing position.[30]

Upon reaching the top, all of the American troops had been spread out along the top of the ridge, Dad explained that two of the four tanks and some infantry were positioned in one area and the other tanks and TDs were situated elsewhere.

After we made the night march and we got to the high ground. We outposted a village, it wasn't really a village, it was two or three houses. In the morning all hell broke loose. The Germans counterattacked us. That was one morning I was scared. We only had eight infantry men and two tanks. We (were supposed to have) one company of infantry (approximately 180 men) but the company of infantry were all wounded or killed (in the attack the day before) except eight men and we were holding a little circle, a little hilltop like. One tank was around the corner to catch the road coming up. Five German tanks were coming up that road and we knocked out the first German tank coming down here, they were trying to get us. It was daylight, just as day was breaking here comes marching over the hill about a battalion of soldiers, almost a thousand German soldiers. We felt we were gone then. We wouldn't of given a nickel for our lives. So what he (my tank commander) did was we called back for artillery fire. He said to hold until they got close enough to us. So they held up until they (the Germans) were about from here to those trees, that's about 200 feet, then we called for the artillery fire. Then the artillery fire came in and it burst at about the height of those trees and we started firing on them and we never had a shot fired back. I don't know if we killed every one of them or if they wouldn't fire back because they knew they would be killed, or if some of them stayed there until night came and got up. We never went and looked.

Whether the artillery shells used were equipped with the radar detonation device, that had been demonstrated to Patton in mid-December, or whether they were ordinary time delayed shells did not matter to Dad or the other troops around him, they were all grateful that the artillery was effective.

Lt Cochran's account of the destruction inflicted upon the Germans on the morning of January 11, is similar.

> (We had) heavy machine gun in position with the rifle companies, where both tanks and TDs were. The Germans attempted to pull out, and when they did we opened up with all we had available. We inflicted many casualties and caused much damage to equipment. Some of it was horse drawn. The horses never pulled equipment again. It did not take long to render this large unit completely ineffective.[31]

As D Company was bringing ammo and supplies to the high ground where the tanks of B Company were situated, C Company tanks along with other elements of the 90th were attacking Doncols and Sonlez from the base of the hill. The attack on Doncols happened with such speed that an entire enemy command post was captured.

During a period of two hours that day during the German counterattack, the tanks of B Company were credited with knocking out thirteen enemy tanks and thirteen self-propelled guns.[32]

Capt. Colby, further commenting on the taking of Hill 490, stated, "It is impossible to estimate what the cost in US soldiers would have been to gain this same ground in daylight action, but it would certainly have been awful."[33]

Patton wrote again in his diary on January 11, "I believe today ends the Bastogne operation. From now on it is simply a question of driving a defeated enemy."[34]

Calling the capture of Hill 490 a great victory in the Ardennes, Toland stated, "The Battle of Bastogne was abruptly over."[35]

German prisoners captured during the battle were some of the same that had faced the 90th and the 712th at the Falaise Gap but had escaped. Because of their encounter with the 90th and the 712th then, documents captured after the battle at Hill 490 revealed the utmost respect accorded the 90th by the Germans.

"It is imperative (said one directive) that steps be taken to ascertain whether or not the American 90th Infantry has been committed. Special attention must be given to the numbers 357, 358, 359 [...] Prisoners identified with these numbers will immediately be taken to the Regimental G-3."[36] The Division that had almost been disbanded in Normandy was now one of the most feared and respected by the German Army.

On January 13, B Company moved back to the town of Surree (southwest of Doncols) for maintenance. The Company also used this maintenance period to whitewash the tanks for winter warfare.

By January 15, some of the towns people of Doncols were returning to rebuild their lives. That same day, the Battalion received fifteen new replacements, all of which were assigned to B Company because of the heavy losses sustained on January 10. B Company resumed the assault on the bulge and moved to the town of Wardin, Belgium (located between Doncols and Bastogne). With the main thrust of the Third Army's attack being toward Houffalize, B Company supporting the flank reached the town of Longvilly, Belgium on January 21.

When other units of the Third Army met at Houffalize with forces of the First Army moving down from the north, the attack shifted eastward toward the German border. B Company having reached the town of Longvilly on January 21, moved next to Boxhorn, Luxembourg on the 24 and Troine on the 26. On January 27, B Company was in Troisvierges, Luxembourg. By the end of January, all of the territory that the Germans had captured in the Battle of the Bulge had been regained; the Battle of the Bulge was over.[37]

CHAPTER 11

The Siegfried Line and Into Germany

Fixed fortifications are monuments to man's stupidity. When mountain ranges and oceans can be overcome, anything built by man can be overcome.

General George S. Patton Jr.

The Siegfried Line was a ribbon of concrete obstacles, called dragon's teeth, along the western German border. Stephen Ambrose provided this description:

> They (dragon's teeth) rested on a concrete mat between ten and thirty meters wide, sunk a meter or two into the ground (to prevent any attempt to tunnel underneath them and place explosive charges). On top of the mat were the teeth themselves, truncated pyramids of reinforced concrete about a meter in height in the front row, to two meters high in the back. They were staggered and spaced in such a manner that a tank could not drive through. Interspersed among the teeth were minefields, barbed wire, and pillboxes that were virtually impenetrable by artillery and set in such a way as to give the Germans crossing fire across the entire front. [...] behind the first row of pillboxes and dragon's teeth, there was a second, and often times a third, sometimes a fourth.[1]

From Troisvierges, B Company advanced to Habschied, Germany and the Siegfried Line. Dad related what happened as his tank approached Germany.

> The Germans had tank traps, what they called dragon teeth, to keep tanks from running (over) them. So it was winter time and it started to get to be spring, and we looked out and you could barely see them. All of a sudden it looked like soldiers (Germans) coming through, it looked like a whole army coming through there. We called back and we waited, we never got any closer and finally around the middle of the day the sun came out strong enough and it was the dragon teeth, the tank traps. The snow was on it, and they were grey and from a distance it looked like men standing there.

Dragon's teeth.

Siegfried Line. (*90th photograph*)

The town of Habschied, Germany was captured on February 6. On February 15, Lt Vutech was officially promoted to Captain; his rank was now commensurate with his duties. Dad was now in a tank commanded by Sgt Charles F. Schmidt. Schmidt landed with the 712th in Normandy and was the most decorated soldier in the battalion and one of the most decorated combat soldiers of World War II, receiving nineteen decorations for valor and heroism.[2] Two of his decorations were awarded personally by Gen. Eisenhower and Gen. Patton. During the course of the war, Schmidt was captured by the Germans three times and managed to escape each time.

On February 27, B Company was alerted to join the 6th Cavalry Group in the taking of the town of Krautshied. When the tanks were moving to this assignment, the infantry guides took the tanks to the wrong town, Bellschied, where they drew fire from a German tank on high ground. Lee Miller, who had won the Silver Star in Dillingen, was killed and two of the tank crew were seriously injured.

By March 8, the 712th was moving through western Germany. This area was an industrial area, particularly coal mines, which were used to run the manufacturing industries further north. This section had never been a Nazi hotbed and more often than not the streets would be lined with cheering civilians, waving flags in much the same way as the French had. But even more gratifying to the 712th was the overflowing joy of the liberated slave laborers as they were released from their miserable camps and cheered the tanks. People from all over Europe who had been taken as slave laborers were found in every town and the roads were soon jammed with these people making their way back to their homelands.[3]

During this period, Jack the Russian left the battalion. Dad stated, "After he went a little distance with us and we liberated towns in Germany he met one of his buddies, one of the kids from his home town so he got out and said 'I'm going home.' He got out and tried to make his way back to Russia.

Dad never saw him again and never knew what happened to Jack.

The Second Moselle Crossing

As the 90th and the 712th continued their eastward movement, they approached the Moselle River, which once again had to be crossed. March of 1945 brought spring rains to Europe and the Moselle River was beginning to overflow is banks again.

Most of the tanks had to be ferried across. Dad described the second crossing of the Moselle on March 14. "One night we had to cross the Moselle River, so they put artificial moonlight so we could see to cross the river. That's the way we made the crossing and the next morning we were over there behind the Germans. It was called 'artificial moonlight,' they would shine two or three powerful air raid search lights up into the air. They got in a certain area in the rear and they would shine on the clouds overhead. It just like the moon. You could see on the ground, just like a good moonlit night."

The opening scene of the movie *Patton* contains one of the most famous quotes of Gen. Patton: "No bastard ever won a war by dying for his country. He won it by making the other poor dumb bastard die for his country."

Dad said he remembered such speeches during training. "In those days they never had, uh, that Rambo (style) so the General gave us a speech to learn how to fight and to fight battles. He said 'Don't try to be a hero, you pay attention to what you learn and you live, because (dead) heroes don't win wars.' And if you stop and think about it that's true."

Dad went on to say that during training they were taught various safety procedures when the tank needed maintenance. For example, occasionally a shell would jam in the 75-mm cannon on the tank. When that happened someone had to get out of the tank and ram a rod down the barrel of the gun from the outside to dislodge the shell casing out of the breech. Dad said when this malfunction occurred, they were taught to turn the turret to the rear of the tank. This maneuver of turning the turret 180 degrees away from the direction of enemy fire was designed to protect the crew member who had to get out of the tank.

As the 712th and the 90th were moving into the town of Mainz, Germany, a shell got lodged in the barrel of the 75 mm in Stanley Muhich's tank. Muhich jumped out of the tank to ram the rod down the barrel and somehow, in the heat of the battle, the turret was not rotated. As Muhich was dislodging the shell, with the barrel still facing the direction of the fighting, a sniper shot him in the back of the head and killed him. Muhich was the last person in B Company killed in battle.

The tank platoon retrieved Muhich's body and withdrew to the little town that had just passed through. Later, a German sniper in a camouflage uniform was captured and brought into town with his hands up. After the capture, another member of Muhich's tank crew took the sniper and marched the prisoner around the back of the tank and out of view and shot him. Dad commented, "I wouldn't want to have to live with that (on my conscience)."

I asked Dad what had happened to the soldier who killed the sniper, and whether he was court-martialed. Dad said nothing happened, no one reported it to the officers, or if they did, the officers just ignored it and did nothing.

Dad said that Muhich's tank mate who shot the sniper even attended a few reunions after the war but no one ever brought up the subject of Muhich's death.

In the tank next to Muhich was a friend of Dad's, Cleo Coleman, one of the original Company H/712th tankers who trained with Dad at Fort Benning.

View from the turret crossing the Rhine. (*Company B photograph*)

Coleman was from Pike County, Kentucky and was descended from the Hatfield clan of the famous Hatfields and McCoys.

Coleman stated he witnessed the sniper being brought into town and saw the member of Muhich's tank crew march the prisoner out behind a stone wall and close the gate. Coleman did not pay much attention, but then heard a gun fire. Someone said, "He shot that prisoner." Coleman and several other went to look. The sniper had a hole between his eyes. Coleman stated, "And he came back through the gate and his face was white. It did something to him when he shot that man in cold blood."[4]

Germany's defeat was inevitable as the 712th and the 90th crossed the Rhine River into the heart of Germany on March 24, 1945, at Mainz. The vast majority of the German Army in the west were killed, wounded or captured during the Battle of the Bulge. Even though the fighting continued, the German Army now consisted of the Volksgrenadiers, or Volkssturm comprised of old men and young boys.[5] Deaths, like Muhich's were occurring needlessly all across the front due to the zealot young German boys who were fighting a vain and useless fight. Lt Cochran of the 359th, expressed the frustration on the part of the American GI:

...while moving through a small village, (we) ran into more Hitler Youth. Several of us were moving down the street, an automatic rifle fired on us. One man was killed. After placing artillery fire on the block, we moved through the buildings. As we neared the block and were on its flank, we opened up and killed three. One youth, perhaps aged 16, held up his hands. I was very emotional over the loss of a good soldier and grabbed the kid and took off my cartridge belt.

I asked him if there were more like him in town. He gave me a stare and said "I'd rather die than tell you anything." I told him to pray, because he was going to die and die now. I hit him across the face with that thick heavy belt. I was about to strike him again when I was grabbed from behind by Chaplain Kerns. He said, "Don't! Let me have him." He took the crying child away. I knew later that the Chaplain had intervened not only to save a life but to prevent me from committing a murder. Had it not been for the Chaplain, I would have.[6]

The Merkers Salt Mines

During its trek across Germany, the Third Army leapfrogged its units; the 90th and 712th would spearhead a movement for several days and then go into reserve as other units passed through them and took the lead position in the advance.

In February 1945, Roosevelt, Churchill, and Stalin had met in Yalta and had made plans for the occupation of Germany at war's end. Each of these Allied nations would occupy a certain sector. By April, the 712th and 90th was once again one of the lead units and had advanced into the German State of Thuringia a sector that would eventually be occupied by the Soviet Union in post-war Germany.

Just before noon on April 4, 1945, the 712th and the 90th entered the small town of Merkers, Germany. There was nothing outwardly unusual about this town other than it was the site of a salt mine. Two days later some chance remarks by German civilians led to the discovery of gold and other riches of the Third Reich. Gen. Patton said that except for the instincts of human decency on the part of two Americans, the Americans might never had discovered the treasure until much of it had been more securely hidden away.[7]

Upon capturing Merkers, the US troops had established a curfew law. Any civilian in the streets after dark was instantly picked up for questioning. In the early morning hours of April 6, Pfc. Clyde Harmon and Pfc. Anthony Kline, two 90th Division military police, observed two women hurrying along a street; they stopped them for interrogation. One woman explained in broken English that her friend was pregnant and needed a midwife. After further interrogation at the Provost Marshall's office, the women's story proved correct. The MPs then intent on helping the pregnant woman picked up the midwife. Sgt Mootz, another MP, then drove the women back to their homes in Merkers. Along the way, Mootz saw a large derrick next to a factory building near the salt mines. In the course of making conversation, Mootz asked what it was. One of the women exclaimed that it was the salt mine in which much gold and art objects were buried. The woman went on to relate that the gold was the German gold reserve and the art objects were brought from the national museum in Berlin for safe keeping. Slave labor had worked for days unloading all of the gold and art and moving it down into the mine

Actually, as soon as the 90th and the 712th entered Merkers, Intelligence Officers had been interviewing displaced foreign workers in the town and several French workers had given reports of gold treasure in the mine. When the news of both stories reached higher level officers, tanks from the 712th and soldiers from the 90th were ordered to guard the various entrances to the mines.[8]

On the morning of Saturday, April 7, Lt-Col. Russell of the 90th Infantry descended deep into the mine on a rickety elevator with a German guide and several other officers. Included in this group was Lt-Col. Kedrovsky and Capt. Forrest Dixon of the 712th Tank Battalion. The elevator took them to the bottom of the main shaft, twenty-one hundred feet beneath the surface.

The find proved to be immense: 110 tons of gold bullion valued in excess of $100,000,000; several thousand burlap bags filled with gold coins from various countries including 711 bags filled with US gold coins. The total amount of gold in bullion and coin totaled $238,490,000. There was also paper currency from various countries including 2,000,000 American Dollars and 5,000,000,000 German Reichmarks.

The mine contained over two thousand priceless paintings and sculptures much of it looted from various European museums. The mine also revealed a darker find: valises full of silverware, cups, candelabra and other treasures looted from families, churches and synagogues, all of which had been hammered flat to fit into the valises. And to the rear of the chamber, the most gruesome discovery, a large quantity of bags, containing pearls and other precious stones, also contained gold fillings and inlays taken from the bodies of the Holocaust victims.

The vast wealth in the mine attracted visits by the highest ranking generals, on April 10, and was described as probably the largest collection of generals of any operation during the war with the exception of the D-Day planning in England.[9]

Generals Eisenhower, Omar Bradley, George Patton, Manton Eddy and Otto Weyland, along with a group of officers entered the mine. As the jittery elevator descended down the pitch-black shaft, with a German operating the elevator, one of the officers was concerned about their safety. Patton, looking at the single cable, said if the cable snapped promotions in the United States

Army would be considerably stimulated. Gen. Eisenhower said, "OK George, that's enough. No more cracks until we are above ground again."[10]

Since Merkers was in territory that the Soviet Union was to occupy in post-war Germany, Eisenhower ordered that the contents of the Merkers mine be transferred to Frankfurt, Germany, within the American sector.

The 90th and the 712th were continuing on the offensive and needed all of its forces. Gen. Eddy had originally ordered only minimal troops be diverted for guarding the mine. After learning the extent of the discovery he countermanded that order and for the next ten days troops from the 357th Regiment of the 90th and three platoons of tanks from the 712th, two from C Company and one from D Company, had a break from combat and were given the assignment of guarding the mine while the treasure was being transferred.

While these three tank platoons remained in Merkers, the remainder of the 712th and the 90th continued in battle trudging their way across the rest of Germany toward Czechoslovakia.

Transfer to Headquarters Company

It was sometime in late March, with only a few weeks remaining in the war, Dad said he was unexpectedly transferred to Headquarters Company. He asked Capt. Vutech, "Captain, why am I being transferred?" Vutech told him, "Louie, you have seen enough action, go back where it is safe."

Dad was upset that Vutech had transferred him to Headquarters Company, although he was perplexed over this development, he followed orders. New replacements were coming in to handle the front line action and there were still important things that needed to be done in HQ Company in order for the battalion to operate smoothly until the end of the war. Dad knew that in HQ Company he was still part of a team.

Dad came to believe that Vutech thought that Dad might have been suffering from some sort of battle fatigue. Dad recalled that before his transfer he had an argument with his tank commander at that time, Sgt Schmidt. Schmidt had called to Dad at his gunner position to fire on a target. Dad looked through the gunner's periscope and didn't see anything, he responded, "What target? I don't see anything." Schmidt said it again; Dad looked again through the periscope and even stuck his head out of the turret to see what Schmidt was referring to but he still didn't see anything. Schmidt yelled at him, "If you want to survive you had better see those targets."

At the time Dad did not believe he was experiencing any effects of battle fatigue.

It is normal for soldiers to experience stress during combat. The adrenaline rush has positive effect on a soldiers body; the physiological and emotional reflexes readies a soldier for battle and enables him to survive, function, and perform tasks under extremely difficult circumstances. Prolonged exposure to the horrors of combat, however, has a detrimental effect on the body increasing the likelihood of becoming emotionally worn down and exhausted. Battle fatigue has been described as basically a temporary overloading and redirecting of psychological defenses. The term described a wide variety of symptoms ranging from disturbance of physical functions such as simple exhaustion, weakness or tremors in limbs, blurred or double vision, ringing in ears, to emotional problems such as anxiety, immense fear, or depression.

Basic training and drill was designed to get soldiers into top physical condition in order to function effectively in combat. The mental and emotional abilities necessary for effective combat performance were just as vital as being in top physical condition. "Battlefield awareness" was the term used to describe this heightened state of mental and emotional conditioning. Yet with all the physical training, the stress produced by the reality of combat caused soldiers to experience many human psychological defense mechanisms.

The War Department was not unaware of the psychological effects of constant combat. In 1944 the Surgeon General issued a report based upon studies of American soldiers under combat conditions. The first page of the report stated, "Just as an average truck wears out after a certain number of miles it appears that the doughboy wore out, either developing an acute incapacitating neurosis or else becoming hypersensitive to shell fire, so overly cautious and jittery, that he was ineffective and demoralizing to the newer men. The average point at which this occurred appears to have been in the region of 200 to 240 regimental combat days."[11] The 712th Tank Battalion far exceeded this point with 314 days in the ETO (European Theater of Operations) combat zone, with 298 days in actual contact with the enemy.[12]

Capt. Colby pointed out:

> ...the feeling of weariness and being unwell was all too familiar among "old" infantrymen who had been in combat since crossing the beach. When we recognized this, which may have been a form of helplessness, we did our best to transfer them to less hazardous duty. When we could not, perhaps because of the situation at the time, it was not unusual that they would soon be killed. Some thought the feeling was a premonition. Whatever it was, it certainly seemed to lead to a letdown of the keenness of perception so essential for survival in combat.[13]

Fighting inside a tank has been described as an even more exhausting and stressful experience. While tankers did not experience the numbing exhaustion of the infantry's foot-slogging experience, tank combat had its own physical demands.[14] "The air inside the cramped confines of the tank became a mixture of sweat, oil, human bodies, and cordite fumes. It was baking hot in the summer and dank and cold in the winter. The interior was dark and the periscopes offered the crew a very limited view of the exterior and was useless at night. The tank was a big and obvious target, therefore, the crew had to keep vigilant eye for enemy anti-tank weapons, like the 88-mm anti-tank gun and the panzerfaust."[15]

No one was immune to battle fatigue, not even a man of the cloth.[16]

Officers learned to recognize signs of fatigue, and perhaps Vutech thought Dad's inability to see the target pointed out by Sgt Schmidt was such a sign and for Dad's safety he transferred him to HQ Company.

Dad said that Vutech had told him to go back to the "safety" of HQ Company, "safety" being a relative term. HQ Company had its share of casualties throughout the war and it was by no means safe. Col. Randolph was killed by artillery fire in the Battle of the Bulge, Lt Marshall Warfield and Sgt Thomas Reilly were killed by machine gun fire near Metz. All in all, HQ Company sustained nine KIA casualties during the war.

Leon Fowler was back with HQ Company around the same time Dad was transferred. Cleo Coleman commented about Fowler's transfer to HQ Company and the emotional stress and reaction to the death of his brother, Harvey Fowler, during the attack on Doncols:

> I seen one boy. What happened, we got replacements. One boy was called to the Army, and his brother volunteered; at that time they let them do this, to stay together. So they came in as replacements while we were in France. Both of them came to our company. One was in the first platoon, and the other was in the third platoon. So the day that one of them would go out and the other didn't, he stayed behind and worried about his brother. Finally, one day, one of them got it – I think the younger one – and the other one, they sent him back behind the lines. It got to him pretty bad. I never did see him anymore.[17]

Even though HQ was not safe, it afforded a higher degree of safety than being on the line in B Company where the tank crews were subject to constant threat of enemy fire. Dad said the remaining weeks of combat were uneventful for him with one exception. Dad and Leon Fowler were ordered to take a bulldozer tank to a front line unit to clear destroyed enemy equipment from the road. Dad explained, "When we traveled these roads we did not know what was lurking around the bend and we had to travel with caution. Even the houses looked deserted. One time I was in a bulldozer (tank) with Leon Fowler and we took off, we were separated from the company. Just he and I were in the tank and we took off down one of these roads and we traveled over a dozen miles and we never saw a thing and we knew we were in enemy territory." They had taken a wrong turn someplace along the way. When Dad and Fowler realized their circumstance, they turned around immediately and raced back in the opposite direction.

As the war was drawing to a close the 712th and 90th approached towns with caution. Usually the residents had resigned themselves to Germany's defeat and would hang white flags from the windows. If no white flags were flying as the tanks approached the town, the lead tank would fire three or four rounds into the town and usually white flags would come out.

Other times the town would contain SS soldiers, Hitler Youth, or fanatical Volkssturm, who would resist until overpowered, and who, more often than not, inflicted casualties on the American troops.

By mid-April, the 712th and 90th were spearheading the Third Army and was near the border between Germany and Czechoslovakia. On April 18, tanks from A Company along with the 358th Regiment of the 90th crossed the border and thus became the first American unit to sever Germany across her waist.[18]

The Battalion's last battlefield KIA casualty occurred on April 30, 1945, in the village of Capartice, Czechoslovakia, eight days before the end of the war in Europe. A platoon from A Company was ordered into the town, two tanks were knocked out by enemy fire. Tec 5 Paul Shannon was killed and six others from A Company were wounded.

In time, Dad came to appreciate Vutech's action in transferring him to HQ Company. It probably saved his life.

CHAPTER 12

V-E Day and Occupation

The one honor which is mine and mine alone is that of having commanded such an incomparable group of Americans, the record of whose fortitude, audacity and valor will endure as long as history lasts.

General George S. Patton Jr., to the Third Army, May 9, 1945

V-E Day, May 8, 1945, found the 712th spread across several towns in Czechoslovakia. A Company was in the town of Stachy; B Company was billeted in a castle at Tynec; C Company occupied a schoolhouse in Maly Bor. D Company was housed at Besiny, while Service Company found itself in the town of Mestys Zelezna Ruda. Headquarters Company had the most luxurious quarters of all in the town of Susice.

For days prior to VE Day, German units were surrendering to American units. Throughout the war, individual German soldiers and small groups of German troops surrendered to Allied forces as they overran the German positions. I questioned Dad on the procedure the tank crews used when the Germans surrendered. He said, "We didn't keep them too long. When we captured them with the tanks, when they came out with their hands up, we made sure that their guns were gone. Then we told them to just go back the road. We didn't fool with them, we couldn't we had to keep on going."

But a mass surrender occurred just days before V-E Day, when the 712th and the 90th first entered Czechoslovakia; a German division wanted to surrender to the Americans. From this point on there are several versions of the surrender.

The B Company History reads: "On May 5th at Kotzing the 11th Panzer Division surrendered intact to our combat team."

The After Action Report of the 712th Tank Bn, reads:

Company "B": [...] 4 May (Kotzting): The Third platoon acted as guides for the 11th German Panzer Division which surrendered to the first platoon and

The Battle Route for the Central Europe Campaign. (*The History of the 712th Tank Battalion*)

second Battalion, 359th Infantry Regiment. C Company commander, Lt Krieg, and first sergeant worked the entire night assembling the vehicles of the 11th Panzer Division in a field. They started at 0930 hours and the vehicles continued to come in until 0900 hours, 5 May.

Dad indicated that, under German military tradition, when a General surrendered his troops, he would only surrender to another General, then afterwards they would sit down and have a drink of wine. Dad, at that time, was with Headquarters Company; the story that he had heard from his buddies in B Company was that Lt Stanley Gagat was at the head of the column when it was approached by the Germans seeking to surrender.

> Gagat got a battlefield commission as a lieutenant, the Germans were trying to get away from the Russians, they didn't want to surrender to the Russians, they were coming into the American lines. So when they got to him, a German General said, "I've got a whole Division I want to surrender."
> So Gagat said, "OK have them throw their guns down."
> The General said, "No, I want to surrender to a General.
> Gagat said, "You either surrender to me or you don't get to surrender."
> The General said again, "Give me a high ranking officer."

Lt Stanley Gaget and new friends. (*Company B photograph*)

Gagat said once more, "You have to surrender to me."

And then he surrendered to Gagat. Gagat was just a lieutenant, that was beneath him, he wanted a high ranking officer, he wanted someone with prestige.

Lt John H. Cochran Jr. of the 359th recounted that day:

The 90th became the Corps reserve as it remained on its objectives near the Czech town of Vseruby, but on the 4th of May the 11th Panzer Division offered to surrender.

A soldier under a white flag of truce approached us. He was brought to me and I heard his demand. He insisted on being taken to the chief of staff of the 90th Division. No German soldier was going to tell me what to do, so I returned him to our perimeter. He was told to return to whence he came. Later, I learned that we were to prepare to receive the 11th Panzer Division into our lines. It was surrendering.

The bearer of the white flag got into the 90th's lines somewhere else, and had a letter with him. He hadn't shown me a letter. It said:

Division C.P. 3 May 1945
 11th Panzer Division Commander

The development of the military and political situation makes it desirable to me to avoid further losses on both sides.

I have therefore ordered the Major, the bearer of this note, to negotiate with you the cessation of hostilities.

Von Wietersheim
Lt-Gen. and Division Commander[1]

The 712th Tank Battalion Operation Journal reads:

> 04 May 45 – 1900 hours – Today the 11th Panzer Division, German, surrendered to the 90th Inf Div, American. B Co and D Co, 712th Tank Bn are assisting in the large task of bringing them in.

It is obvious that Dad's friends in Co. B had embellished the story about Gagat when relating it. No doubt, the German Major had approached Gagat after being rebuffed by Lt Cochran. After receiving the same rebuff at the hands of Gagat and obviously frustrated that these American lieutenants were not aware of the proper protocol for receiving an enemy surrender, and, in order to avoid capture by the Russians, he provided Gagat with the letter he had not displayed to Lt Cochran. After reading the letter, Gagat, in all probability, forwarded the letter back up the chain of command.

Gen. Earnest was now in command of the 90th and he "referred the matter up to the Third Army and Gen Patton approved. All of this took a couple of days."[2]

The History of the 712th records the event,

> And then, just as the Division prepared to go into reserve on Corps order, General Von Weitersheim of the 11th Panzer refused to surrender to any other unit but insisted on having "the honor" of surrendering to the "elite 90th Div." On 3 May he met Gen'l. Earnest and unconditionally surrendered his entire outfit which consisted of close to 10,000 men and over 2,000 vehicles. B Co. and 359 were hard put marshaling these troops as they poured into the American sector.[3,4]

The History of the 90th Division detailed the surrender indicating that the German officer bearing the surrender note was blindfolded and taken to the 90th Division Command Post, where the arrangements of the "unconditional surrender" of the 11th Panzer Division were completed. Lt-Gen. von Wietersheim arrived at Vseruby later that afternoon to confirm the terms of the surrender. One hour later the long columns of the surrendered division poured in.[5]

Remembering Dad's amusing story about basic training, how tankers considered themselves the toughest soldiers in camp, it seems that the tank crews in both armies were alike. In giving his account of the surrender of the 11th Panzer Division, Capt. Colby stated that the only potential troublemakers in the German column were their tankers, who did not like the idea of surrendering. The German tank crews drove into the road block area with the barrels of their tank guns elevated as though on parade and the tank commanders standing in the turrets at stiff attention. The American captors had to have the German commanding officer order one crew to exit the tank in order for the Americans to enter and disarm the tank guns.[6]

And then the day arrived – on 7 May 1945, Headquarters received Field Message #95, 90th Inf. Division which contained the following paragraphs:

> A representative of the German High Command signed the unconditional surrender of all German land, sea and air forces in Europe to the Allied Expeditionary Force and simultaneously to the Soviet High Command at 0141 Central European Time 7 May 45 under which all forces will cease active operations at 0001 9 May 45.
>
> All offensive operations by Allied Forces will cease. Troops will remain in present positions. Due to difficulties of communication there will be some delay in similar orders reaching enemy troops so full defensive precautions will be taken. No release will be made to the Press pending an announcement by the heads of the Three Governments.[7]

Although all hostilities were to officially end on May 9, 1945 at 1 second past midnight on May the 8th, V-E Day has officially been recognized since as May 8, 1945.

Dr McConahey wrote:

> One of the telephones rang. An officer answered it and then turned to us and said: "The war is over!" No one cheered. No one fired off his gun. The news was too big for that – too awesome. We simply stood there looking at each other and saying, "The war's over at last!" Then the telephone rang again, and we received the division orders. We were to remain in place, take any German prisoners who came in, and not fire unless fired upon.[8]

Dad, along with the rest of Headquarters Company, was in Susice, Czechoslovakia on that day. The people in Czechoslovakia were celebrating and welcoming the American troops. It was a double cause for celebration for them – they were liberated from the Nazis, and the war had finally ended.

> The simultaneous arrival of American troops and the promise of a lasting peace aroused a frenzy of jubilation among the Czechs who played host to the Americans with all the enthusiasm and hospitality that can spring from gratitude.

V-E Day and Occupation

Susice Czechoslovakia. (*Author's collection*)

Czechoslovakian girls in native dress. (*Author's collection*)

Ed Swierzcyk sitting on a Jeep at the V-E Day celebration. (*Company B photograph*)

Each city and village was garlanded with flowers, dances and parties and street festivals were the order of the day. The girls dressed in colorful native costumes, while musicians sang and played until the hours of the dawn.⁹

The Americans soldiers had been told the war was over, but Dad was still skeptical whether all the German soldiers had received the same news. He explained, "V-E Day, I was in Czechoslovakia. And they said the war was over, well we knew it was just about over. They said at night you can use your flashlight on guard duty. I said 'You're nuts, if you think I'm going to let some stupid German shoot me with a light.' I pulled guard duty without a light."

Shortly after V-E Day, the Soviet Army arrived in the towns occupied by the 90th and the 712th.

On May 15, the occupation zones had been determined by the Allied leaders and the 712th had to move 118 miles west, back across the Czechoslovakian-German border to Amberg, Germany. The liberation of the above towns in Czechoslovakia by the 712th and the 90th was short lived; their occupation was ceded to the Soviet Army. Immediately after World War II, the Iron Curtain fell across Eastern Europe and Czechoslovakia remained under Soviet domination until the fall of communism in December of 1989.

Czechs greet the Soviet Army in May 1945. (*Company B photograph*)

Amberg, Germany

After V-E Day, the 712th was ordered to pull back into the American sector of occupied Germany, to the town of Amberg. Dad and I included on our itinerary a brief stop in this town where Dad was stationed during the occupation.

In 1945, Amberg was a quiet little Bavarian town with an estimated population of 30,000. It was founded in the year 1034 and its name originates from the brook that slowly flows through the town, called the Am. The town had been virtually undamaged by the war and retained much of its old world charm, with narrow, crooked streets, tiny dark alleys, an ancient moat and wall, battlements and arched gates at every entrance. Around the outside of the Stadtmauer or city wall, there was a long, shady promenade, and quiet parks with benches.

During the occupation, the 712th Tank Battalion was assigned to occupy a German World War I camp in Amberg, known as Metzer Kaserne. It was home to a glass factory, then an ordinance factory between the wars, and the barracks in the camp housed a German artillery unit at the beginning of World War II.

Although Amberg was virtually unscathed during the war, American bombers did damage the glass factory located in the camp, as well as the roofs and windows of the barracks buildings. The first night the 712th moved in there was no water available. The first order of business was to make the camp livable. Civilian labor was utilized for fixing windows, shingling the roofs, carting away the rubble and trash, scrubbing the floors, and removing all Nazi decorations. Among the mass of junk in the surrounding warehouses, the 712th found sufficient chinaware and silver, and a full size Battalion Mess was in place, in operation with cooks from all companies as well as German cooks. On Saturday evening June 2, 1945, one of the camp's necessities had been built from scratch and became operable – a beer tank.

An elaborate system of underground wiring connecting all nearby camps was discovered and repaired and eventually a switchboard was put in operation. "Mudholes were filled in and graveled over [...] civilians took care of policing up so that the men of 'old Blood and Guts' were thus relieved of mud and butts and could turn their attention to more interesting pursuits."[10]

The new home of the 712th was named Camp George B. Randolph in honor of the Battalion's late commander. Flanked by the tanks and other vehicles which formed the "armored fist" of the famed 90th Infantry Division throughout its combat days, the officers and men of the 712th were addressed by Brig.-Gen. Joseph M. Tulley during ceremonies on June 13, 1945.

"You men formed a vital and important cog in the 90th Division team!" Gen. Tulley asserted, after reviewing the history of the 712th. "From the time you joined us until the final hour of our victory – in the hedgerows, through France, at Metz, during the river crossings, in the Bulge, in the Siegfried Line, across Germany and into Czechoslovakia – you have served us ably and well."[11]

Gen. Van Fleet, who commanded the 90th during the Battle of the Bulge, wrote to the 712th, "No fighting division ever had better armor support than did the 'Tough Ombres'; in fact, in many engagements the tankers were attacking and the other arms were in support. I do know there was a great feeling of loyalty and mutual respect among our several fighting elements – the tanks, the TD's, the artillery, the doughfeet, the air. These were the major combat units which made up the team of the 90th Division along the front line."[12]

Combat was the only thing the battalion was engaged in between June 28, 1944 and May 8, 1945. Now there was time to burn. To keep time from moving too slowly, the men turned to sports. Volleyball courts, horse shoe pits, and soft ball diamonds were soon established in and around camp. Being summer, the men also enjoyed swimming, first at a lake about 3 km east of camp and then in a pool in Amberg; finally a concrete water reservoir behind the Mess Hall was converted into a pool. A stable was refurbished and horses obtained for horseback riding. Sightseeing tours were organized to visit the various resort spots in the vicinity of Amberg. Hunting and fishing was available for the outdoor enthusiasts.

Tanks at Camp Randolph. (*Company B photograph*)

A dark room was built for the many GIs who now possessed German cameras and photography classes were offered. On June 18, the first issue of the camp newspaper, *Tank Tracks*, was published. It contained news of the various events around camp, it included a sports section, as well as general information and army news.

By the end of June a full service laundry and tailor shop was operational, complete with pressing machines to provide crisp military neatness in the tanker's uniforms.

Time was also spent repairing and refurbishing the military equipment that had just come through the war. "The Germans were a beaten people, they gave us no trouble," Dad said about the days in Amberg. To make sure the Germans maintained a healthy respect for the American occupiers, military parades were held through Amberg from time to time. The first such parade took place on June 29. The parade was an "impressive sight with the infantry looking quite military and 'sharp'; the tanks looking like they just came off the assembly line."

On July 13, Jack Benny brought a USO show to the area and entertained the troops of the 90th and the 712th. Along with Benny, movie star, Ingrid Bergman, and others entertained the troops in an open field. Gen. Earnest got a huge round of applause when he rejected the chairs that had been set up for him and sat down on the grass like all of the troops in attendance.

Jack Benny with Joe Roush. (*Company B photograph*)

Ingrid Bergman. (*Company B photograph*)

The USO entertains the 90th and the 712th. (*Company B photograph*)

Fall In – You're still in the Army. (*Company B photograph*)

Above: Barracks at Camp Randolph. (*Company B photograph*)

Left: Military Road to Camp Randolph. (*Author's collection*)

V-E Day and Occupation

Above left: Cpl Gruntz at Main Gate to Camp Randolph. (*Author's collection*)

Above right: Inside Camp Randolph. (*Author's collection*)

Bob Kellner, Joe Roush, Eugene Baum, and Woody Mercer with liberated haberdashery. (*Company B photograph*)

HQ Company friends with Nazi souvenirs. (*Company B photograph*)

The Park Theater. (*Company B photograph*)

The 712th Downbeats: Cpl John Doherty, pianist; Cpl L. J. Buzzeo, clarinet; T/5 Wes Hitchcock, drummer; T/4 Roland Frenett, guitarist; Pfc. Myron Johnson, trombonist; Clem Crumm, bass fiddle.

Joe Roush, Circus Ringmaster. (*Company B photograph*)

Felix the Strongman. (*Company B photograph*)

Originally a barn within the camp was converted into a makeshift movie theater. Near the camp there was a theater, the Park Theater. Constructed in 1938, it was refurbished and was converted exclusively for the GIs, to replace the makeshift barn theater. The first screening was in mid-July. It was also equipped with a stage to conduct live performances.

Joe Roush was in his glory at Camp Randolph; he was placed in charge of entertainment, he organized vaudeville shows, circus performances and a minstrel show. Joe had been in combat until he was wounded during the action at Falaise Gap. After recovery he had returned to B Company as a cook. The 712th was also entertained by their own, the musicians in the battalion formed a band, the 712th Downbeats.

When Dad and I visited Amberg in 1994, most of the buildings that comprised Camp Randolph were boarded and the entire facility was fenced to prevent entry. The site was under renovation and today houses a community technical college for the Amberg area.

Munich

Following our stop in Amberg, Dad and I traveled to Munich. The 712th did not go through Munich during the war, but Dad went there after V-E Day. During the summer of 1945, while he was stationed in Amberg, just north of Munich, Dad and another soldier from HQ Company, Edmund Keady, were assigned the duty of bringing one of the officers from the battalion to the airport in Munich. For safety reasons, American GIs never traveled the German countryside alone even after the hostilities ended. Since the officer was leaving on a flight, he had two escorts in order that there be two soldiers in the jeep on the return to Amberg.

Keady had a brother in the Army who was stationed in Garmisch-Partenkirchen, a resort area south of Munich. In addition to getting a chance to see the sights in Munich while bringing the officer to the airport, Keady and Dad were also given permission to go to Garmisch-Partenkirchen to visit Keady's brother.

When I looked through Dad's war photos as a boy, I remember him showing me a photograph of him standing outside of the beer garden in Munich where Hitler made his first political speech. In the summer of 1945 that beer garden had been converted into a Red Cross Canteen for American servicemen stationed in Munich.[13]

Dad in front of Bürgerbräukeller. (*Author's collection*)

Ludwigstrasse. (*Author's collection*)

During our visit in 1994, Dad did not recall its location, however, we did tour several other spots in Munich that Dad had visited and photographed in 1945. We spent the afternoon in Marienplatz, the square in front of Munich's Town Hall. The town square is named after the column of the Virgin Mary at its center. The facade of the Town Hall houses the Glockenspiel, a mechanical carillon and clock with near life-sized figures performing a dance and jousting match three times a day.

We also walked to Ludwigstraße, a large boulevard upon which the German Armies from the time of King Ludwig I in the first half of the nineteenth century paraded in military formation.

After seeing all the medieval architecture in Munich, my first reaction was that Munich survived the war unscathed. But Dad quickly pointed out that such was not the case. His photographs taken during his visit in 1945 show extensive destruction. Dad and I toured a museum near the center of town, one room was devoted to photographs taken after the war; these photographs showed the damages sustained by the museum and the restoration efforts that took place after the war.

Concentration Camps

At Flossenbürg, men of the 90th learned that propaganda and truth are sometimes the same. It was here that they saw with their own eyes a vivid example of the cruelties of which the enemy was capable. Flossenbürg, one of the most infamous concentration camps in all Germany, was first encountered by the 90th. Bodies of former inmates were stacked grotesquely like cords of wood. The ovens used for disposing of the bodies were on display. More than 1,100 inmates living under indescribably hard conditions, were liberated by troops of the 90th, to whom the nature of the enemy was now revealed fully and graphically.[14]

The Flossenbürg concentration camp was a German prison constructed in 1938, in the Oberpflaz region of Bavaria. The camp's site was selected so that the prisoners could be used as free labor to quarry the granite found in the nearby hills.

Prisoners were forced to work in the Flossenbürg camp quarry and in armaments-related production. Malnutrition, disease, and exhaustion from hard labor was rampant among the prisoners being held. Combined with the brutality of the guards, this treatment was the cause of thousands of prisoner deaths.

German military officers involved in the failed 1944 assassination attempt against Hitler were confined at Flossenbürg. In early April of 1945, as American forces, including the 90th Infantry Division and the 712th, were approaching the camp, the SS executed these military officers.[15] The SS then began the forced evacuation of 22,000 prisoners, leaving behind only those too sick to walk. On the death march to Dachau the SS guards shot any prisoner too sick to keep up. Before they reached Dachau, more than 7,000 prisoners had been shot or had collapsed and died. The 90th Infantry Division and the 712th liberated Flossenbürg on April 23, 1945.

Dad said that other troops in the 712th had liberated Flossenbürg. He had heard of the sights but he did not personally go into the concentration camp.

The Dachau concentration camp, the camp where the poor souls of Flossenbürg were forced to march was closer to the itinerary Dad and I had planned in 1994. Therefore, the morning we left Munich, we traveled a short distance to Dachau.

Dachau is a small quaint town located about 10 mile northwest of Munich. Ironically, the infamous concentration camp that bears its name is located just outside of the town limits, within the territory of the adjoining village of Prittlbach. Yet, because of the evil, barbarity and terror of the Nazi regime which occurred within the concentration camp, the name Dachau will forever be synonymous with those transgressions against humanity.

The former concentration camp at Dachau is now preserved as a memorial to the tens of thousands of people, of various nationalities, who suffered and

Fence and guard tower at Dachau. (*Author's collection*)

died there at the hands of the Nazis between 1933 and 1945. The exhibits and museum located there give testimony of darkest depths of man's inhumanity to man.

It was the first of the concentration camps, opened by the Nazis on the grounds and facilities of a munition factory during World War I. The original intent was for Dachau to serve as a work camp, and although it was not operated as an extermination facility like Auschwitz, tens of thousands died within its walls. In the closing months of the war, the Nazis tried to eliminate evidence of the atrocities that occurred; in the four months preceding the liberation of the camp by the American Army, over 13,000 prisoners died.

During its twelve years in operation, the main area consisted of row after row of barracks which housed the inmates. These barracks no longer exist except for the outline of their foundations. However, two of the barracks have been recreated in order to show today's visitors the horrific cramped conditions in which the prisoners lived.

The brick and stone buildings which served as the gas chamber, the crematoriums, and the prison where the Nazis conducted torture still exist. The main gate, through which the inmates were marched in, contains the cruelly misleading words *Arbeit Macht Frei* (Work Makes You Free). The German headquarters building now houses the museum, which contains photographs and films of what occurred within Dachau.

Creamatorium at Dachau. (*Author's collection*)

The most disturbing aspect of the brutality was the medical experiments performed on the prisoners. There was a photograph of a man who was taken up in a plane at high altitudes and his skull was cut open in order to observe the affects high altitude had on the human brain; the experiment ended in the man's death. Other experiments involved taking prisoners at high altitudes without oxygen masks. The object of the experiment was to determine the effect of lack of oxygen on the human body. The information was used to design equipment for German aviators for high altitude flights. The time it took for these prisoners to die was recorded as part of the experiment. Prisoners were also submerged in freezing water to determine how long a person could survive before dying of hypothermia.

The crimes committed by the Nazis was not limited exclusively to the Jews. Others that the Nazis considered undesirable were thrown into the concentration camps. I was very surprised to learn that over 2,500 Catholic priests were confined in the Dachau Concentration Camp. The first German priest incarcerated at Dachau was Father Franz Seitz,

In a booklet describing the atrocities of Dachau, Dr Johannes Neuhäusler describes Father Seitz's induction into the camp:

> Scarcely had he arrived at the camp when the SS-man pulled a rosary from the priest's pocket and mockingly placed it on his head so that the cross hung over

his forehead. Thus he led him up and down the camp, kicking him and striking him with clenched fists, and screaming wildly: "The first pig from the Old Reich has arrived!" Seitz had a picture of Pius XII in his breviary. The SS-man held the picture under the nose of several prisoners and called out: "The Roman head priest will be locked up in Dachau with all the other prisoners after the war. Then the Catholic swindle will be finished forever." A picture of Our Lady gave this miserable Nazi an opportunity to crack vulgar jokes about the maternity of Mary, blasphemies which no pen dare to repeat.[16]

When the 90th Division entered Bavaria, Father Murphy wrote, "we are in Bavaria now, all the people are Catholic. All hate the SS as being "Gottlose" (Godless)."[17]

The vast majority of the photographs and news film from that era was black and white. This black and white photography, more than anything, portrayed the foreboding feelings of hopelessness, despair and horrid existence of those poor unfortunate souls.

The morning of our visit was bright and clear, it was a colorful autumn day. But once inside the dreary gray walls, it was as if all color had disappeared. It seemed as if there was a perpetual gray cloud overshadowing the concentration camp and that it would forever be devoid of color and the connotation of joy or happiness that vibrant colors suggest. It was virtually impossible to perceive those bleak surroundings as anything but gray and colorless. From all corners of the camp, the gruesome remnants of its operational days maintain the feeling of horror that seems to permeate every object within its walls.

After the Dachau Concentration Camp was liberated in 1945, the Americans occupied it and converted it and the adjoining SS camp into a prisoner of war facility to intern up to 30,000 officers from Nazi party organizations and the German army. The post-war military tribunals for war crimes, as depicted in the movie *Judgment at Nuremberg*, were not restricted to the city of Nuremberg. Nazi personnel from various concentration camps were also prosecuted in a series of trials conducted by the US Army at Dachau.

Capt. Clifford Merrill, the commanding officer of A Company when the battalion landed at Utah Beach, had been seriously wounded after only several weeks of battle in Normandy and was sent home to recuperate. Following his recovery, he returned to Europe during the occupation and was a member of the tribunal at the Dachau war crimes trials. Capt. Merrill also served as provost marshal at the prison compound established at the former concentration camp compound. Capt. Merrill made the Army his career; he served in both Korea and Vietnam, where he was again wounded. He and his wife were among the group that came to Mom and Dad's home following the 712th reunion in 1985.

After our somber tour of Dachau, Dad and I headed back toward France. We arrived in a village on the outskirts of Saarbrücken, Germany at just about dusk and decided to find a hotel and spend the night. After renting a room, we noticed a small sign on the street outside of the inn give directions to a Katholische Kirche nearby. By this time we had become a little adroit at deciphering German and realized that there was a Catholic Church nearby. Since it was Saturday evening, we also noticed that we had enough time to attend the weekend vigil Mass.

I imagine that this part of the town did not get many American tourists; when the altar boy passed by with the collection basket, we were low on German currency so Dad and I put American currency into the basket. That little boys eyes got as big as saucers when he saw American money.

After Mass, Dad said that it was a small town similar to this during the war where he attended Mass one Sunday. It was right about the time they had moved into Germany and at that time, the 90th and the 712th were leapfrogging with the armored divisions in the move across the country. The 90th and the 712th would advance and then stop and let the armored division move through. It was during one of these stops that the opportunity arose for the GIs to go to Mass that Sunday. Dad explained:

> When we got into Germany, in about the first or second town, it was a Sunday morning and we wanted to go to church. And so we went to church. The American soldiers sat on one side of the church and the German people sat on the other side of the church. I was sitting next to an army buddy of mine (Sgt Gunther Jahnke) and he spoke German. They wouldn't even look at the Americans, they were scared to death of us; they looked straight ahead in church. And so the parish priest announced something to the German congregation in German, and when he finished speaking they looked around and smiled at all the soldiers. When that happened, I asked Jahnke, "Jahnke, what did he say?" Jahnke said, he told them, "These men are soldiers of God, you don't have to be afraid of them."

Toward the end of the war, and afterwards, many Germans claimed that they had no idea that the concentration camps existed. The Catholic population in this town, however, knew well how brutal the SS troops and the Gestapo were to the German civilian population. The priest that celebrated Mass that Sunday morning in early 1945 obviously also knew about the atrocities being committed by the Nazis to not only Jew in the concentration camps but Catholics as well. The townspeople's fear and mistrust of all military personnel were obvious and the sincere testimonial by that German priest was welcomed by both the German civilians and the American GIs at that Sunday Mass.

CHAPTER 13

Alsace and Ancestors

To forget one's ancestors is to be a brook without a source, a tree without a root.

Chinese Proverb

As Dad and I headed back to Paris, we made a slight detour in eastern France into Alsace in search of ancestors. Since my grandfather died when my Dad was a boy, the only family history Dad knew was that our Gruntz ancestors emigrated to America in the late 1800s from Alsace. Dad's grandfather was a boy of about seven years of age when he arrived in New Orleans with his father, stepmother and brothers and sisters.

My genealogy research in the months prior to our trip proved to be beneficial. I had discovered the birthplace of my great-great grandfather. He was born in the little French village of Franken, located in the Department of Haut Rhin (southern Alsace) not far from the location where the French, German, and Swiss borders meet.

We spent the night in Colmar, the capital of Haut Rhin. There are no telephone books in France like we were accustomed to back home, but the hotel clerk was very helpful in doing a computer search and generating a list of about forty Gruntz families that still resided in that area that is known as the Sundgau region of Alsace.

The next morning, Dad and I visited the government archives in Colmar and to our surprise we were able to obtain a copy of the record of the birth of our ancestor, Louis Gruntz, who was born on November 27, 1825, nearly a century before Dad. At this point, we also gained information on one more generation back, his parents' names were Ludwig Gruntz and Catherine Schmitt. With my passion for genealogy, I could have spent a week in Colmar doing extensive research, but we were on a time schedule and after a couple of hours, Dad and I were back in the car on our way to the village of Franken.

Franken is a small farming village with relatively few homes, we knocked on a few doors but no one answered except for one home, but the lady in that house spoke no English. To the best of our knowledge there were no longer any Gruntz families in this village. We visited the village church and the surrounding cemetery but did not find any Gruntz tombstones. I took a picture of an ancient tomb marker dating back to the 1600s, because of its age and condition. I discovered later when we were back home that this ancient tombstone belonged to the Baümlin family, from which we are descended through a maternal line that married into the Gruntz family.[1]

Dad was particularly thrilled to be in the village of his ancestors; I was happy that I was able to play a small part in making this possible. We realized that we were the first descendants of Louis Gruntz to return to his village in over 120 years.

With the aid of the Gruntz telephone list we acquired from the hotel clerk, we made a brief stop in the town of Hesingue, which had the most Gruntz names listed. Unfortunately, our inability to speak French, coupled with our inability to locate someone who could speak English prevented us from making any contact with any of the Gruntz families.

Although we were unable to make contact with any distant relatives during our trip, in the subsequent months after our trip I sent dozens of letters (translated into French) and received return correspondence from several Gruntz families who were surprised to discover that there was a Gruntz family in America.

Alsace has been battled over between the French and the Germans for several hundred years and even though the people speak a dialect of German, the majority of the population was more sympathetic to the France than to Germany. In 1871 Germany annexed the area of Alsace, in the Rhine valley on the west bank of the Rhine River and on the east side of the Vosges Mountains.

My ancestors were apparently on the losing side of that conflict or they were merely tired of war, but Louis Gruntz and his family emigrated to Louisiana in 1873.

The territorial entity of Elsass (the German name for Alsace) was created by the German Empire in 1871 and remained under German domination until the Armistice after World War I. In the Treaty of Versailles, Germany had to cede the territory back to France. When the Germans invaded France during World War II, they immediately occupied Elsass and quickly drafted most of the able body men into the service of the German Army. Many were sent to Normandy. Dad said that he had always wondered if he had fired upon any of his distant cousins during the war. That question remains a mystery.

CHAPTER 14

The Last Time I Saw Paris

...the freedom of Paris is associated with a persistent belief that nothing ever changes. Paris, they say, is the city that changes least. After an absence of twenty or thirty years, one still recognizes it.

Marguerite Duras (1914-1996)

Dad and I began the final leg of our journey by automobile. By midday, we had arrived at the outskirts of Paris.

Since it was a Sunday afternoon, I presumed that the traffic would be light and so we ventured into the middle of Paris in our rented automobile. I presumed incorrectly. Before long, we found ourselves hopelessly trapped in the traffic circle, circling the Arc de Triomphe.

After what seemed an eternity, I was determined to position our car on the outer lane of the traffic circle and exit at the first available street. I eventually accomplished this maneuver, but was even more disturbed to find us on the Champs-Elysées. After several blocks, I spotted a sign for a parking garage off on a side street and quickly found the entrance and we parked the car. As we were walking down this prestigious Parisian boulevard toward the Arc de Triomphe, by chance I caught sight of a plaque near the entrance to 92 Champs-Elysées. It was the building in which Thomas Jefferson resided when he was the United States Ambassador to France from 1785 to 1789.

After visiting the tomb of the Unknown Soldier in the middle of the Arc de Triomphe, we did a little shopping and then made our way back to the car. In the safe confines of the parking garage, we studied the map to determine the best way back toward the airport. Our plan was to find a hotel near the airport, return our rental car and use the subway as our means of transportation to continue our tour of Paris.

Finding a hotel room that night near the airport was relatively easy. After unloading all of our belongings from the car, we returned it to the rental agency at the airport the next morning. We circled the airport traffic ramps several times in frustration, before we were able to see the small sign indicating the entrance to the rental return lot. After the last day and a half in Paris traffic we were truly happy to be saying goodbye to our automobile.

Dad and I boarded the subway train at the airport for our first full day of sightseeing in Paris. While walking through one of the subway stations as we were transferring trains, I was taken aback at one of the sights. Several French soldiers in camouflage fatigue uniforms, armed with Uzi sub-machine guns were patrolling the subway station. In those days prior to September 11, 2001, that was a strange and an amazing site for this American to experience in a public facility.

For the next two days we experienced Paris as typical American tourists. We shopped for souvenirs, visited the Eiffel Tower, Invalides. We visited Notre Dame Cathedral, one of the most revered Catholic sites in France, where I was dismayed to see a sign at the entrance, "Beware of pickpockets".

We also found the Opera House and the adjacent Grand Hotel where Dad once stayed during the war. Between the capture of Metz and the assault on Dillingen, there was a lull in the battle for the 712th. When this occurred, Dad wrote home to Mom and told how he came to be in Paris:

November 29, 9 p.m.
  Darling I promised to write you a blue letter yesterday, but I didn't get chance to. Just as I sat down and started to write they came around and said the fellows were going to draw for a pass to Paris. 2 fellows out of the Company were allowed to go. Well I won one of the passes. I am in Paris now. I just got here so I can't tell you much about it as it is dark. But I will write and tell you about it tomorrow Love. I am going to be here until the day after tomorrow…

Troop transport trucks picked up soldiers going on furlough at the forward areas and drove them to Paris. Sgt Edward Dowgiert was the other member of B Company who won a pass; he was in the truck with Dad. In Paris, the transport trucks pulled up next to the Grand Hotel near the Paris Opera House. The hotel had been opened to Allied troops in October, only one month prior to Dad's stay. A Life Magazine reporter and photographer were there doing a story about soldiers on leave in Paris. The photographer snapped a picture just as Dad and Dowgiert were getting out of the truck. That picture ran in the February 26, 1945 edition of Life. Standing next to the truck was an old Frenchman. Dad said that the Frenchman was dealing in the black market and was trading for cigarettes. Dad traded a carton of cigarettes for a silver bracelet which he sent to Mom.

I asked him what was Paris like during the war. "It was just like another world. It was like back home. They (the Parisians) were celebrating, they were still celebrating. Everything was wide open, all the stores were open again, but we never had any money. But they never had much stuff to sell."

Above left: Life cover.

Above right: Cpl Gruntz in *Life Magazine*.

Cpl Gruntz in Paris. (*Author's collection*)

> Nov. 22
>
> Darling
> Here is a little Xmas card I bought over here. It isn't very pretty Darling. But it does let you know I am thinking of you and always will. Darling I also hope you have a Merry Xmas and I hope and pray to God long before next Xmas I am home with you. Merry Xmas Darling.
> All My Love
> Forever. Your Baby.

1944 Christmas cards home. (*Author's collection*)

It was the first time in months that Dad was able to sleep in a bed with sheets. The hotel housed 850 soldiers per night with the cost of the room being approximately $0.40 per night. When Dad and I visited the hotel, Dad inquired about the room rates. They had increased considerably since 1944 – the rate was now approximately $400.00 per night.

The hotel managers had opened the grand ballroom of the hotel to the GIs where they could enjoy a hot meal. The French were not as hospitable to the German soldiers billeted at the hotel during the Nazi occupation; the French managers kept them out of the grand ballroom telling them that the huge chandeliers were likely to fall during air raids.

I inquired as to whether Dad bought any other souvenirs. "No. I had a picture taken on one of those two-bit cameras that I sent to Mom. I looked like a French refugee."

The back of these pictures indicates it was taken on November 29, 1944. I asked Dad what he did while he was in Paris. He said, "I went sightseeing. We went to eat in the dining hall."

Dad got to be in Paris a total of 36 to 48 hours. "We got there one evening, stayed that night, went to see Paris, stayed another night, and then the next morning at 7:00 o'clock we were on the trucks to go back."

Even though Dad could not reciprocate Mom's daily letters to him, Dad wrote home to Mom every chance he had. In late November, particularly while he was in Paris, he took the opportunity to mail several Christmas cards to Mom in order that she would receive them by Christmas. The cards were some of the few souvenir items he was able to purchase while shopping in Paris.

CHAPTER 15

Going Home

I, for one, know of no sweeter sight for a man's eyes than his own country.

Homer, *The Odyssey*

Dad and I spent our last night in Paris, packing all of our gear and preparing for the long flight home the next day. In a matter of hours we would be home, unlike Dad's trip home in 1945. What took us only hours in 1994 took weeks in 1945.

The day after the war in Europe ended, Mom clipped a news story headlined as "Pacific is No Tank Country". An Associated Press story from Washington DC stated:

> The tank carried the load in the European war; in the Pacific, it will be the doughboy and his bayonet […]
>
> Europe was tank country, for such end-run generals as Patton, Hodges and Simpson, with wide flanking movements, big pincers operations and lightning stabs.
>
> The Pacific is totally different. The home islands of Japan do not lend themselves to tank warfare. […] in a campaign where the terrain is overcome by the yard instead of the mile, it is the foot-slogging doughboy with his rifle and bayonet who must carry the burden.

Earlier news stories throughout the war had indicated that tanks had been used in various island campaigns in the Pacific Theater of Operations (PTO). Mom had hoped and prayed that the May 9 newspaper assessment was correct.

I asked Dad if the 712th Tank Battalion was ever considered for transfer to the PTO to fight the Japanese. He replied, "Well they said about sending the troops from Europe over to Japan because they had to invade it, you see. But then when the atomic bomb came out and they dropped that. I didn't want to think about that (being sent to Japan). I had to start counting up my points, anyone who had 85 points didn't have to go. And I had 85 points. So we felt like we were going to go home."

America's use of the atomic bomb, ended all concerns of being deployed to the Pacific. The camp newspaper, Tank Tracks, described the mood on August 15, 1945:

> The tense waiting of the men was rewarded today as headlines screamed the war was over and radio broadcasts kept repeating Japan had surrendered. There was no change in the camp's activities. It seemed like any other day. The change was great though. It was the change that took place inside. It was the feeling of joy and silent prayer. It was all over. It meant home was much closer – so much closer now.
>
> It is hard for one to realize what the end actually meant. To those who were fortunate enough never to see a day of it, there was great celebration. A screaming, crazed exhibition of joy without realizing its true meaning. To the man who knows, there was no shouting or screaming just a prayer inside thanking God he was spared and hoping never again will he be part of the game of death. Yes, it was accepted casually but inside was that little prayer, "Thank God, it's over."

Later, when I asked Mom about the events back home in New Orleans when the war ended, she told me about V-E Day, "When the war was over many in our neighborhood went to Canal Street, they were celebrating. They had dances and everything. I wasn't in the mood for all of that. I was still home crying because I didn't know if Dad was still alive. So until he came home, I didn't celebrate. I don't remember V-J Day because I was just concerned about Dad."

The Army had developed a formula by which troops earned points. Points were awarded for each medal awarded, and for each month of service. 85 points was the lucky number; once anyone received that amount, he was shipped home. Shortly after arriving in Amberg, most of the Battalion was just below the magic number. But replacement troops, who had just arrived toward the end of the war and had fewer than 65 points were reassigned to other units to remain in Germany for the occupation. Those with more than 85 points waited in anticipation for the news that they would be going home.[1]

That word came in mid-September of 1945. The joyous atmosphere that surrounded the news however, was shattered several days later. When one hears of a soldier's death during the years 1941-1945, one naturally assumes the death occurred in combat, but accidents occurred not only in the combat zone but also in the occupied territories after hostilities ceased. The final Battalion casualty was Andrew Lampman of B Company. He had survived combat; he is even pictured in the post-war company photograph taken at Camp Randolph, yet on September 15, 1945, Andrew Lampman was killed

Waiting to come home – killing time playing solitaire. (*Author's collection*)

in a truck accident four days after the Battalion received orders that it was being sent home. Death did not take a holiday because the war ended. Just as civilians had to be safety conscious, Lampman's death pointed out that all of the 712th had to remain vigilant to prevent accidents.

Even Gen. Patton suffered this cruel irony. After surviving the war, he died as a result of injuries sustained in a post-war automobile accident in Germany in December of 1945.

On September 11, 1945, the redeployment took place. Those few with less than 85 points were reassigned to the 90th.

> The 712th was still a Tank Battalion on paper, but the 712th of FORET DE MONT CASTRE, FALAISE GAP, MAISIERES, METZ, DILLINGEN, OBERWAMPACH, THE SIEGFRIED LINE, and CZECHOSLOVAKIA was a thing of the past. The "best tank battalion in the US Army" that the Boche could hurt but never whip, an outfit that never retreated in the face of the enemy – broken up by the point system.[2]

The 712th Tank Battalion moved by motor convoy and train to Camp Detroit in southern France and then to the Calais Staging Area near Marseilles.

On October 15 all personnel loaded the troop transport ship for the voyage back home to America. Dad said, "They loaded us on the USS George Washington and I stayed up on the deck all the time. I slept on the deck and all, it was warm. I didn't want to go down in the hole, plenty of them got seasick on the way home."

Left: Cpl Gruntz at Camp Detroit. (*Author's collection*)

Below: Camp Detroit. (*Company B photograph*)

Camp Detroit. (*Company B photograph*)

USS *George Washington* in Marseilles Harbor. (*Author's collection*)

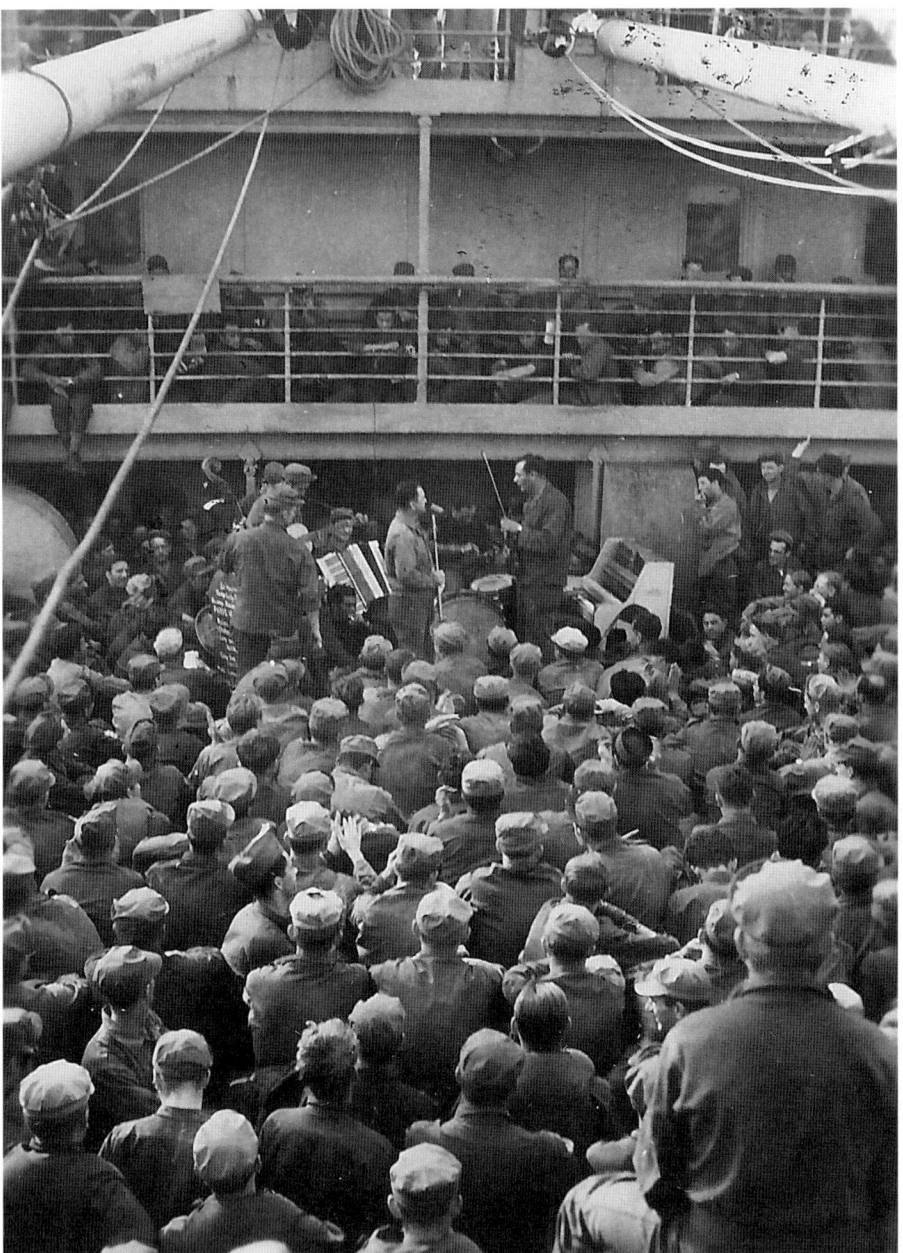

The voyage home. (*Company B photograph*)

Going Home

On October 25, the voyage ended in New York; and the 712th was taken to Camp Joyce Kilmer. "Here the Battalion finally passed out of existence and in no time at all trains, buses, planes and autos were carrying the ex-tankers toward home and civilian life."[3]

From New Jersey, Dad traveled by train to Camp Shelby, in Hattiesburg, Mississippi. Now that he was being discharged, the Army was giving him the hobo accommodations. The train car from New Jersey was a boxcar outfitted with about sixteen bunks. Dad and fifteen others rode and looked at the sights out of the open boxcar door. When it rained, they had to shut the door to keep from getting wet.

At Camp Shelby, he had to turn in his uniform that had been issued to him in Europe. It was a new and comfortable style. In its place he was issued an old woolen uniform that was very uncomfortable. Dad said that it felt like it had been made in World War I.

On November 1, 1945, All Saints Day, Dad was discharged and he had a bus ride home to New Orleans. In a few hours he was back home in Louisiana. After arriving at the bus station on Canal Street, Dad caught a taxi-cab home. Dad said, "I was so excited to get home, I got out of the cab and ran into the house." After greeting Mom, Dad, realized that he didn't have his discharge papers. "Oh my God I dropped my discharge papers. We called the taxi company and they found them in the back seat of the cab. So they dropped them in the mail to me."

On our flight home in 1994, we had the good fortune of having a relatively empty plane; I, therefore, took a window seat. As we crossed the coast of France, I could see all of the little square hedgerow fields. My thoughts turned to eleven days earlier when I was viewing these fields close-up, and how my perception of war had been altered during that intervening eleven- day period. My perception of war as a glamorous adventure, which had been deeply imbedded in my youth, was now supplanted by the more realistic depictions provided by my father.

Following the Civil War, US General William Tecumseh Sherman described War as being Hell. This graphic assessment seems appropriate for all wars. War is Hell for the combatants, it is Hell for the civilian populace in the path of opposing combatants, and it is Hell for the combatants' families back home.

CHAPTER 16

Other Casualties and a Never Ending War

In war, there are no unwounded soldiers.

Jose Narosky

During this trip and in the years that followed I continued to learn more and more about members of the 712th Tank Battalion and World War II in Europe.

I accompanied Mom and Dad to the annual 712th reunions. And in June of 2000, I had the privilege of having a repeat trip to Europe with Dad. Once again Dad told his story as we traveled the battle route of the 712th. The occasion for this trip was the dedication of a World War II monument in Périers, France. This time Mom joined us along with my two youngest children, David and Becky.

The monument being dedicated in Périers depicted four soldiers who were killed in action in the town's liberation, Virgil J. Tangborn, Andrew J. Speese, Richard E. Richtman of the 90th Infantry Division and Tullio Micaloni of the 712th. These four were representative of the more than 1,000 troops of the 90th killed in the fields and hedgerows near and around Périers.

This was a special occasion for Dad, not only was he attending the ceremony as the official representative of the 712th, but he was there for the dedication of a monument honoring his friend, Tullio.

There were five of us in a medium size car with luggage in the trunk and on the roof. Dad was now eighty-one years old and a knee injury he sustained early in life was now debilitating; he could not walk any great distance without being in intense pain. Whenever we traveled, we brought along a wheelchair to increase Dad's mobility. We brought the wheel chair to Europe along with an automobile bicycle rack. Due to the luggage taking up most of the space, we had the wheel chair mounted on the bicycle rack on the rear bumper. Traveling down the roads of France, we looked like the opening scene of the Beverly Hillbillies.

Prior to this trip, Paul Wannemacher, President of the 712th Tank Battalion

Dad next to statue of Tullio Micaloni. (*Author's collection*)

Association asked our assistance in a project that the 712th Association was undertaking, locating the grave sites of all of the 712th members killed in action.

Obtaining the grave sites of the soldiers buried in the various American Cemeteries in Europe was a relatively easy task. While in Europe, I obtained a printout from the three cemeteries from Leland Atkinson, the Superintendent of the Luxembourg Cemetery. We were very surprised to learn that he was born and raised in Gulfport, Mississippi, practically a stone's throw from our family's summer cabin in Waveland, Mississippi. Atkinson worked for several years at the Normandy Cemetery as the Assistant Director and knew Henri and Janet Levaufre very well. He was stationed in Normandy during the time that Steven Spielberg was filming the cemetery scene in *Saving Private Ryan*. We spent more than an hour visiting with Atkinson discussing the exploits of the 90th Infantry Division and the 712th Tank Battalion.

Atkinson advised us that in 1948 and 1949 the United States Government offered each family the option of having their loved one's body exhumed and returned to the United States for re-interment in cemeteries of the family's choice. Many families took advantage of this offer. Finding the final resting places of the members of the 712th that were returned home proved to be a daunting task which took over three years to accomplish. I considered it an

Dad and Leland Atkinson. (*Author's collection*)

honor to be able to assist Paul Wannemacher with this task.

Through the years I came to know several of the 712th members in the later years of their lives. In talking with Dad and other members of the 712th and in researching obituaries from a half a century ago, I came to know these soldiers vicariously as young men in 1943 and 1944. Those young men who had their whole future taken from them. As I learned the details of each death I became saddened by their deaths. The obituaries and facts surrounding each death had such profound sadness and revealed that the families back home in the United States were also casualties of war. They had no physical wounds, only emotional wounds. The casualties of World War II, like all wars, were neither limited to the battlefield nor to the period of hostilities.

One of the last grave locations I discovered was that of Tec 5 Fred Becker of B Company, who died on July 8, 1944. The only means of obtaining his grave location was through a request under the Freedom of Information Act for his IDPF (Individual Deceased Personnel File). Approximately one year after making the request, a copy of Becker's file finally arrived in the mail. The information not only provided the cemetery in which he is now buried but also correspondence between his mother and the War Department.

In the file was a handwritten letter written by Becker's mother:

> Dear Officer:
>
> I know how very busy you all are so I am grateful for your time. My son, T/5 Frederick W. Becker 11102404 was killed in action on July 8, 1944 and I would so much like to know where he is buried so I am asking that favor, Please.
>
> I have tried before to find out and now have been referred to this address. Please let me know whatever you can, Thank you so much.
>
> /s/ Mrs Grace Becker

A similar letter appears in the IDPF of Dee Johnson – Johnson was with Dad at Sainte-Suzanne and was wounded. Like Dad, he returned to action but was killed in the Battle of the Bulge in January 1945. On December 5, 1947, nearly three years later, Johnson's mother wrote inquiring about when the body of her son would be returned home.

> To the Quartermaster
>
> Please give me all the information you can about when the remains of the soldiers buried at Foy Bastogne Belgium, it's been so long since we had any word regard to when it will be so please let me know if you can.
>
> A broken hearted mother
> /s/ Mrs Ben S. Johnson

For many Americans back home there was little joy in V-E day and V-J Day, the horrible consequences of war lived within their hearts for many years and for some the rest of their lives. The letters of Mrs Becker and Mrs Johnson exemplify the unending pain these families had to endure.

The Request for Disposition of the Remains for Dad's friend, David Dickson, contains the following request by Dickson's father:

> It is requested that the remains of my son, David H. Dickson be returned for burial in the grave of his brother George H. Dickson [...] who was a veteran of World War I and is now buried in the Philadelphia National Cemetery...

Now that I have sons of military age, I can only imagine the unbearable grief and sorrow that these parents endured when they received word of their sons' demise. The movies of my youth did not portray this aspect of war. The brief yet poignant scene in *Saving Private Ryan* when the Army Officer and the minister arrive at the Ryan home can only partially convey what the parents of KIAs went through.

Two other 712th KIA, whose final resting place I researched, were Lt Marshall Warfield and Major Ira Hawk of Headquarters Company. Warfield, who was the nephew of Edwin Warfield, Governor of the State of Maryland from 1904 to 1908, was killed in action on September 17, 1944. With the assistance of a genealogists in Maryland, I discovered that Warfield was buried in a private cemetery in Howard County Maryland. The cemetery was identified as the Governor Warfield Cemetery. Major Ira Hawk of Headquarters Company was killed in action on July 23, 1944 and was re-interred in the Baltimore National Cemetery.

I had occasion to visit Maryland on several occasions since my son, David, was enrolled as a student at the University of Maryland in College Park. On one such visit in May of 2003, I took the occasion to spend a few extra days to locate the two 712th grave sites in Maryland. Visiting Ira Hawk's burial site was relatively easy. Finding Warfield's final resting place was a little more formidable. The Governor Warfield Cemetery is located off of Jennings Church Road, a not well traveled country road, in Howard County Maryland. The cemetery and its gate is well camouflaged from the roadway by a small wooded area and I drove past it three times before seeing the gate. After a short walk through the wooded area I came upon the small cemetery surrounded by a stone fence in the middle of a farm field.

After a few minutes I located Warfield's headstone, the inscription reads:

>
> In Memory of
> Lt Marshall T. Warfield
> April 17 1917
> September 17, 1944
> Killed in Action
> East of Metz France
> Brought Home December 8, 1948
> His Wife
> Olga Gannon Warfield

I noticed that there was no date of death for his wife nor was there any other gravestone bearing her name anywhere near his grave. I assumed that she had remarried after the war and was buried elsewhere. My visit to this out of the way cemetery only aroused my curiosity to learn more about this family.

When I returned home, I began searching the internet for information on Gov. Warfield. My search led me to a bulletin board where an inquiry was posted by Stephanie Rockford for information on Lt Marshall Warfield who was killed in World War II. Assuming that she was a relative of Warfield, I immediately contacted her. Mrs Warfield, was a good friend of Stephanie's grandmother and consequently she and Mrs Warfield also developed a close relationship; then I was astonished to learn that Mrs Warfield was still alive and, now in her 90s, resided in Virginia. Through correspondence and a delightful telephone conversation with Mrs Warfield, the story of Lt Marshall Warfield unfolded.

Warfield grave. (*Author's collection*)

The Warfield family was a very prominent political family in Howard County. Several members were elected to a variety of offices, including Edwin Warfield as Governor. The cemetery, is situated on land that the Warfield family received by land grant from the King of England during the colonial period. Mrs Warfield also corrected me on the name of the cemetery. Although it is called the Governor Warfield Cemetery because of the Governor, its correct name is the Cherry Grove Cemetery

When the war first started, Marshall and several friends enlisted. He was a sergeant when he met and fell in love with Olga. She rebuffed his original proposal of marriage because of his rank. He, not to take no for an answer, enrolled in Officer Candidate School and after completion of training was commissioned a 2nd Lieutenant. After seeing the ends he would go to, Olga said yes the next time he asked. She told me that she enjoyed the life of an officer's wife. There were dances virtually every weekend at the officer's club and they both enjoyed to dance.

She was devastated at the news of his death and spent many years not knowing how he died. After many inquiries to officers she had met in 1943, she finally learned the circumstances of that fateful day, September 17, 1944. Warfield along with Sgt Tom Reilly were in the HQ Reconnaissance Platoon. They were patrolling an area near Thionville, just north of Metz, when they were ambushed by fire from a German machine gun nest.

Olga never remarried. Stephanie told me that she still has a picture of her beloved Marshall hanging prominently in her living room.

Unlike Olga Warfield, life took a different path for Richard Williams' widow, Opal. Aunt Opal kept in touch with Mom for many years after the war. But her life continued to be marred with tragedy. Following Richard's death in 1945, she remarried after the war to another military man. He was killed in the Korean War.

I believe she remarried and was divorced once or twice after that. Her last visit to us that I recall was in 1968 for my wedding. Then for some inexplicable reason she ended her relationship with my mother. During a 712th reunion in Kentucky in 1976, Mom and Dad visited Opal's parents, at which time they brought Mom and Dad to meet Richard's parents.

After Richard was killed, the only information his family received was the telegram from the War Department notifying them of his death. It had been over thirty years since his death and during that visit from Mom and Dad, they learned for the first time the details of the battle for Doncols that occurred on January 10, 1945, and how Richard had died.

Dad said that he and Mom spent several days visiting both of these Kentucky families. When Aunt Opal heard of Mom and Dad's visit to Richard's family, she became angered and wrote Mom a long letter. She returned all photographs and wanted no more contact with Mom. Needless to say, Mom was dumbfounded. She has never heard from her since, yet Mom still has fond memories of the good times the four of them had in 1943. We can only imagine what painful memories were resurrected in Aunt Opal to prompt such a response.

The stories of casualties sustained by the military during war often overshadow the fact that civilians living in the war zone are exposed to many of the same dangers and are also casualties of war.

The story of the liberation of Périers offers another example of how the French civilians suffered during the war. Following four years of harsh domination by the Nazis, in June of 1944, the people of Périers found themselves in the middle of the advancing path of the United States Army. Several days prior to its liberation, the United States Army shelled and bombed the town. The photographs of the town taken in July of 1944 show that this softening of enemy resistance practically leveled the town. The German troops evacuated the town prior to the bombing, but 128 townspeople were killed by the shelling and bombing. The hardship and suffering, amidst the destruction and debris of their town, plagued the civilians long after the troops had moved the war eastward.

Henri Levaufre later told me about one of his personal encounters with danger. Henri's father had about twenty-five cows on his farm before the invasion. Shortly after Périers was liberated, Henri was helping his father gather the eight remaining cows that survived. His father was walking along a path pulling the lead cow tethered on a rope. Henri was following the last cow, when it suddenly stopped to nibble on grass. Henri gave him a slight tap on the rump with a stick to get the cow moving again. When the cow moved, it stepped on a land mine. When the explosion shattered the pastoral silence, Henri's father turned around and looked in horror to see his son covered in blood, fortunately, all of the blood belonged to the cow. Henri did not have a scratch, the cow had absorbed all of the blast. Henri said that the countryside around his home was littered with live German mines well into 1949 and that several French citizens were killed by them long after the war had ended.

The monument dedication of the four US soldiers, in June of 2000, marked the beginning of a several year project to convert the old abandoned train station, which Dad had captured, into a museum and a memorial park honoring the 128 citizens of Périers killed during the war.

There is only one small hotel in the town, consequently, housing for all of the American guests during the dedication ceremonies was a logistic problem easily solved by the townspeople. Each French family opened their homes and housed an American family during the several days of the event. The display of appreciation to America and Americans even after fifty-six years was overwhelming. The heartfelt appreciation of the citizens of Périers to America for liberating their town from Nazi rule was a truly moving experience considering the destruction of their town in 1944 and the deaths of their fellow citizens was caused by American bombs and shelling.

That spirit of gratitude is not unique to Périers. Several days after the dedication ceremony, we traveled to the city of Tours to visit Christian and Evelyn Levaufre, Henri and Janet's son and daughter-in-law. While staying in their home, Dad became seriously ill and required medical attention. A physician made a house call to the Levaufre home to attend to Dad. After Dad had passed the danger and the doctor was beginning to leave, I offered to pay the doctor for his visit. He politely told Christian in French that he would not accept any payment; for personal reasons he said that he would not charge an American veteran in need of medical treatment.

The suffering and hardship that the French suffered at the hands of the Nazis produced a deep and lasting gratitude these people have for their American liberators. Even the sharp political differences between the United States and French governments in 2003 over the American invasion of Iraq does not seem to have shaken the gratitude for the American soldiers sacrifices in 1944. On the occasion of the two-hundredth anniversary of the Louisiana Purchase on December 20, 2003, Jean David Levitte, the French Ambassador to the United States, speaking on the historical significance of that 1803 transaction stated, "France wanted to help your nascent republic to emerge as a powerful and friendly ally on the other side of the Atlantic Ocean. In return, America saved

France twice last century. We will never forget. Dear friends, we will never forget. And next year, on the 6th of June, we will commemorate, in the most solemn and moving way, the 60th anniversary of D-Day."

Continuing Battles

V-E Day may have marked the end of hostilities in Europe, but, for many soldiers, it did not mean the end of their private battles.

The stress on the human mind caused by the emotional wear and tear of witnessing horrible carnage, violence and death did not end on the battlefield. Some soldiers returning to civilian life experienced a delayed onset of the disorder by experiencing a host of problems which are now considered symptoms of Post-Traumatic Stress Disorder (PTSD).[1] Both the immediate onset of this syndrome on the battlefield as well as the delayed onset has been known by many names; it was known as soldier's heart in the Civil War, shell shock in World War I and battle fatigue during World War II. Regardless of the name attached to this condition, they all essentially describe the same phenomenon.

Most returning soldiers tried shutting out memories of the war, but some, nevertheless, had disturbing memories or experienced recurring nightmares, others became compulsive gamblers, still others exhibited a simmering rage or anger, losing their temper for no reason at all, many experienced depression, anxiety, and alcohol abuse. A few experienced difficulty with functioning in social or family life, they suffered loss of jobs, marital problems and other family discord, which often led to divorce. And death still hovered over the 712th tankers. The first veteran to succumb to this post-war fate was Richard Grable, Dad's barracks mate at Fort Benning. On April 9, 1946, six short months after returning home from war, Grable was killed in an automobile accident.

Dad admitted that beginning in 1945, upon his return home, and for many years thereafter he had nightmares about the war. While others also suffered from nightmares, Dad said that some combat veterans endured far more than nightmares.[2] He explained that the war affected everyone differently.

> Now something happened to people – (one of the sergeants who received a battlefield commission) stayed in France after the war and then went to college. He came back home and became a drunkard. He worked in the iron mills in Cleveland, Ohio. And when we passed through there after the war, when we had our reunions, they called him up, Kellner called him up, to ask him to come have supper with us at the hotel. His wife said "He can't talk to you, he doesn't want to talk to you." He was drunk. That's how it affected him.

After our return in June of 2000, I attended the 712th reunion with Mom and Dad in Wichita, Kansas. We brought the photographs of our European trip and Dad recounted all of the details of the monument dedication for the other attendees. John and Rose Ockenga had planned to attend the reunion but were unable because John was ill. At the conclusion of the reunion, we drove to Wakeman, Ohio to visit the Ockenga family.

John Ockenga was a Technical Sergeant in B Company whose duties were to make the front line repair the tanks. Although the 712th Tank Battalion had a Service Company, which performed major repairs to broken or disabled tanks well to the rear of the front lines, each combat company had several service personnel to assist tank crews on the front line with minor repairs and sometimes to retrieve disabled tanks and bring them to the rear.

We spent several days in Ohio; Dad and Mom shared with John and Rose details about the reunion and all that had transpired since their last visit. Naturally, during our visit, we pulled out the photographs of our trip to Europe. When we came to the pictures taken in Sainte-Suzanne and Dad indicated the site where his tank was knocked out and where Willinger was killed. John said that he remembered that event vividly.

When Dad's tank was disabled, John had to go to the front line to retrieve the tank after Lloyd Sparks brought it back into the American side of the front. John said that he had the grim job of removing Willinger's body from the tank. A few minutes later, John began to weep over this memory. We put the pictures away and neither the war nor the trip were discussed again. Rose indicated that on several occasions she had mentioned to John about returning to Europe like Dad and I had but that John was not interested. All through their married life, he rarely mentioned anything about the war. She said that the only time he enjoyed the service was before the war when he was in the 11th Cavalry stationed in California and when he rode border patrol on horseback.

Capt. Belton Cooper described the gruesome task of service personnel in recovering and repairing tanks.

> When a tanker inside a tank received the full effect of a (shell), sometimes the body, particularly the head, exploded and scattered blood, gore, and brains throughout the entire compartment. It was a horrible sight. The maintenance crews had to get inside and clean up the remains. ... With strong detergent, disinfectant, and water they cleaned the interior of the tank as best they could so men could get inside and repair it. After the repairs were completed, the tanks' fighting compartment would be completely painted. In spite of this, the faint stench of death sometimes seeped through.[3]

I can only imagine the horrible memories our discussion and photographs conjured up for John that evening. Our visit to the Ockenga farm in September of 2000 was the last time we saw John. He passed away several months later.

As I mentioned early on, the reticence of veterans to speak about their experiences was a common characteristic of combat veterans. Paul Wannemacher once told me, "We never talked about the war because people who weren't there would never believe all the things that we saw." In an interview with Aaron Elson, Otha Martin of the 712th once said, "A lot of people say veterans never talk to them. The reason they don't talk is they couldn't get the picture over to somebody that wasn't there. Somebody that wasn't there, he would think that you're making that story up."

This silence among veterans was not unique to World War II combatants. In 1869, the poet Edgar Lee Masters authored a poem entitled "Silence". In it the inability of Civil War veterans to talk about combat experiences is described. In one stanza, Masters writes:

> A curious boy asks an old soldier ...
> "How did you lose your leg?"
> And the old soldier is struck with silence, ...
> And the boy wonders, while the old soldier
> Dumbly, feebly lives over
> The flashes of guns, the thunder of cannon,
> The shrieks of the slain,
> And himself lying on the ground,
> And the hospital surgeons, the knives,
> And the long days in bed.
> But if he could describe it all
> He would be an artist.
> But if he were an artist there would be deeper wounds
> Which he could not describe.

Besides the psychological wounds from the war, many soldiers also faced physical disabilities. Jim Flowers was wounded on July 10, 1944 after only one week in battle. Yet he had to cope with his physical wounds for the rest of his life. After being wounded, he spent several months in hospitals in England before being returned to the States. Flowers spent the next three years in Army hospitals in rehabilitation and being fitted with prosthesis for both legs. He was discharged from the Army in November, 1947. He had been in the Army for a little more than five years, the majority of that time was spent in the hospital. After his discharge, Flowers went to work in the prosthetics section of the Veteran's Administration Hospitals in Waco, Texas and then Dallas Texas.

Louis Gruntz, John McDaniel and Jim Flowers at 90th Reunion, Little Rock, Arkansas, 2002. (*Author's collection*)

In August of 2002, the 90th Regional Support Command named a building at its Texas facility in honor of Jim Flowers. Dad was invited to attend the ceremony. Dad, Mom and I, along with the wheel chair flew to Dallas. I had been introduced to Jim briefly at other 712th reunions, but this was the first time, I actually had the opportunity to "meet" him.

Less than thirty days later, the Gruntz family and Jim Flowers were once again in each other's company. The occasion was the 90th Infantry Division reunion in Little Rock, Arkansas, and the dedication of the Henri Levaufre Heritage Center at the 90th RSC Headquarters in Little Rock.

We saw Jim for a third time at the 712th reunion in Fort Lauderdale Florida one month later in September. Jim was a fiercely independent person, more so after his wife, Jeanette passed away. Despite being in his eighties, and having two prosthetic devices, Jim traveled alone to Little Rock and Fort Lauderdale. Jim also was never one to hold back his words, at times he could be very brusque. His friends in the 712th took this in stride because they knew Jim.

One day in the hospitality room at the 712th reunion, Jim was sitting in an cushioned armchair, the kind you sink into when you sit down. I was sitting to his right and Orin Bourdo was sitting directly across from Jim. As Jim was trying to get up out of the chair, he was having a little difficulty and he asked Orin to give him a hand. Orin, also in his eighties, used a cane to get around so I jumped up to assist Jim. In a somewhat harsh tone, Jim told me to get my hands off of him. I was startled by his response, but was not offended. Others nearby also were startled at the response. Orin later explained that Jim could only be assisted from the front, if someone helped him from the side he would lose his balance. With respect to the harshness of his tone, Orin said, "That's just Jim." Orin also explained that he believed that Jim's rough exterior at times was his way of coping. "He always felt personally responsible for losing all those men under his command."

The next day, I was again in the hospitality room but I was sitting across from Jim. When he went to arise, he asked me to help him, which I immediately did. He then paid me a huge compliment. He stated that he believed that my Dad was a very fortunate man to have a son like me to help him in his travels. Perhaps this was Jim's way of apologizing for the incident the day before, but in my mind, no apology was necessary.

The reunion in Fort Lauderdale was the last time Dad and I saw Jim. He died two months later, over the Thanksgiving holidays of 2002.

In the late 1990s, Mom, Dad and I met Bob and Edith Levine, friends of Henri and Janet Levaufre. Henri and Janet were staying at Mom and Dad's home during one of their biennial trips to the US to visit friends in the 90th and 712th. On this occasion, Bob and Edith, also happened to be in town on another matter and were straying in a local hotel.

Bob was in the 90th Infantry and fought on Hill 122. He was captured by the Germans and while being moved further behind German lines, he was wounded by artillery on July 11th, 1944. The German doctors had to amputate his foot just above the ankle.

Bob stated that every July 11th after that he would always imagine where he was on that day in 1944 and he would "start getting in his combat mode." After many years he thought he was over this annual malaise, but fifty years later, on July 11, 1994, he went to movies to see Forrest Gump, believing it to be a comedy. During the Vietnam scene, when Lt Dan lost both of his legs, Bob said to his wife:

> "I don't believe it Edith, what are we doing here?" Of all days, the crucial day, we go see this thing...
>
> It was very similar to Hill 122. It was real wild, sheer chaos. Going through the woods, down the hill, was like that. Shell bursts, and guys yelling and screaming, then I heard, you could hear tanks...
>
> So I realized at that point that maybe traumas like that just don't go away forever.[4]

After learning some of Dad's wartime experiences, I felt somewhat ashamed for my inquisitive behavior as a child. At that time in his life, in 1954, Dad was trying to forget all of the horrible aspects of war. He kept his physical memorabilia of the war out of sight in a box in the dark recesses of his closet. Likewise, he was also trying to keep all of those vivid memories hidden and tucked away in the dark recesses of his mind. My relentless questioning as a small boy caused him to relive those memories. At the age of eighty-four, when he voluntarily talked about the war, at least those memories emerged at a time and under the circumstances of his choosing.

Reunions

The World War II veterans eventually realized that images and events they tried to forget in the late 1940s and the 1950s was a virtually impossible task. Recalling these events at the time and circumstances of their choosing became easier as they attended reunions.

The 90th Infantry Association has long considered members of the 712th Tank Battalion their own. And although the members of the 712th also consider themselves part of the 90th, they remain fiercely proud of their status as an "independent" battalion. In fact, Dad once jokingly told some 90th members, "The 712th wasn't attached to the 90th… the 90th was attached to the 712th."

Dad had joined the 90th Association and paid dues over the years but the first reunion he attended was in August, 2002 in Little Rock, Arkansas. The reasons were two-fold for attending this reunion: the 90th Regional Support Command, the successor of the 90th Infantry, has its headquarters in Little Rock; during the reunion, the 90th RSC was opening the Henri Levaufre Heritage Center. The center is to house research materials and other items of the 90th and its support units and was named in honor of Henri who collected a wealth of information over the years regarding the 90th's battle history in Normandy. Henri and Janet were present for the occasion. Secondly, the 90th RSC was premiering a documentary film it had produced on the 90th, Dad and Mom had been interviewed for possible inclusion in the film. Although their interview ended on the cutting room floor, two still pictures of Dad, during the war, were included in the final cut.

Over 1,000 people attended this reunion, several like Dad, were attending for the first time. During one dinner, we sat at a table with another first timer, Leonard Patulski from Milwaukee, Wisconsin. With many of Dad's friends from the 712th hailing from Milwaukee, the conversation naturally turned to mentioning the names to see if he knew any. Although Leonard did not recognize any 712th members by name, Dad and Leonard quickly engaged in discussions about the war.

Patulski was in the 359th Regiment of the 90th during the Battle of the Bulge. He had recalled riding on the outside of the tanks on a few occasions.

Louis Gruntz and Leonard Patulski. (*Author's collection*)

He then mentioned that one of those tanks contained a Russian, and all that Russian wanted to do was kill Germans. Dad was flabbergasted; he quickly exclaimed, "You were riding on my tank." Dad then proceeded to tell him about Jack the Russian.

Of all of the banquet tables set in the hotel ballroom, what providence had led these two first time attendees of the reunion to sit at the same table?

Another strange occurrence happened in July of 2003. In gathering the audio tapes of our journey in 2000, my trip journal from 1994, and other source materials for putting Dad's story on paper, I also pulled from Dad's closet the box of his memorabilia from the war. I also discovered a separate box belonging to Mom, containing all of the love letters she received from Dad during the war. Until this time, I had never opened that box that Mom hadn't opened in decades. Mixed in among Dad's letters was a letter that Dad received from Joe Mack Reeves in 1943, the young boy on the farm where Dad's tank broke down during maneuvers in Tennessee. I also brought out the two photographs of Joe Mack that were in Dad's box of memorabilia. Neither Mom nor Dad realized that Joe Mack's letter was inadvertently mixed in with Dad's love letters that Mom had secreted away.

In that 1943 letter, the little boy tells Dad about recent developments on the farm, he also wrote:

Joe Mack, 1943 letter. (Author's collection)

> Alexandria Tennessee
> Aug. 23 - 1943
>
> Dear Gruntz,
>
> I missed you so much after you left, wish I could see you.
>
> You should see my little dog, he has grown a lot. We have nine little white pigs now. They are so pretty.
>
> We will start to school Friday I will be glad. I am planning on going to the Fair Saturday and see the Rodeo. Wish you were here to go with me.
>
> What have you been doing since you left here? Guess you will soon go back to Camp. When you get back to Camp send your address and I will send you my picture.
>
> Write me sometime soon
> I love you,
> Joe Mack

I missed you so much after you left, I wish I could see you. Write me sometime soon, I love you,

Joe Mack

When Dad was being shipped overseas at the beginning of 1944, he had sent several personal items home with Mom and during this process young Joe Mack's letter had been misplaced among Mom's letters.

Dad had always lamented that he had lost contact with this little kid and that he could not find his address after the war to see what had happened in his life. Even though sixty years had passed since Dad's tank broke down on the Reeves farm, I made an attempt to locate Joe Mack Reeves. With only this skimpiest of information, I did an internet research and found over a dozen Joe Reeves' in Tennessee, but only one named Joe M. Reeves who was the right age and who lived in Murfreesboro, TN, not far from Alexandria.

I wrote to this Joe M. Reeves on July 21, enclosing a copy of little Joe Mack's letter along with a copies of the photos. In my letter I asked if he was the boy in the pictures. I received a four page letter in response, Joe Reeves wrote, in part:

Dear Mr Gruntz,

I am the Joe Mack Reeves you are looking for. I'm so glad you put forth this effort which truly brought tears to my eyes as I read your letter.

On Friday night, July 18, my wife Nancy and I were with three couples of friends and the subject of the World War II maneuvers came up. I quickly injected my lingering thoughts about Gruntz and what happened to him after he departed our farm. I have thought many times about whether he survived the war. I'm delighted to know that he survived and has been blessed with this life span.

Of all the soldiers who participated in exercises and/or camped on our place, Gruntz is the only name I have remembered. My parents often related to others my pain and crying when he departed. Ours was one of those somewhat rare occasions in life when one truly bonds with another without analyzing the reason [...]

I share Tom Brokaw's conclusions that the World War II participants were our greatest generation. I have thanked God for the sacrifice made by so many for the rest of us. [...] Having observed the maneuvers, listened to the nightly news reporting on the progress of the war, and seeing the dead and wounded arriving home, my life was impacted and shaped forever by World War II. [...]

Gruntz is one of the very special people in my life and I'm thankful [...] you who took this initiative. Tell him I still love him.

Sincerely, best wishes and God's blessing
/s/ Joe Mack Reeves

I telephoned Joe to learn if he would be receptive to the idea of seeing Dad again. I explained that Mom, Dad and I would be passing through Tennessee in the fall in order to attend the annual 712th Tank Battalion Association reunion, being held that year in Fort Mitchell, Kentucky. Both Joe and Dad were excited about seeing each other again after all these years and our plans for this unique reunion were made.

CHAPTER 17

The Final Battle

> Old soldiers never die, they just fade away.
>
> Gen. Douglas MacArthur

Dad had been an outpatient at the Veterans Hospital in New Orleans for over thirty years. During this thirty-year period, his most serious ailment had been angina which was under control with medication His final battle began in November, 2002, when he went for a regular checkup. During the routine examination he complained of feeling completely exhausted and short of breath

Dad's primary care physician at the VA informed Dad that he would order an echogram to see if his heart was getting weaker and that he was also ordering a breathing test. He also had an x-ray taken of Dad's chest.

Several days later, the doctor called and said that there were two suspicious spots on Dad's lung but not to be alarmed because he was ordering CT scan in order to see more clearly this suspicious area on the x-ray.

Dad received word from the VA Hospital, at the end of November informing him his appointment for the CT Scan would be January 29, 2003. Mom complained about having to wait two months for this critical test and was told that he could have the CT scan done on December 27 when he came for the echogram.

The entire month of December was unsettling. On December 27, 2002, Dad and Mom arrived early for the echogram, which was scheduled for 8:00 a.m. only to be informed that the echogram would not be performed that day and it would have to be rescheduled. They were advised that department was short one employee that day and that the employee that was on duty would only perform six echograms that day and did not have time to perform our scheduled appointment. They were both devastated and outraged by this news. At ages eighty-three and eighty respectively, it was difficult for them to get to the VA Hospital, and then after arriving at that early hour only to be informed that an important diagnostic test, which had been ordered one month earlier was cancelled without their knowledge.

Since Mom and Dad were at the hospital, Dad proceeded to have the CT scan performed. After having the CT scan, Dad had a heaviness in his chest and the doctor performing the CT scan recommended that he go to the emergency room for a cardiogram. The emergency room personnel had Dad admitted to MICU for fear that he was on the verge of a heart attack. He stayed for two days in MICU and it was suggested that he undergo an angiogram. Our family has had two unfortunate incidents with members who have undergone angiograms, one died on the operating table and the other had a massive stroke while undergoing the procedure. Because of this fear, Dad hesitated in having this procedure and wanted more time to consider the necessity and to discuss it with his primary care physician upon the doctor's return from his vacation. But Dad told the doctor in MICU that if he really needed to have one, he would consent to it. Since the heaviness that he had felt in his chest at the time of the CT scan had subsided and not returned, Dad was released from MICU and sent home.

On December 31, 2002, at 8:00 a.m., Dad received a telephone call from someone at the VA with the results of the CT scan. He was told, "You need to have a biopsy because you have cancer."

Despite the fact that the CT scan showed a growth on Dad's lung and that a biopsy would have to be performed, the doctors insisted that his heart condition was more serious and that they could not perform the lung biopsy until he underwent an angiogram. Therefore, Dad consented to having the angiogram performed. When Dad's primary care physician returned from his vacation during the first week in January, he put in the order for the angiogram to be performed. Again Dad was told that we would be informed of the appointment date and time for the angiogram. He went the entire month of January without receiving any word from the VA Hospital about when this would be done.

Meanwhile Dad's coughing and breathing conditions worsened; he became so short-winded that on January 31, Dad, Mom and I went to the emergency room at the VA Hospital. The male nurse who was on duty in the emergency room said that he knew Dad was sick and needed help. Dad saw his primary care physician later that afternoon. His physician examined him and stated that Dad's lung was beginning to collapse.

Dad's physician called for the cardiologist to meet with Dad on Monday, February 3, 2003. He informed us that it didn't look good for Dad and that nothing could be done until Dad had the angiogram to see if his heart was able to withstand the biopsy procedure. Dad's blood oxygen level was 93%. On Monday morning, February 3, the three of us arrived at the VA early for the 12:30 p.m. appointment with the cardiologist. We met with a nurse practitioner. She indicated that Dad's lung needed attention more than his heart. She felt that hospitalization was the quickest way for him to receive the necessary treatment. She could see how sick Dad was and that he was having a terrible time breathing, he had a terrible cough and she could not hear air in his left lung. She made several phone calls trying to have him admitted to the VA Hospital. While awaiting responses to her phone calls we returned to the waiting area, because she was getting behind schedule on seeing other patients. About an hour later, after consulting with the cardiology and pulmonary specialist she came to the waiting area she told us that those physicians indicated that Dad's medical condition at that time did not qualify him for admission to the hospital. In other words, physicians who had not even seen Dad, determined that he was not sick enough to be admitted to the VA Hospital. She then had Dad scheduled for an angiogram over a week later, on February 11, 2003, and sent us home.

Needless to say we were all not only disappointed but furious for not only this treatment by the VA staff that determined that Dad was not sick enough to be admitted, but also for their constant delays in providing Dad vital medical attention. How could employees of the Veterans Administration have such a cavalier attitude to someone who had gallantly served his country?

Upon leaving the VA Hospital I immediately proceeded to our local hospital, East Jefferson General Hospital. After the triage nurse at East Jefferson saw Dad and discovered his blood oxygen level was 86%, Dad was admitted at once. He was put on oxygen and his breathing difficulties subsided considerably in only about five minutes. X-rays there revealed that his left lung was collapsed and that he had fluid in or around his lung. Cardiology exams revealed that although he had angina, his heart was healthy enough to withstand any testing for his lung condition. On Wednesday, February 5, 2003, over 1400 cc of fluid were removed from his lung cavity in order to improve his breathing. The biopsy was performed on this fluid. The doctors informed us that the tumor on Dad's bronchial tube was malignant.

He began radiation therapy on Friday afternoon, February 7, 2003 and the oncologist assigned to him was successful in having Dad accepted into program for an experimental drug being tested. The drug was a form of chemotherapy but is administered orally by pill; it does not have all of the side effects of regular chemotherapy. The doctors were hopeful that this combination of radiation therapy and oral chemotherapy would prolong Dad's life.

Dad remained too weak from this ordeal to be released from the hospital and he was transferred to the skilled nursing facility until he completed his initial sixteen radiation therapy treatments.

Dad began a regimen of the oral chemotherapy and the initial prognosis was promising. Although he was still able to get around, he was now constantly tethered to an oxygen tank.

After several weeks, however, it appeared in subsequent x-rays that the cancer had spread to other parts of his lung. Dad then progressed to regular chemotherapy but after only three weeks the injections were collapsing his veins and making him terribly sick. Dad made the decision to cease this treatment and return to the oral chemotherapy in hope that this was retarding the spread of the cancer even if it was not stopping it. Although ill, Dad's spirits were still high and, on May 10, he celebrated his eighty-fourth birthday and he and Mom's sixty-first wedding anniversary. Although he was saddened to learn several days later that his friend, Les Vink, had passed away on May 10.

Dad had a regular visit with his pulmonary specialist in June. The date was June 6, 2003, the fifty-ninth anniversary of D-Day. The doctor broke the news to Dad that the cancer was still spreading and at such a rate that Dad would probably survive the summer but he would not see Christmas. Dad's response was, "Fifty-nine years ago, I would not have bet you a dollar that I would live this long." Dad further expressed his belief that he would still beat this thing and be around longer than his doctor predicted.

Dad was still feeling strong and made plans to attend the 90th Infantry Association reunion in August. The reunion was scheduled to take place in St Louis. Dad had also made plans to attend the 712th Battalion Association reunion in September in Fort Mitchell, Kentucky. I scheduled vacation days at work for these two events, planning to drive Mom and Dad to these two functions.

It was during the month of July that I located Joe Mack Reeves and during our conversations, we made plans to stop and visit with Joe and his family in Tennessee on our way to Fort Mitchell.

By August, however, Dad strength was beginning to wane. He cancelled plans to attend the 90th reunion and hoped that he could regain his strength to travel to Kentucky and visit Tennessee to reunite with Joe Mack.

In the beginning of September, Dad's oncologist thought he could make the trip and administered medication to provide him additional strength to make the trip. Unfortunately, Dad had an adverse reaction to the medication and became gravely ill, he was so dehydrated that he required hospitalization. Dad never fully bounced back from this setback. Our plans for attending the reunion in Fort Mitchell had to be cancelled.

Both Joe Reeves and Dad were looking forward to meeting again. The story of Dad and Joe reuniting after sixty years was such a compelling human interest story that newspapers both in New Orleans and Murfreesboro ran articles on how they met during the war and had not seen each other in sixty years.

I called Joe to inform him of our trip cancellation and explain that Dad's health had worsened. Without hesitation he asked if he could come to New Orleans to visit Dad. I naturally agreed and Joe scheduled his visit for the same weekend we would have been traveling to Fort Mitchell.

Right: The *New Orleans Times Picayune* newspaper heralds the reunion.

Below: Cpl Gruntz and Joe Reeves' reunion. (*Author's collection*)

We were all anxiously awaiting the arrival of Joe and his wife, Nancy. Despite the passage of sixty years, that bond that had formed between a young soldier and a small boy was still there. After catching up on what had occurred in each other's lives, they began talking about the farm in Tennessee as if the occurrences of 1943 had just happened.

Dad's doctor had indicated in July that Dad's desires and abilities would slowly begin to disappear. His mobility would gradually be reduced, and his desire for foods would dissipate. Finally, the natural instinct to live would be diminished; the intellect eventually would determine that there must be a better existence on the other side. By the middle of September, the physician's predictions were beginning to come true. Dad was fading away; he came under the care of hospice.

Dad's world was growing smaller. By the time of Joe Reeve's visit, Dad no longer left the house. We all looked forward to Thanksgiving with hope but with the realization that it would be our last Thanksgiving together. Dad gave us hope and still maintained that he wanted to celebrate Christmas as a family.

To buoy Dad's spirits, I bought a Christmas tree on November 11. All of my children and grandchildren helped to decorate the tree in the sun room next to the kitchen. Dad's bed was in the sun room where he could be near to all the activity in the house.

We had a small quiet Thanksgiving dinner; Dad was still able to traverse the few steps from his bed in the sun room to the nearby kitchen table. Although Dad's condition was beginning to fade fast, he still maintained that he would be with us for Christmas.

As the word of Dad's illness spread to his old Army buddies, he had been receiving calls from many wishing him well. As Christmas approached, Jim Cary called to extend holiday greetings and wish Dad the best. Dad told Jim. "If I can make it through Christmas, I will feel that I have accomplished plenty."

Dad made it through Christmas and New Year's, but his world was continually shrinking. He was no longer able to walk and I had to lift him from his chair to his bed and vice versa. Eventually, his world became the bed. As his doctor predicted, his desire for food gradually disappeared.

I had moved back in with Mom and Dad several months earlier and as I was leaving for work one morning shortly after Christmas, Dad asked where I was going. He said he wanted me to be there when he died. I told him that I would be there when that time came but that he was not going to die that day. Dad's tolerance for pain that he had endured in the field hospital in August 1944 was still with him fifty-nine years later. Throughout January, the hospice nurse indicated that the dosage of pain medication for someone in Dad's condition was 200 mg; Dad was only taking 50 mg.

By February 4, 2004, however, Dad had slipped into a coma. On the morning of February 7, 2004 we awoke and Dad's breathing, even with oxygen, was labored. Mom and I were next to the bed. She left the room for a moment to take an insulin shot for her diabetes. Dad then breathed his last. I called Mom to tell her and I looked at my watch; it read 7:12 am.[5] The number that been so significant to him in life, 712, was with him even in death.

Dad was buried with traditional military honors. The grave side scene of a military funeral is often depicted in the movies, but this familiarity hardly prepares one for the reality of experiencing the haunting echo of Taps and the meticulous folding and presentation of the flag for your own family member. At Mom's request, the Honor Guard handed me the flag with the customary Army protocol:

> This flag is presented on behalf of a grateful nation and the United States Army as a token of appreciation for your loved one's honorable and faithful service.

Retracing Dad's battle route with him had indeed altered my perceptions of war. If those words had been uttered to me before our trip a decade earlier, the deep significance of their meaning would have escaped me. As my eyes welled up, it was with grief and sorrow I received the flag, but also with a deep sense of pride and admiration.

EPILOGUE

Thanks Dad

Gratitude is the memory of the heart.

French Proverb

When the last troops from World War II came home, after the parades ended and the GI returned to civilian life, there seemed to be a collective societal effort to put the war years in the past. Patriotism seemed to be talked about in platitudes and was somewhat of a cliché. As I was growing up, there seemed to be an almost complacent attitude about veterans, perhaps because there were so many of them. Recognition of the sacrifices of America's Greatest Generation was put on hold for far too long. The National World War II Memorial honoring the sixteen million who served and the more than 400,000 who died was not opened until almost sixty years after D-Day, long after many veterans it is meant to honor had passed away.

At the end of the 1970 film *Tora! Tora! Tora!*, about the attack on Pearl Harbor, Japanese Admiral Isoroku Yamamoto is portrayed as having said "I fear all we have done is to awaken a sleeping giant and fill him with a terrible resolve."[1] During my school years it seemed as though the giant had fallen back asleep.

But following that day "which will live in infamy", the reaction of the American public was swift and strong. The Japanese attack on Pearl Harbor sparked something in all Americans that day. In movies depicting that period, as well as stories and newspaper accounts depicting the mood and reaction of the American public, one immediately gets the sense of the emotions of the day – fear of the unknown future, anger and hatred toward the attackers, and an enormous swell in patriotism and a fierce determination to achieve victory. But for one born after that date, these depictions provide only a sense of emotions from that period. As Dad once told me, "No amount of words can describe what it feels like to be shot at. The only way you will know what it feels like is when someone aims a gun at you and fires a shot."

The full impact of Dad's statement about understanding his wartime experiences became clearer as the events of September 11, 2001, unfolded. History will both compare and distinguish these two dates, December 7, 1941, and September 11, 2001, but for anyone born after 1941, we can now more fully appreciate and understand the depth and intensity of the emotions our parents and grandparents experienced that fateful Sunday in 1941. My generation and my children's generation now have a benchmark upon which we can compare and equate the beginning of World War II.

Having never been in the military, much less in combat, I realize that I can hardly expect to fully comprehend the emotions and feelings my father and other combat veterans of World War II and other wars have endured. My life experiences provide me no comparable event with which to relate. I can only expect to have knowledge of facts and only a small sense of his experiences.

Knowledge of all of the facts does not equate to a complete understanding or full comprehension of all of the emotions associated with battle. Movies filmed decades after World War II, such as *Saving Private Ryan*, provide more graphic visual and audio depictions of battle. The movie experience, however, cannot come close to the actual experience. The movies cannot provide the smells associated with war -- the putrid odor of decaying flesh, the smell of five men confined in a tank for days on end, or the smell of tank exhaust fumes or expended ammunition. Nor can one spending two to three hours viewing a movie or reading a book experience the full range of emotions that a combat veteran experiences in battle twenty-four hours per day for weeks or months at a time. My reaction on viewing the movie *Forrest Gump* does not come anywhere close to emotional experience that Bob Levine experienced during the Vietnam scene. The full understanding of those aspects of combat, which will forever elude me, is reserved for that relatively small fraternity of American service men and women who have actually experienced combat.

Even though I will never know the full feelings of combat, hearing Dad's story brought me out of the darkness of complete ignorance regarding the harsh realities of battle. At least I now have a small sense of the reality of war and what my father endured during World War II.

In the years following our trip, I accompanied Dad to his 712th reunions. I, like Aaron Elson, the son of another veteran, was welcomed into their inner circle and I came to know and respect all of the 712th comrades. After Dad passed away I continued to attend their reunions and was entrusted with the inevitable task of handling the legal affairs associated with disbanding their organization as their numbers were beginning to dwindle more rapidly and it became too difficult for them to travel. It was with extreme sadness that their final farewells were made at the last reunion in 2007.

Echoes of the sadness I felt on Dad's passing have revisited me whenever I learn of the death of one of his 712th brothers – Reuben "Goldie" Goldstein of A Company, Tony D'Arpino of C Company, Al Kruszewski, Wayne Hissong

Cpl Gruntz at D-Day Museum in 2002. (*Author's collection*)

and Joe Fetsch of Service Company, Dale Albee of D Company, and Dan Diel, Orin Bourdo, Zygmund Kaminski, Ed Swierczyk and Cleo Coleman of B Company.

Patton once said that there should be no mourning of the fighting men who died. "Rather we should thank God that such men lived." Although I could not help but mourn the passing of the men of the 712th Tank Battalion, I am thankful that such men lived.

All Americans owe a debt of gratitude to all veterans for the freedoms we enjoy, a debt that can never be fully repaid. My journey with Dad strengthened and increased my respect and admiration for the men and women in the armed forces and for all veterans. I have come to more fully appreciate not only the sacrifices made by Dad and the other men of the 712th tank Battalion but also all combat veterans of not only World War II, but Korea, Vietnam, Desert Storm, Iraqi Freedom, and Operation Enduring Freedom in Afghanistan.

As I reflect on the hardships my parents had to endure as children and young adults, I realize what a privileged life I have been given. But, of all the gifts Dad gave me throughout my life, none can compare to that gift in October of 1994 – when he finally answered my boyhood question, "What did you do during the war, Daddy?" His sharing the story of his experiences in World War II with the 712th Tank Battalion is a gift that I will forever cherish.

Endnotes

Prologue

1. Even after Hurricane Katrina in August of 2005, New Orleans celebrated Mardi Gras in February 2006.
2. The 1973 movie about the struggles of a first-year law student balancing his coursework and personal life.

Chapter 1

1. Hodding Carter and Gerald K. Smith, *The New Republic*, February 13, 1935, pp. 11-15.
2. Unemployment rates fluctuated between 10 percent and 20 percent. Even if one could find a job, they may only have been employed for two or three days a week earning only a few dimes per hour.
3. In addition to national policies regarding the implementation of the Selective Service System there was public sentiment against drafting fathers who had a wife and young children to support, however, the ultimate decision on who would be drafted in a community was left to the local draft board.

Chapter 2

1. A Gallup poll that year reportedly showed that 96 percent of Americans opposed entering the war.
2. *Citizen Soldiers*, by Stephen E. Ambrose, p. 22.
3. *The Patton Papers 1940-1945*, by Martin Blumenson, pp. 56-57.
4. *Citizen Soldiers*, by Stephen E. Ambrose, p. 22.
5. 175,000 Regular Army and 225,000 National Guard.
6. Although we were not related by blood, she became known to me as Aunt Opal because of her close friendship with Mom.
7. German submarines roamed the Atlantic Ocean in packs attacking vessels bringing supplies to England (this German Naval tactic was known as the *Rudel* or "wolf pack" because teams of U-boats would gang up on convoys and simply overwhelm the merchant vessels and the defending warships accompanying them.). After Germany declared war on the US on December 11, 1941, the Kriegsmarine unleashed its submarine pack in American coastal waters; from May 1942 until December 1943, the Nazis launched an offensive in the Gulf of Mexico, codenamed Operation Drumbeat (Paukenschlag). The German Navy

successfully attacked seventy-two merchant ships in the Gulf. Fifty-six ships were sunk by U-boat and an additional fifteen vessels were damaged. The greatest concentration of attacks and sinkings was just off the mouth of the Mississippi River because New Orleans was a shipbuilding center and the major United States port for access to the agricultural and manufacturing products in mid-America.

8. *The Tigers' Tale*, Vol II, No. 4, August 26, 1943, "Somewhere in Tennessee" Blue T/4 Tells All, by T/4 Louis R. Stockstill.
9. 712th Tank Bn. Operational Reports – History – ARBN 712-0.1.
10. The Reconnaissance Company, designated Troop E of the old 11th Cavalry, was incorporated into a new unit designated the 90th Cavalry Reconnaissance Squadron, Mechanized, also attached to the 10th Armored Division. Headquarters and Headquarters Troop of the old 11th Cavalry was re-designated as Headquarters and Headquarters Troop of the 11th Cavalry Group, Mechanized on April 19, 1943; the remainder of the 11th Cavalry Group consisted of the 36th and 44th Cavalry Reconnaissance Squadrons reassigned from other divisions.
11. The name Samuel was dropped at a young age. He was known as Whitside and later Whit.
12. From a memorial to Samuel 'Whit' Whitside Miller submitted to the US Military Academy and subsequently published in the West Point Assembly and posted on the internet.
13. *Tanks for the Memories*, 2nd Ed. by Aaron Elson, pp. 64-70. Aaron Elson, conducted a series of interviews of 712th veterans in writing his book. Several men related stories regarding the reasons why Col Miller had been relieved of his command and Randolph appointed in his stead.

Chapter 3

1. *US Army Tank Crewman 1941-45*, by Steven J. Zaloga.
2. *Sherman Medium Tank 1942-1945*, by Steve Zaloga and Peter Sarson, pp. 3-4.
3. When production of the Sherman tank ceased in June 1945, 49,234 had been built, more than the combined British and German tank output.
4. This strategy was first put forward by Col. John Fuller, the chief of staff of the British Tank Corps, at the end of World War I. Fuller's ideas, entitled Plan 1919, were developed in more detail in his books, *Reformation of War* (1923) and *Foundation of the Science of War* (1926). Unfortunately, Fuller's ideas were ignored by the British Army but were studied in Germany and further developed for use in 1939.
5. The technical classifications and models of the German tanks progressed as improvements and modifications were made. Panzer I (Panzerkampfwagen I [PzKpfw I]) produced in 1934, was quickly succeeded by Panzer II (Panzerkampfwagen II [PzKpfw II]) in 1935.

    Various models of the Panzer III (Panzerkampfwagen III [PzKpfw III]) were produced between 1937 and 1943: Sd. Kfz. 141 – Ausf. A-H (1937-1941); Sd. Kfz. 141/1 – Ausf. J-M (1941-1943); and Sd. Kfz. 141/2 – Ausf. N (1942-1943).

    A series of the Panzer IV (Panzerkampfwagen IV [PzKpfw IV]) models were likewise introduced between 1942 and 1945: Sd. Kfz. 161 – Ausf. A-F (1937-1942); Sd. Kfz. 161/1 – Ausf. F2/G (1942-1943); Sd. Kfz. 161/2 – Ausf. G-J (1943-1945). Panther Tanks (Panzerkampfwagen V [PzKpfw V]), Sd. Kfz. 171, were brought into battle beginning in 1943. The Tiger Tanks (Panzerkampfwagen VI [PzKpfw VI] Sd. Kfz. 182 were produced from the latter

part of 1943 until March 1945.
6. *The Sherman Tank*, by Roger Ford, p. 19.
7. Panther and Tiger series.
8. *Citizen Soldiers*, by Stephen E. Ambrose, p. 63, and *Sherman Medium Tank 1942-1945*, by Steve Zaloga and Peter Sarson, p. 3.
9. *Sherman Medium Tank 1942-1945*, by Steve Zaloga and Peter Sarson, pp. 3-4.
10. *Ibid.*, p. 24 and *Citizen Soldiers*, by Stephen E. Ambrose, p. 63.
11. *Death Traps*, by Belton Cooper, p. 40.
12. *Sherman Medium Tank 1942-1945*, by Steve Zaloga and Peter Sarson, pp. 3-5.
13. *Citizen Soldiers*, by Stephen E. Ambrose, p. 63.
14. *Sherman Medium Tank 1942-1945*, by Steve Zaloga and Peter Sarson, pp. 14-15.
15. *Citizen Soldiers*, by Stephen E. Ambrose, p. 63.
16. Id. p. 63.
17. Id. p. 63.
18. Of the more than 88,000 tanks produced by the US during World War II, over 49,000 Sherman tanks, compared to the entire German production of all models of tanks between 1934-1945, totaling less than 28,000. In addition, Great Britain had produced more than 24,000 tanks.
19. *The Sherman Tank*, by Roger Ford, p. 35.
20. *Ibid.*, p. 38.
21. *Ibid.*, pp. 37-40.
22. *US Army Tank Crewman 1941-45*, by Steven J. Zaloga, p. 22.

Chapter 4

1. General Absolution in place of Confession and Communion as Viaticum – with the "no fast" privilege replaced the regular Church rules for Confession and fasting before communion until VE Day, *War from the Ground Up*, by Colby, p. 470.
2. *712th Tank Battalion Operational Journal* – ARBN 712-0.7, p. 1.
3. While in England, all Allied tanks were waterproofed and equipped with snorkels in order to allow them to be deposited by the landing crafts in the water rather than having to bring the craft onto the shoreline.

Chapter 5

1. *Bringing Up Father – Diary of a WWII Chaplain*, by Revd Donald J. Murphy, p. 18 (unpublished).
2. *Citizen Soldiers*, by Stephen E. Ambrose, pp. 18-19.
3. *Patton and His Third Army*, by Gen. Brenton G. Wallace, Stackpole Books, pp. 33-34.
4. *Death Traps*, by Belton Y. Cooper, pp. 49-50.
5. *Bringing Up Father – Diary of a WWII Chaplain*, by Revd Donald J. Murphy, p. 29. (unpublished)
6. *A History of the 90th Infantry Division in World War II*, p. 11.
7. During the Normandy Campaign, parts of the 712th were also attached to the 8th Infantry Division on a few occasions.
8. *A History of the 90th Infantry Division in World War II*, p. 1.
9. *Bringing Up Father – Diary of a WWII Chaplain*, by Revd Donald J. Murphy, p. 17. (unpublished)
10. Less A Company, which was attached to the 82nd Airborne Division.
11. Jim Cary was a Captain in C Company when the battalion landed in Normandy but he was wounded during the first few days. After his recovery, he was assigned to B Company.
12. *Tanks for the Memories*, by Aaron Elson, p. 29.

13. 712th Tank Battalion After Action Report, 3 July 1944.
14. *A History of the 90th Infantry Division in World War II*, p. 11.
15. *Bringing Up Father – Diary of a WWII Chaplain*, by Revd Donald J. Murphy, p. 25. (unpublished)
16. Charles Cragg Jr., Charles Davidson, Edward C. Dowgiert, Henry James, William Land, Frank Merritt, Edward Pomeroy, William Ross, Raymond Searcy, Rodford Stroup, Bruno Vercillo, and Juel Winfrey.
17. Harry Neuhauser, brothers, Leon and Harvey Fowler, Doye Smith, William Bilger, and Orville Dame.
18. Catholic Chaplain, Fr. Joseph J. Esser, Salvation Army Chaplain Edgar H. Stohler, and Disciples of Christ Chaplain, James M. Hamilton.
19. *War from the Ground Up*, by John Colby, p. 25, 496; *A Soldier's Story* by Omar Bradley, p.295-297; *The Patton Papers 1940-1945*, by Martin Blumenson, p. 497. The members of the 90th also devoted a full chapter in *War from the Ground Up* in providing a brutally frank and honest assessment of the senior officers that led them in battle.
20. *Citizen Soldiers*, by. Stephen E. Ambrose, p. 35.
21. *Ibid.*, p. 45.
22. 712th Tank Battalion After Action Report, 27 July 1944.
23. 'St. Lô, France – Breakthrough or Breakout?' by J. J. Witmeyer, *Purple Heart Magazine*, Vol. LXVIII, No. 3, May/June 2003.
24. *Patton Unleashed*, by Tim Ripley, p. 77.
25. *A Soldier's Story*, by Omar Bradley, pp. 295-297.
26. Dwight D. Eisenhower spoke of Patton In an interview with Brenton Wallace while Wallace was writing the book *Patton and his Third Army*, Stackpole Books.
27. *Patton – A Genius for War*, by Carlo D'Este, p. 332
28. *Ibid.*, pp. 332-333.
29. *Ibid.*, p. 387.

Chapter 6

1. *August 1944, the Campaign for France*, by Robert A. Miller.
2. *Patton Unleashed*, by Tim Ripley, p. 76.
3. *War As I Knew It*, by George S. Patton Jr., p. 342.
4. *Bringing Up Father – Diary of a WWII Chaplain*, by Revd Donald J. Murphy, pp. 29-30 (unpublished).
5. *Patton and His Third Army*, by Gen. Brenton G. Wallace, Stackpole Books, pp. 200-201.
6. *The Patton Papers 1940-1945*, by Martin Blumenson, p. 497.
7. *A Soldier's Story*, by Omar Bradley, p. 297.
8. *War As I Knew It*, by George S. Patton Jr., p. 99.
9. *Battalion Surgeon*, by William M. McConahey, MD, p. 73.
10. *The History of the 712th Tank Battalion*, p. 20.
11. The capture of Mayenne was the subject of an advanced infantry officers course taught by Capt. Boyd L Brown at The Infantry School of Fort Benning following World War II.
12. Vutech held the rank of Lieutenant at the time of the capture of the bridge at Mayenne. Later in the war he promoted to the rank of Captain.
13. In *War from the Ground Up*, Capt. John Colby gives an accurate and detailed account of the action involving the bridge at Mayenne, however, his account contains one slight erroneous fact. Colby misidentifies the tank commander as Lt Lombardi from C Company. Normally, C Company of the 712th was assigned to the 357th Regiment and B Company of the 712th was assigned to 359th

Regiment, however, on August 5, 1944, a platoon of tanks from B Company was the closest to handle the mission at the bridge.
14. *Tanks for the Memories*, by Aaron Elson, p. 199.
15. Hamilton held the rank of Major at the time of the capture of the bridge at Mayenne. Later in the war he promoted to the rank of Lt-Col.
16. *War from the Ground Up*, by Colby, pp. 181-184.
17. *Ibid.*, pp. 177-178.

Chapter 7

1. *Death Traps*, by Belton Y. Cooper, p. 263.
2. The award ceremony took place after VE Day in Amberg, Germany. Sparks did not receive a copy of his Silver Star citation for almost 60 years; he received a copy in 2004 when it was discovered in the records of the 90th Inf. Division, not the 712th's records.
3. *Battalion Surgeon*, by William M. McConahey, MD, p. 77.
4. *A Soldier's Story*, by Omar N. Bradley, p. 375.
5. Hamilton held the rank of Major during the battle of the Falaise Gap. Later in the war he was promoted to the rank of Lt-Col. before retiring from the Army.
6. *Below the Salt*, by John A. Busterud, Foreword.
7. *Tanks for the Memories*, by Aaron Elson, pp. 192-193.
8. Leslie Vink was a sergeant during the battle at the Falaise Gap, but was later promoted to lieutenant.
9. *Tanks for the Memories*, by Aaron Elson, p. 199.

Chapter 8

1. *The Patton Papers, 1940-1945*, by Martin Blumeson, p. 522.
2. *War As I Knew It*, by George S. Patton Jr., p. 340.
3. There were five kinds of Army rations: A, B, C, D, and K
   A – which was practically all fresh or frozen food served in camp or permanent quarters; fresh meat, vegetables, fruit, bread, butter, etc.
   B – '10 in 1' – enough food for three meals for ten men for one day – powdered eggs and powdered milk, cereal, coffee, canned butter, canned roast beef and other meats, canned fruit, dried vegetables, crackers, jam, etc. Two hot meals could be served out of this ration which was all packed in one box or carton.
   C – small cans of mixtures of meat and vegetables, beans, jam, crackers, powdered drink, sugar, cereal, etc.
   D – an emergency ration of solid rich chocolate.
   K – done up in a neat, waterproof cardboard package about the thickness of an average book but narrower. The outside was camouflaged so that if left on the ground it would not show from the air. Each package contained one meal for one man and was marked Breakfast, Dinner, or Supper. Breakfast contained fruit bar, Nescafé, sugar, crackers and a small can of cooked ham and eggs. Dinner and Supper contained a can of cheese or potted meat, crackers, orange or lemon powder, sugar, chocolate or other candy, cigarettes and chewing gum.
   Both C and K rations could be eaten cold, or heated if the GI had the opportunity to heat it up.
4. *Patton and His Third Army*, by Gen. Brenton G. Wallace, Stackpole Books, pp. 206-207.
5. *The Patton Papers, 1940-1945*, by Martin Blumenson, p. 531.
6. *The Siegfried Line 1944-45*, by Steven J Zaloga, p. 12.
7. *The History of the 712th Tank Battalion*, p. 30.

Chapter 9

1. Brig.-Gen. Raymond McLain was promoted to the rank of Major General on September 22, 1944. On October 15, 1944, Brig.-Gen. James Van Fleet was named commanding officer of the 90th Infantry Division.
2. *The History of the 90th Infantry Division in World War II*, p. 34.
3. *The History of the 712th Tank Battalion*, p. 33.
4. *War from the Ground Up*, by John Colby, p. 301.
5. *The History of the 90th Infantry Division in World War II*, p. 39.
6. *The History of the 712th Tank Battalion*, p. 35.
7. *Bringing Up Father – Diary of a WWII Chaplain*, by Revd Donald J. Murphy, p. 61 (unpublished).
8. *Battalion Surgeon*, by William M. McConahey MD, p. 99.
9. *Death Traps*, by Belton Y. Cooper, pp. 133-134.
10. *Bringing Up Father – Diary of a WWII Chaplain*, by Revd Donald J. Murphy, p. 66 (unpublished).
11. *712th Tank Bn. B Company History*.
12. *Tanks for the Memories*, by Aaron Elson, p. 228.
13. *A History of the 90th Infantry Division in World War II*, p. 48.
14. *Tanks for the Memories*, by Aaron Elson, p. 229.
15. *Ibid.*, p. 230.
16. *Patton and His Third Army*, by Gen. Brenton G. Wallace, Stackpole Books, pp. 135-136.
17. *Citizen Soldiers*, by Stephen Ambrose, p. 136.
18. *War As I Knew It*, by George S. Patton Jr., p. 184.
19. *Ibid.*, p. 184-185. In a footnote, Col. Paul Harkins elaborated:

> On or about the fourteenth of December, General Patton called Chaplain O'Neill, Third Army Chaplain, and myself into his office in Third Headquarters at Nancy. The conversation went something like this:
>
> General Patton: 'Chaplain, I want you to publish a prayer for good weather. I'm tired of these soldiers having to fight mud and floods as well as Germans. See if you can get God to work on our side.'
>
> Chaplain O'Neill: 'Sir, it's going to take a pretty thick rug for that kind of praying.'
>
> General Patton: 'I don't care if it takes a flying carpet.'
>
> Chaplain O'Neil: 'Yes, sir. May I say, General, that it usually isn't customary among men of my profession to pray for clear weather to kill fellow men.'
>
> General Patton: 'Chaplain, are you teaching me theology or are you the chaplain of the Third Army? I want a prayer.'
>
> Chaplain O'Neil: 'Yes, sir.'
>
> Outside the Chaplain said, "Whew, that's a tough one!
>
> What do you think he wants?'
>
> It was perfectly clear to me. The General wanted a prayer – and he wanted one right now – and he wanted it published to the command.
>
> The Army Engineer was called in, and we finally decided that our field topographical company could print the prayer on a small-sized card, making enough copies for distribution to the army.
>
> It being near Christmas, we also decided to ask General Patton to include a Christmas greeting to the troops on the same card with the prayer. The General agreed, and wrote a short greeting, and the card was made up, published, and distributed to the troops on the twenty-second of December.

20. *Battle, The Story of the Bulge*, by John Toland, pp. 206-207.
21. *Ibid.*, p 218.
22. *Ibid.*, p.219.
23. *War As I Knew It*, by George S. Patton Jr., p. 186.
24. From the *Review of the News*, 6 October 1971.
25. Training Letter No. 5

Chaplains of the Third Army,

At this stage of the operations I would call upon the chaplains and the men of the Third United States Army to focus their attention on the importance of prayer.

Our glorious march from the Normandy Beach across France to where we stand, before and beyond the Siegfried Line, with the wreckage of the German Army behind us should convince the most skeptical soldier that God has ridden with our banner. Pestilence and famine have not touched us. We have continued in unity of purpose. We have had no quitters; and our leadership has been masterful. The Third Army has no roster of Retreats. None of Defeats. We have no memory of a lost battle to hand on to our children from this great campaign.

But we are not stopping at the Siegfried Line. Tough days may be ahead of us before we eat our rations in the Chancellery of the Deutsches Reich.

As chaplains it is our business to pray. We preach its importance. We urge its practice. But the time is now to intensify our faith in prayer, not alone with ourselves, but with every believing man, Protestant, Catholic, Jew, or Christian in the ranks of the Third United States Army.

Those who pray do more for the world than those who fight; and if the world goes from bad to worse, it is because there are more battles than prayers. 'Hands lifted up,' said Bosuet, 'smash more battalions than hands that strike.' Gideon of Bible fame was least in his father's house. He came from Israel's smallest tribe. But he was a mighty man of valor. His strength lay not in his military might, but in his recognition of God's proper claims upon his life. He reduced his Army from thirty-two thousand to three hundred men lest the people of Israel would think that their valor had saved them. We have no intention to reduce our vast striking force. But we must urge, instruct, and indoctrinate every fighting man to pray as well as fight. In Gideon's day, and in our own, spiritually alert minorities carry the burdens and bring the victories.

Urge all of your men to pray, not alone in church, but everywhere. Pray when driving. Pray when fighting. Pray alone. Pray with others. Pray by night and pray by day. Pray for the cessation of immoderate rains, for good weather for Battle. Pray for the defeat of our wicked enemy whose banner is injustice and whose good is oppression. Pray for victory. Pray for our Army, and Pray for Peace.

We must march together, all out for God. The soldier who 'cracks up' does not need sympathy or comfort as much as he needs strength. We are not trying to make the best of these days. It is our job to make the most of them. Now is not the time to follow God from 'afar off.' This Army needs the assurance and the faith that God is with us. With prayer, we cannot fail.

Be assured that this message on prayer has the approval, the encouragement, and the enthusiastic support of the Third United States Army Commander.

With every good wish to each of you for a very Happy Christmas, and my personal congratulations for your splendid and courageous work since landing on the beach, I am, [...]

signed The Third Army Commander.

26. *Patton and His Third Army*, by Gen. Brenton G. Wallace, Stackpole Books, pp. 158-159.

Chapter 10

1. 600,000 Germans, 500,000 Americans, and 55,000 British.
2. British had 1,400 with 200 killed, the Germans had 100,000 killed, wounded or captured.
3. *War from the Ground Up*, by John Colby, p. 502.
4. *Tanks for the Memories*, by Aaron Elson, p.230.
5. *Battle, the Story of the Bulge*, by John Toland, p. 287.
6. Ibid., p. 296.
7. Ibid., p. 314.
8. Ibid., p. 336.
9. Ibid., p. 350.
10. On January 8, 1945, the day before the attack by the 90th and the 712th, Gen. Patton wrote in his diary, "I passed through the last battalion of the 90th Division moving in by truck. They must have been riding in the cold, blizzard weather in open trucks for many hours, but were in splendid form and cheered and yelled as I drove past. It was a very inspiring sight."
11. *Battle, the Story of the Bulge*, by John Toland, p. 350.
12. *The History of the 712th Tank Battalion*, p. 46.
13. Father Murphy writes about how bitterly cold it was while saying Mass one day that January, "Mass at 10 in the Church for the people I buried yesterday. It was so cold the water froze as it hit the chalice, and the water in the cruet froze too", *Bringing Up Father – Diary of a WWII Chaplain*, by Revd Donald J. Murphy, p. 80; see also *War from the Ground Up*, by John Colby, p. 401.
14. *Tanks for the Memories*, by Elson, pp. 230-231.
15. *War from the Ground Up*, by John Colby, pp. 380-381.
16. *Battalion Surgeon*, by McConahey, pp. 103-104.
17. During one of the 712th reunions I attended subsequent to my trip with Dad.
18. Cary had been in command of C Company when he was wounded in Normandy and when he returned to the battalion he was assigned to B Company to replace Capt. Jack Galvin, who had been wounded.
19. *Tanks for the Memories*, by Elson, pp. 233-234.
20. Dale Albee received a battlefield commission and was promoted to 2nd Lieutenant soon after this incident.
21. D Company, 712th Tank Bn. Journal.
22. *Patton and the Battle of the Bulge*, by Michael and Gladys Green, p. 147.
23. *War from the Ground Up*, by Colby, pp. 374-377, comments by Pfc. Jack Ammons in the 359th Regiment of the 90th Infantry Division.
24. *Surprise Night Attack – 1945*, Brig.-Gen. (Ret.) Raymond E. Bell Jr., unpublished.
25. *War from the Ground Up*, by John Colby, p. 365.
26. *Surprise Night Attack – 1945*, p. 4.
27. Talbott eventually retired from the Army as a Lieutenant General.
28. *War from the Ground Up*, by John Colby, p. 365-366.
29. The Americans discovered later that road upon which they were advancing was the division boundary between the German 5th Fallschirmjaeger (Parachute) Division and the 9th Volksgrenadier (Infantry) Division.
30. *War from the Ground Up*, by John Colby pp. 368-369.
31. *War from the Ground Up*, by John Colby, p. 369.
32. *The History of B Company of the 712th Tank Battalion*, p. 6.
33. *War from the Ground Up*, by John Colby, p. 370.

34. *The Patton Papers, 1940-1945*, by Martin Blumenson, p. 622.
35. *Battle, the Story of the Bulge*, by John Toland, p. 357.
36. *History of the 90th Infantry Division in WWII*, p.52.
37. This epic battle also has the distinction of being the only combat action of World War II in which all three elements of the old 11th Cavalry Regiment were involved:
   1) 1st and 2nd Squadron – The 11th Tank Battalion, as part of the 10th Armored Division, was defending Bastogne from within along with the 101st Airborne Division.
   2) Headquarters & Headquarters Troop – The 11th Cavalry Group, assigned to the Ninth US Army and attached to the XIII Corps. relieved the 406th Infantry Regiment of the 102nd Infantry Division and soon found itself charged with the defense of the entire sector on the northern shoulder of the bulge, previously held by the entire 102nd Infantry Division.
   3) 3rd Squadron – The 712th Tank Battalion, attached to the 90th Infantry Division was part of the Third Army's relief column punching its way into Bastogne.

Chapter 11

1. *Citizen Soldiers*, by Stephen E. Ambrose, p. 144.
2. Schmidt's decorations included a Distinguished Service Cross, four Silver Stars, a Soldier's Medal, three Bronze Stars, seven Purple Hearts, a Croix de Guerre (French), a Croix de Guerre (Belgium) and a King George Medal (Great Britain).
3. *The History of the 712th Tank Battalion*, p. 57.
4. *A Mile in Their Shoes*, by Aaron Elson, p. 225.
5. The Volksgrenadier divisions were a more manpower-economical version of the standard Grenadier divisions. The name Volksgrenadier ("grenadier of the people") was chosen for propagandistic effect. These divisions were hastily trained and comprised remnants of destroyed divisions, inexperienced conscripts, wounded returning from the hospitals, and transfers from the Navy and the Luftwaffe.

    The Volkssturm ("People's storm") was the militia consisting of children and old men formed to defend the Fatherland. They usually had no training and were often sent into battle with a Panzerfaust and a reassuring speech.
6. *War from the Ground Up*, by John Colby, p. 447.
7. *Ibid.*, p. 453.
8. *Below the Salt*, by John A. Busterud, pp. 107-108.
9. Id., p. 154.
10. 'Nazi Gold: The Merkers Mine Treasure', by Greg Bradsher, Prologue, *Quarterly of the National Archives and Records Administration*, Spring 1999, vol. 31, no. 1.
11. SGO Central File, 1943-1945, '710-Psychoneurosis', Record Group 112. Records of the Surgeon General. National Archives, Washington DC, Report of Norman T. Kirk, Surgeon General, dated 16 September 1944.
12. 314 days in the ETO combat zone – June 28, 1944 to May 8, 1945. *Tank Tracks*, Vol. 1, No. 1, June 18, 1945, p.2 (Ch 30) lists the days in combat as 310. The discrepancy in the count is due the Tank Track editors beginning the count on July 3, 1944, the date the battalion first officially engaged the enemy.
13. *War from the Ground Up*, by Colby, p. 345 – statement by Billie Breedlove, a medic in the 358th Rgt.

14. *US Army Tank Crewman 1941-45*, by Steven J. Zaloga, p. 27.
15. *Ibid.*, Gen. Bruce Clarke described the life of tankers in combat in World War II:

> The failure of many armored division commanders was the failure to appreciate that an armored unit produces a tremendous workload on its men [...] It just isn't possible to fight men in a tank day-after-day, day-after-day. The tank gives you claustrophobia – they are crowded in there with ammunition right up against them. The place is dark. The tank is noisy and it vibrates [...] You fight inside a tank 12 hours a day and that's pretty debilitating, well it's not like an infantryman in the open air [...] Then at night, you've got to haul the ammunition, probably over several hills, because you aren't located where a truck can drive right up to you and give it to you. And you've got to haul your fuel in five-gallon cans. You have to check your tracks and all that sort of business. And you have to provide local security to keep the damn enemy from coming and throwing a grenade in the turret.

16. *Bringing Up Father – Diary of a WWII Chaplain*, by Revd Donald J. Murphy, p. 65 (unpublished).
17. *A Mile in Their Shoes*, by Aaron Elson, p. 220.
18. *The History of the 712th Tank Battalion*, p. 67.

Chapter 12

1. *War from the Ground Up*, by John Colby, pp. 466-467.
2. *Ibid.*, p. 467.
3. *The History of the 712th Tank Battalion*, p. 69.
4. *War from the Ground Up*, by John Colby, pp. 466-467.
5. *The History of the 90th Division in World War II*, p. 82 and 83.
6. *War from the Ground Up*, by John Colby, pp. 466-467.
7. *712th Tank Battalion Operational Journal*, ARBN 712-0.7, pp. 267-268, 7 May 1945.
8. *Battalion Surgeon*, by William M. McConahey, MD, p. 152.
9. *A History of the 90th Infantry Division in World War II*, p. 85.
10. *The History of the 712th Tank Battalion*, p. 71.
11. *Tank Tracks*, Vol. 1, No. 1, June 18, 1945, p. 1.
12. *Tank Tracks*, Vol. 1, No. 12, September 4, 1945, p. 2.
13. Bürgerbräukeller was the site of Hitler's Beer Hall Putsch on November 8, 1923. It is where he attempted for the first time to seize control of the German government. This initial attempt ended in failure and Hitler was imprisoned for a short time. After Hitler emerged from prison and eventually gained power, this beer hall became a symbolic location for the Nazi party and was the site of annual celebrations each November 8. It was also on this site that a failed assassination attempt on Hitler's life occurred on November 8, 1939. After giving a speech, Hitler left the location a few minutes before a bomb exploded.
14. *The 90th Infantry Division in World War II*, p. 80.
15. Gen. Hans Oster, Admiral Wilhelm Canaris, Revd Dietrich Bonhoeffer, Dr Karl Sack, Dr Theodore Struenck and Gen. Friedrich von Rabenau.
16. *What Was It Like in the Concentration Camp at Dachau*, by Dr Johannes Neuhäusler, p. 50 (citing Goldschmitt: Zeugen des Abendlandes, p. 36).
17. *Bringing Up Father – Diary of a WWII Chaplain*, by Revd Donald J. Murphy, p. 104.

Chapter 13

1. Catherine Schmitt's mother was Catherine Baümlin.

Chapter 15

1. Each active duty person would have an Adjusted Service Rating Card issued on which the point score would be recorded. Points were earned as follows:
    i. Service Credit – One point for each month of duty between Sept. 16, 1940, and May 12, 1945.
    ii. Overseas Credit – One point for each month overseas between the same dates.
    iii. Combat Service Credit – Five points for each of the following awards:
        a. Distinguished Service Cross, Legion of Merit, Silver Star, Distinguished Flying Cross, Soldier's Medal, Bronze Star Medal, Air Medal, Purple Heart, and Bronze Service Star.
        b. For Navy Personnel, the Navy Cross, Distinguished Service Medal, Legion of Merit, Silver Star, Distinguished Flying Cross, Navy and Marine Corps Medal, Air Medal, and Purple Heart.
    iv. Parenthood Credit – Twelve points for each child under 18 years of age. The initial critical score for separation was set at 85.
2. *The History of the 712th Tank Battalion*, p. 74.
3. *The History of the 712th Tank Battalion*, p. 78.

Chapter 16

1. Post-Traumatic Stress Disorder (PTSD) became known as such in the 1970s due to problems some Vietnam veterans were experiencing. Many studies have shown that the more prolonged, extensive, and horrifying a soldier's exposure to war trauma, the more likely it is that he would become emotionally worn down and exhausted.
2. Cleo Coleman expressed having similar problems. *A Mile in Their Shoes*, by Aaron Elson, pp. 226-227.
3. *Death Traps*, by Belton Y. Cooper, pp. 21-22.
4. *They Were All Young Kids*, by Aaron Elson, p. 182.
5. The coroner recorded Dad's death on the death certificate as 7:55 a.m. This was the time the telephone call from the hospice nurse was received in the coroner's office informing the coroner of Dad's death.

Epilogue

1. Although there is no evidence that Yamamoto made this statement on December 7, it seems to represent his true feelings about the attack after it was over. Yamamoto believed that Japan could not win a protracted war with the United States. He is also known to have been upset by the bungling of the Foreign Ministry which led to the attack happening while the countries were technically at peace, thus making the incident an unprovoked sneak attack that would certainly enrage the enemy.

    Almost one year earlier, Admiral Yamamoto, in a letter to Ogata Taketora on January 9, 1941, did state: "A military man can scarcely pride himself on having 'smitten a sleeping enemy'; it is more a matter of shame, simply, for the one smitten. I would rather you made your appraisal after seeing what the enemy does, since it is certain that, angered and outraged, he will soon launch a determined counterattack."

Bibliography

Books

Ambrose, Stephen E., *Citizen Soldiers* (New York: Touchstone, 1997).
Bell Jr. (Ret.), Brig.-Gen. Raymond E., *Surprise Night Attack* (Unpublished, 1998).
Blumenson, Martin, *The Patton Papers 1940-1945* (Boston: Houghton Miflin, 1974).
Brokaw, Tom, *The Greatest Generation* (New York: Random House, 1998).
Bradley, Omar, *A Soldier's Story* (New York: Random House, 1999).
Busterud, John A., *Below the Salt: How the Fighting 90th Division Struck Gold and Art Treasure in a Salt Mine* (Philadelphia: Xlibris, 2001).
Colby, John, *War From the Ground Up: The 90th Division in World War II* (Austin: Nortex, 1991).
Cooper, Belton Y., *Death Traps: The Survival of an American Armored Division in World War II* (New York: Ballantine Books, 2003).
D'Este, Carlo, *Patton: A Genius for War* (New York: Harper Collins, 1995).
Ford, Roger, *The Sherman Tank* (Osceola, WI: MBI Publishing, 1999).
Green, Michael and Gladys, *Patton and the Battle of the Bulge* (Osceola, WI: MBI Publishing, 1999).
McConahey, M. D., William M., *Battalion Surgeon* (Rochester, MN: Privately Pub, 1966).
Miller, Robert A., *August 1944: The Campaign for France* (Norvato, CA: Presidio Press, 1996).
Murphy, Revd Donald J., *Bringing Up Father: Diary of a WWII Chaplain* (Unpublished, 1945).
Neuhäusler, Dr Johannes, *What Was It Like in the Concentration Camp at Dachau*
Patton Jr., Gen. George S., *War As I Knew It* (Boston: Houghton Miflin, 1947).
Ripley, Tim, *Patton Unleashed: Patton's Third Army and the Breakout from Normandy, August, September, 1944* (St Paul, MN: MBI Publishing, 2003).
Toland, John, *Battle, the Story of the Bulge* (New York: Random House, 1959).
Wallace, Gen. Brenton G., *Patton and His Third Army* (Mechanicsburg, PA: Stackpole Books, 2000).
Zaloga, Steve & Sarson, Peter, *Sherman Medium Tank 1942-1945* (Boxley, Oxford, UK: Osprey Publishing, 1978).
Zaloga, Steven J., *US Army Tank Crewman 1941-45 European Theater of Operations 1944-45* (Boxley, Oxford, UK: Osprey Publishing, 2004).
Zaloga, Steven J., *The Siegfried Line 1944-45* (Boxley, Oxford, UK: Osprey Publishing, 2007).

Bibliography

Magazines & Periodicals

Carter, Hodding and Smith, Gerald K., *The New Republic*, February 13, 1935
O'Neill, Msgr. James H., *Review of the News*, October 6, 1971
Witmeyer, J. J., 'St Lô, France: Breakthrough or Breakout?', *Purple Heart Magazine*, Vol. LXVIII, No. 3 (May/June 2003).
Tank Tracks, Vol. 1, No. 1 (June 18, 1945).
Tank Tracks, Vol. I, No. 3 (July 2, 1945).
Tank Tracks, Vol. I, No. 12 (September 4, 1945).

Archives & Company Histories

712th Tank Battalion: "B" Company History
"D" Company, 712th Tank Battalion Journal
The 90th: A History of the 90th Infantry Division in World War II (Nashville, TN: Battery Press, 1999)
The History of the 712th Tank Battalion (1945)
National Archives, Washington DC
– 712th Tank Bn. Operational Reports, History, ARBN 712-0.1
– 712th Tank Battalion Operational Journal, ARBN 712-0.7
– 712th Tank Battalion After Action Report
– Records of the Surgeon General. Report of Norman T. Kirk, Surgeon General, dated 16 Sept., 1944
– SGO Central File, 1943-1945, *710-Psychoneurosis*, Record Group 112